creative
kids' murals
you can paint

creative
kids'
murals
you can paint by Suzanne Whitaker

NORTH LIGHT BOOKS
Cincinnati, Ohio
www.artistsnetwork.com

Creative Kids' Murals You Can Paint. Copyright © 2006 by Suzanne Whitaker. Manufactured in Singapore. All rights reserved. The drawings in this book are for the personal use of the decorative painter. By permission of the author and publisher, they may be either hand-traced or photocopied to make single copies, but under no circumstances may they be resold or republished. It is permissible for the purchaser to paint the designs contained herein. No other part of this book may be reproduced in any form or by any electronic or mechanical means, including information storage and retrieval systems, without permission in writing from the publisher, except by a reviewer, who may quote brief passages in a review. Published by North Light Books, an imprint of F+W Publications, Inc., 4700 East Galbraith Road, Cincinnati, Ohio 45236. (800) 289-0963. First edition.

Distributed in Canada by Fraser Direct
100 Armstrong Avenue
Georgetown, ON, Canada L7G5S4

Distributed in the U.K. and Europe by David & Charles
Brunel House, Newton Abbot, Devon TQ12 4PU, England
Tel: (+44) 1626 323200, Fax: (+44) 1626 323319
Email: mail@davidandcharles.co.uk

Distributed in Australia by Capricorn Link
P.O. Box 704, Windsor, NSW 2756 Australia

Other fine North Light Books are available from your local bookstore
or art supply store, or direct from the publisher.

10 09 08 07   5 4 3 2

    Library of Congress Cataloging-in-Publication Data

Whitaker, Suzanne.
    Creative kids' murals you can paint / Suzanne Whitaker.-- 1st ed.
        p. cm.
    Includes index.
    ISBN-13: 978-1-58180-805-6 (pbk. : alk. paper)
    ISBN-10: 1-58180-805-4 (pbk. : alk. paper)
  1. Mural painting and decoration--Technique. 2. Children's rooms. I. Title.
    ND2550.W47 2006
    751.7'302430523--dc22
                                                    2005034588

Editors: Holly Davis and Gina Rath
Production Coordinator: Greg Nock
Art Director/Designer: Clare Finney
Interior Layout Artist: Barb Matulionis
Photographers: Tim Grondin, Al Parrish and Christine Polomsky

Metric Conversion Chart

TO CONVERT	TO	MULTIPLY BY
Inches	Centimeters	2.54
Centimeters	Inches	0.4
Feet	Centimeters	30.5
Centimeters	Feet	0.03
Yards	Meters	0.9
Meters	Yards	1.1
Sq. Inches	Sq. Centimeters	6.45
Sq. Centimeters	Sq. Inches	0.16
Sq. Feet	Sq. Meters	0.09
Sq. Meters	Sq. Feet	10.8
Sq. Yards	Sq. Meters	0.8
Sq. Meters	Sq. Yards	1.2

About the Author

Suzanne Whitaker is a professional artist and former production artist and illustrator for F+W Publications. She has a degree in Fine Arts from the University of Cincinnati's Design, Architecture, Art and Planning Program, and has painted murals all over the greater Cincinnati area. Her work appears in private homes, shops, doctor's offices, Procter & Gamble research rooms and day-care centers.

Suzanne, who owns and runs the business, "Murals by Suzanne," feels that being a mother has given her special insight into what appeals to children. She now lives in Phoenix, Arizona, with her husband, Ken, and her son and daughter, Ean and Sedona.

Dedication

To Mom and Dad
For the paint and permission to let my adolescent energy create a jungle in there!

Acknowledgments

I am grateful to so many…thanks to Holly Davis and Gina Rath for their vision and clarity in words; thanks to Clare Finney and Christine Polomsky for their vision and clarity in graphics; and thanks to Jamie Markle, Kathy Kipp and Amy Jeynes for seeing the potential of it all.

Thank you to all the wonderful kids and their parents for allowing the "picture-takers" into their homes to show off their rooms for this project.

A big thank-you to my favorite technical adviser, my sister Rose Whitaker, for dispensing endless knowledge and making me laugh hard all the while (We will do that book together someday!); and to Josh Knarr, who is number-one spouncer and precision striper; and to my friend, Connie Musuraca, the ideamaker with a generous heart; and also to Mary Pat Burke, Tracey Seibert and Eileen Bord for the years of giving great love and care to my children so that my brush could roam. And thanks to the balance of my siblings, Jim, Rita, Colette and Sharon Whitaker, for unending support over the years. Thanks also to "Cath" and "Mr. Price" for their quiet, guiding spirits and to Oprah, of course, for being my contemporary spirit guide.

Special, special appreciation goes to my husband, Ken, for loving me and enduring my never-ending spastic moments and to my children, Ean and Sedona, whose young, inventive minds and vision never cease to amaze me!

contents

introduction

Children's rooms are the perfect place for your creative spirit to take flight because children are amazed at and genuinely appreciative of your creativity.

What I most enjoy about creating for children is listening to their ideas. In their minds' eyes there are no boundaries! A child clearly envisions dinosaurs and volcanoes of long ago—and even hears the sounds they make. Ideas blossom just by listening to a preschooler's account of a family of bunnies having tea with their friends in the garden. Absorb these creative morsels and transform them into a visible environment the child will love.

My hope is that this book will motivate you and give you the tools needed to transform your child's personal space into a magical wonderland—just follow your heart.

Suzanne Whitaker

A few words of encouragement: When attempting something new, my young son often gets discouraged if he is unable to perfect it immediately. When this happens, I always encourage him to start with what he knows and practice that first—then work up to the next level.

As an adult I sometimes have to remind myself to practice what I preach. We all want to immediately "get it," but when attempting something new, we're always better off beginning simply and working our way up.

I've tried to keep the projects in this book simple and easy to follow. At first glance, some may appear to be detailed, but if you look closely, you'll see that each project is broken down into simple steps that anyone can accomplish. If, however, you've never picked up a brush and still feel a bit hesitant about jumping into those projects that appear detailed, then turn to page 116 and check out the section called "Easy Designs." This might be the place for you to start. Try one of these quick and easy designs, and not only will your child have a fun and colorful room, but also you'll loosen up and feel confident to tackle other designs in the book.

Remember, it's just paint—and paint can always be painted over. Time to pick up that brush!

materials

Paint

For painting kids' rooms, I mix true primary and secondary colors to achieve the colors I need. I prefer water-based latex, acrylic paints and purchase mine at Sherwin-Williams or Miller Bros. paint stores. However, you don't have to use a specific brand of paint; you can go into any paint store and cross-reference the colors I have listed on the opposite page with almost any other brand of paint. With latex paint I can't always achieve the color saturation that I need. Therefore, I also use Liquitex brand tube acrylics. Liquitex acrylics are fully saturated, pure colors and can be found at most craft stores.

On the next page are lists of the Sherwin-Williams and Liquitex true primary and secondary colors I most often use for mixing.

I usually buy quarts of Sherwin-Williams Satin Interior paint from the Bright and Energetic paint-swatch deck in the following colors:

SW6871 Positive Red
SW6903 Cheerful (Yellow)
SW6959 Blue Chip
SW6887 Navel (Orange)
SW6925 Envy (Green)
SW6983 Fully Purple

For white I prefer Sherwin-Williams SuperPaint Luminous White, which I purchase off the shelf in gallon cans.

A true saturated red is very difficult to find in a latex paint because latex reds lean toward a fire red (kind of orange in color) and are too transparent. When I need a pure application of red, I like Liquitex Cadmium Red Deep Hue. For a bright Magenta, Liquitex Medium Magenta is best. Liquitex colors I frequently use are these:

Cadmium Red Deep Hue
Cadmium Yellow Medium
Ultramarine Blue
Hooker's Green
Light Green
Dioxazine Purple
Raw Sienna
Raw Umber
Acra-Magenta
Medium Magenta

Polycrylic

Whether using latex acrylic or the Liquitex tube acrylics, I always mix my paints with Minwax Polycrylic Protective Finish in Clear Satin. I love Polycrylic mixed in with my paints. The Polycrylic works as a medium, is incredibly durable, and the mixture can be translucent when needed. Because I mix it with all my paints, I rarely have to use it as a finishing coat (for which it is advertised). Sherwin-Williams and Home Depot stores carry this brand name.

You Don't Have to Mix

In this book I don't go into detail about how to mix the colors for each project. I don't want to get into specific colors and/or mixtures because every kid's room is different. Even if the wall color is similar to what is shown in the book, something else, such as the trim, furniture or bedding, will differ.

The colors I have listed on this page are what I specifically use for mixing. I love to mix my own colors, but I know that many people don't. If you don't like to, don't worry; I have a simple suggestion for you. You can use acrylic craft paints (the ones easily found in all craft and many department stores). Bottled acrylic paints come in hundreds of colors, making it easy to find the perfect color to match any room décor! And with my method of mixing every color with Polycrylic, you won't need to buy a whole lot of paint.

To keep the durability, make sure there is always more Polycrylic than water. Add only enough water to achieve proper fluidity.

The amount of pigment differs in every paint brand; I think you'll find it helpful to practice mixing the paint and Polycrylic (and water if needed) until you achieve the translucency or opacity you want.

Whether I'm glazing, washing or filling in a shape that requires more opacity, I almost always thin my paints with Polycrylic and water in varying amounts (always use more Polycrylic than water). It's rare for me to use a pigment straight out of the container.

Basecoat

Always begin with a good-quality basecoat. The quality of the basecoat paint is very important and a washable flat or eggshell is best. Personally I have found that the basecoat paint a builder sprays on a new home is usually a very thin coat of flat paint and is much too absorbent for my needs.

Brushes

I have a range of brushes that I use for many purposes. It's important that a brush is comfortable to use—it should feel good in your hand. But even more important for me is that it has to be *cheap*! I can be pretty hard on brushes and sometimes have been known to abuse a brush by soaking it too long in a bucket of sludge water. In these instances, if the brush is too far gone, it may have to be thrown away. However, if the brush isn't completely destroyed, it can be excellent for scribbling (such as for texture or grasses).

Typically, I use Royal Soft-Grip brushes, which are inexpensive and durable. They can be bought at craft stores and many department stores, either singly or in a variety pack. For the bulk of my mural work, I use no. 8 and no. 12 flat brushes. Brushes of these sizes are used mostly for laying in colors in areas or shapes about 2 to 8 inches (51 to 200mm) square in size.

I use a small, no. 2 round Soft-Grip brush for outlining and a larger no. 8 round brush for painting flower petals, etc. I also like to have a no. 8 filbert on hand

when I need to paint soft edges.

I invest in only one or two really good 1- to 2-inch (25-51mm) soft, acrylic bristle brushes found at artists' supply stores. I use them for larger areas, and since they are soft, they allow me to achieve a smooth surface.

Wide and very wide wooden-handled chip brushes with natural bristles—from

2 to 5 inches (51 to 125mm) in size—are great for painting textured areas, such as the grassy background of Cat & Dog (pages 74–76). They're very inexpensive and can be found in many stores. When working with small stencils, I use a spouncer brush, which fits nicely in the palm of the hand.

Always Inspect Sponges

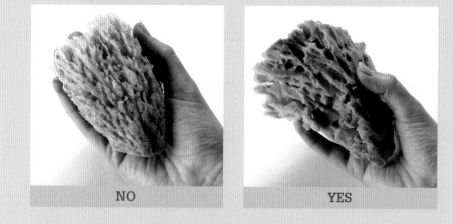

NO	YES

Inspect a sponge before you buy it. The best ones have large pores.

No. 12 flat   No. 8 round   No. 2 round   No. 8 filbert   Soft bristle   Chip   Spouncer

Sponges

I'm really picky about the sponges I use. Not all sponges are alike or good for the job. The best are natural sea sponges. Many craft stores and even some paint stores sell them. Take a look at a sea sponge and you'll notice that it has spikes and pores. Always take time to inspect them. Spikes that are not too close together make large pores, which provide a more believable or interesting texture for wildflowers in a field, moss on a tree or a cirrus cloud.

Rags

I'm particular about the rags I use for painting. I always use a soft, white cloth—T-shirt cotton is best. White is important because any other color can transfer dye to your work surface. When working, always have a dry and a wet rag on hand.

Tape

For taping off areas on walls, 1-inch (25mm) blue painter's tape is good. But when taping off a ceiling, I've found Easy Mask KleenEdge is most successful at *not* lifting ceiling paint in corners or edges. Never use cheap, tan masking tape because it lifts the paint from the wall.

A Handy Holder

For each job, I premix my paint colors in separate plastic cups. Placing these cups in a cupcake tin makes them easier to transport and keeps them from tipping over. The cups fit into the tin perfectly!

Miscellaneous

Below are several additional miscellaneous materials I use when creating murals:

Paper for sketching

No. 2 pencil

Kneaded eraser

Tape measure

Tracing or graphite paper

Ladder or stepladder

Level

Craft knife

Plastic cups/containers
   (small and large)

Mixing tray or paper plates

Paper towels

Bucket

Drop cloth

Paint Consistency
Most of the time a thin, but not runny, consistency is desirable.

Mixing Paint
You can mix paint to the opacity you need. Just mix paint, Polycrylic and water until you reach the desired consistency.

Wash Consistency
Mix a small amount of pigment with Polycrylic and water to a watery consistency. The amount of pigment can be increased or decreased depending on the translucency you need.

techniques

Mixing Paint

As previously mentioned, whether I use paint from a can or tube, I always mix my mural paints with Polycrylic and water.

For most applications you want the consistency of your mixture to be thin but not runny. You'll know the mixture is too thick if the brush doesn't flow smoothly across the surface and too thin if the paint runs.

The image you are painting further dictates how thick or thin the mixture must be. When the paint needs to be opaque (see "Mother Goose," pages 42-44), you'll need a thick mixture with more pigment (and usually two applications of paint). When painting an airy, somewhat translucent dress of a fairy (pages 54-55), you'll need a thin mixture with less pigment.

Blocking In

Blocking in is simply laying down the initial layer of paint in a loose, usually transparent manner. I think of this as the initial statement of my work.

Washes

Anytime it's necessary to describe something in very subtle terms, a thin, transparent paint layer (wash) will execute that effect most successfully.

A wash mixture incorporates a small amount of pigment with the Polycrylic and water (use less water than Polycrylic), and is applied with either a rag or brush. I use washes for many things: to add a background to a character, to give depth to a landscape or trees and shrubbery, to warm

Applying a Wash with a Brush
A wash is applied in a free-flowing manner. You want the background color to show through. The brush marks can remain, or you can brush them smooth, depending on the look you want.

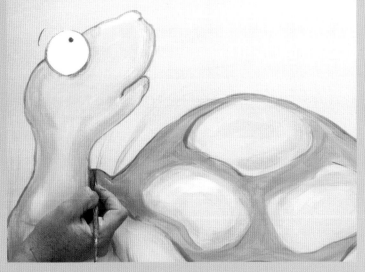

Outlining and Gesture
Using a small round brush and a small amount of black with green, I outlined this turtle using free-flowing, fun lines that varied in width.

Use gesture to bring out the personality of your painting. Doesn't this little guy seem expressive and full of life?

up a skin tone or to simply add an interesting design element, such as texture.

Having a dry rag on hand is helpful for catching a too-runny wash.

Outlining

You will see throughout the book that I use outlining in various ways. Often I create a thin black mixture using black pigment, Polycrylic and water (roughly one-third of each). The mixture should flow easily but not be runny.

Outlining is often the final touch, used to define a given area or to create a clean edge to a shape. It can also be used to show motion or to add interest or texture, such as with a rippled line. You can vary the width of the line or smudge the line in some places. The line should be alive, not static, and it doesn't always need to connect—the viewer's eye will naturally fill in the open areas.

I've found that it's best to work from top to bottom, so you don't unintentionally smear the lines as you make them.

Keep the mural colors unified. If the dominant color of the entire mural is green (as in murals with lots of green foliage and grass), I add a bit of green to the black outline mixture.

Gesture

Without a doubt, gesture is the most basic structure or element of any composition. When I refer to gesture throughout this book, I am describing the very essence of the pose of a character or object or the rough layout structure of a composition. It's important to keep the essence shining through to the very end, or sadly, your art will appear to be overworked and stiff!

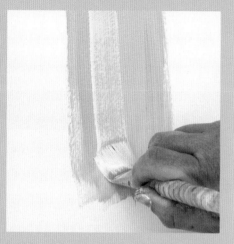

Drybrushing

To drybrush, use a brush with very little water. The object is to leave unpainted areas.

Smooshing

The circular motion used in smooshing adds soft texture while allowing the base color to show through.

Smudging

Your finger is a handy tool for softening or blending an area.

Drybrushing

Drybrushing is applying paint to a dry surface, using a brush with very little water. The paint is applied quickly, leaving areas of the surface unpainted. Often I use this technique when I'm adding a highlight to an item.

"Smooshing"

Smooshing (my own term) is applying paint with the brush, using a somewhat circular motion. Smooshing can add a soft texture while still allowing the base color to show through.

Scumbling

For scumbling you need less paint on your brush than for smooshing. Use scumbling in a scribble-like manner to add a texture to an area.

Smudging

Smudging is essentially finger painting. For example, with a brush I may apply a light pink onto the cheek of a character. Then I use a finger or two to soften the color. I like the "impressionistic," less-defined imprint of this technique.

Smoothing Brushstrokes

When you want the freshness of the brushstrokes to show texture or to describe something with a little extra emphasis, use a brush with stiff bristles.

To achieve a less-distracting appearance, you want smoother brushstrokes. For these, use a soft-bristled brush.

Removing Tape

As mentioned previously, I only use blue painter's tape or, for ceilings, Easy Mask

Removing Tape
Remove tape slowly, always staying within a few inches of the surface.

Cutting Out a Stencil
Using a sharp craft knife helps you achieve clean, crisp stencil edges.

KleenEdge. When removing tape, it's all too easy to lift paint from areas you never intended. To avoid this, always lift the tape carefully, slowly and with your hand staying within just a few inches of the wall or molding surface. Never use cheap, tan masking tape—it's the worst offender!

Making a Stencil

Because I generally prefer the freedom of freehand painting, there are few instances when I need a stencil. But stencils do come in handy for painting symmetrical, exacting or repetitive shapes.

I make my stencils using either bristol board or thin acetate sheets. I use the bristol board when I only have a few repeating shapes, but for a shape that I must repeat over and over, I use fairly thin acetate. You can find both in fine art or craft stores.

To make a symmetrical stencil such as the one I used for "Scroll Border" (see pages 98-99), fold a piece of bristol board in half and draw half of the shape (centerline on the fold). Then cut out the half shape with a very sharp craft knife and unfold. Voilà—you now have one perfectly symmetrical shape to trace or paint!

For stenciling small shapes, I sometimes use a spouncer brush (found at most craft stores). But when I need a more opaque coverage of paint, I trace the shape with a pencil and paint the shape in carefully.

Creating a Template

A template is similar to a stencil, but it's usually used only one time, so it can be made of paper or thin posterboard.

For "Fairyland" (see pages 50–55), I used a large, symmetrical oval template as a guide for the overall shape of the mural. To make a template like this, first cut off a rectangle of brown paper large enough to cover the area you intend to paint. For "Fairyland" I used a 3' x 4' (91cm x 122cm) piece. Fold the rectangle into quarters and then cut a slight curve on the open ends of the folded quarters. Unfold, and you have an oval that you can tape to the wall and lightly trace around the edges. Before cutting out large templates like these, you might find it helpful to practice with a smaller scrap of paper.

Ragging

Ragging an area creates texture. For this technique, I use a rag dipped in a mixture of Polycrylic and pigment.

This method was used for laying in the basic foundation for tree foliage in "Soft Realistic Tree" (see pages 58–59).

Ragging Soft Foliage

The softness in this tree's foliage is achieved by first ragging in the background greenery with diluted color. The leaf clusters that are more defined are then brushed in (see "Soft Realistic Tree, pages 58-59).

Ragging: Apply the First Color

Dip a moist rag (white, cotton T-shirt fabric is best) into a mixture of paint, Polycrylic and water, and apply the first color with a circular motion lightly and quickly. The background color should still show through.

Ragging: Apply a Second, Lighter Color

For more interest and dimension, add a second, lighter color in the same manner.

Ragging can also add to the interest and balance when used to create a decorative, repetitive faux texture. A textured band or border can help tie a room together, especially a large room.

To apply a ragged border, dip a damp rag into a mixture of pigment, Polycrylic and water (1:1:1, adjusting proportions if necessary) and, with a circular motion, apply pressure lightly and quickly to the wall. Rag about two feet (61cm) at a time, moving and turning the rag in various directions throughout.

Following are a few tips for achieving a good ragging effect:

- Be careful not to get your mixture too runny or watery, or it will not hold the ragging texture.

- Practice—paint a sheet of cardboard with the basecoat color, figure out the paint proportions you need, and then practice applying the mixture.

- As you work, check for small bubbles and blow on them to prevent pits in the dried paint.

Ragging Off/Buffing Out

There are times when you want a subtle effect. You can achieve this by adding paint to a surface and then subtracting it by touching or blotting with a dry or nearly dry rag. I call this ragging off or buffing out.

Troubleshooting

Even professionals have to correct mistakes or clean up spills once in a while. Over time I've found the following helpful:

- Be sure to have some of the base (wall) color paint for touch-ups. Use a small brush to apply the paint. Then, using a circular motion, fade it out (or softly blend it) into the wall color. You can sometimes get away with using a small roller for these touch-ups, but only if the paint is an exact match. I have found that brushes blend a little better.

- Much to my dismay and despite my best efforts to cover with a drop cloth, I have dripped paint on a client's carpeting. (I won't tell you about the large spills!) For small areas I have had the most success with Resolve carpet cleaner. Be sure to follow the directions on the label.

- OOPS! cleaner is good for removing drips on painted surfaces, such as molding.

what works spatially

To begin painting a room you must first consider the wall area as a whole. In other words, how much wall space or ceiling space (if applicable) is available? Also, decide what you want to accomplish in the room. Are you working from a predetermined focal point? Are you adding a decorative accent (or border) or trying to tie several elements together?

The Focal Point

In most children's bedrooms the bed or crib is the main focus. Therefore, when designing a theme such as bunnies in a flower garden, you could start the design above the bed and then take an element from the design, such as the flowers, and repeat this in other visible places in the room. Areas around the chest of drawers, above a doorway or near a rocking chair are usually good places to add elements.

Consider a Tree

A tree is a great element to consider when you want to frame a corner or bring attention to a reading area in a child's room. You can paint a tree any size, shape or color that you need for a particular area. And a tree can be as simple or realistic as you

want; it can even have a face or a secret door—don't be afraid to be creative!

Be Flexible

If wall space is limited, you might consider a decorative border around the top portion of the wall. One child's room had furniture that consisted of a tall bookshelf unit, an armoire, a desk with an adjoining hutch as well as a bed with a tall headboard, leaving little space for painting. I solved the problem by painting a colorful border.

On the flip side, a room so large that the furniture seems to swim in it might benefit from both a border and an accent wall to tie it all together (see page 112). Be flexible and allow the placement and/or size of the furniture to help you create a room the child will love.

Finding Inspiration

With most themes you may need inspiration for ideas or reference material to paint something convincingly. Do a little research. Never underestimate searching for photos and creating your own inspiration file to help spark ideas.

I carry a wealth of reference books, mostly children's picture dictionaries and

the works of children's illustrators that I like. The concept that an artist is able to simply work from memory is a myth (not to mention a pet peeve of mine).

You can always go to the library for inspiration or to find a picture of that perfect locomotive. Search the Internet for the correct safari lion's face or even better, photograph the climbing clematis in your own backyard. Inspiration is everywhere!

Find Inspiration in Your Backyard

This photo of my clematis and trellis is the inspiration behind "Trellis," (above and pages 104-109).

sketching it out

Sketch it Out

When planning a mural for a room, a sketch is a useful communication tool. Conveying your ideas with only words can be difficult, since not everyone has the ability to visualize verbal descriptions. Sketches are also invaluable for preventing or working out problems.

Above and to the right are examples of two themes that were planned and

sketched beforehand to solidify the ideas.

The layout of the nursery rhyme room (see illustration above) was such that the crib wall was the last thing you noticed. The wall with the hutch was much more visible, so the right side of the hutch seemed a perfect location for Mother Goose. Although a few elements changed from my original sketch, one great element remained—the apple tree. The bright apple

tree depicting the Rock-a-bye Baby theme happily framed the sleeping child in the crib until the crib was outgrown.

For "Mr. Froggy Goes A Courtin'" (see illustration on opposite page), my client and I discussed how elements in the poem could be portrayed on the walls of the room. We decided that the first wall to the left of the entrance would show Mr. Froggy going a courtin' on his horse, facing in

(Left page) Sketch and mural elements for the nursery rhyme room.

(Above and right) Sketch and mural from the "Mr. Froggy Goes A Courtin'" wall sequence.

(Below) A scaled grid breaks a design into smaller parts for easier enlarging and transferring.

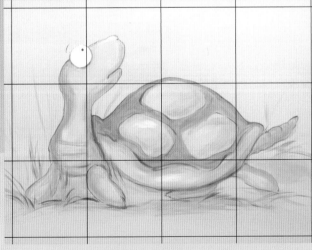

the direction of the next wall. The second wall, divided by two good-sized windows, would depict Ms. Mousie's cottage in the tree. The inevitable conclusion to the story, the wedding banquet, would be placed as the focal point above the child's bed on the wall to the right of the entrance.

Enlarge with a Grid

You can use a grid to enlarge and transfer a picture or photo to a wall surface. Here's how:

1) Divide your sketch or photo into equal parts—1-inch (25mm) square sections on your sketch easily translate into 1-foot (31cm) square sections on a wall.

2) Pencil a 1-foot (31cm) grid lightly on the wall, using a yardstick and a level.

3) Simply transfer the information from each 1-inch (25mm) square grid section on your photo to the same 1-foot (31cm) square grid section on the wall.

If you need to preserve the original reference photo, protect it by covering with an acetate overlay or tracing paper.

Pastel Room
The soft colors in this room have a calming effect, sometimes preferred in a bedroom.

color

Usually the predominant color in a mural will be the color that the client has specified or the colors of the mural image(s) you are painting. When your choice is more open, an easy way to approach color in a room is to match the bedding fabric. For instance, one of my clients has a daughter who loves pink, so we let the predominant pink in her striped bedding determine the color used for the pink flowers, pink fairy dresses and pink lettering painted on the walls of her room. I also added some of the less dominant colors from the bedding and the color of her furniture to a castle and a pond that I painted on her wall.

Unify and Personalize

If you have white furniture or white, sheer curtains in a room, unify the room by adding some of that white to a mural figure, such as a horse. If you're painting a tree and the color of the crib frame in the room

is natural wood, you can add the natural wood color to the tree trunk.

Another way to customize or personalize the images in a child's room is by matching a character's hair color or skin tone to the child whose room you are painting, as I did with the fairy in "Fairyland" (see opposite page and pages 54-55).

Create a Mood

Use color to create the mood of the room. Whether you use soft or bright colors purely depends on what you're trying to achieve. Some children (or their parents) might prefer a bedroom with the calming effect of pastel colors, such as soft pink, lavender, light blue or soft yellow. On the other hand, in a playroom, the bright, primary colors of pure red, blue and yellow can be used to create a fun, energetic atmosphere for activity.

Primary Color Room
Bold, energetic colors convey that this is a room for fun and play.

backgrounds

The wall color is not the background color. In every instance of mural painting, you'll begin with a wall color (perhaps white), which might be referred to as a background color. However, when I use the term background throughout this book, I'm generally referring to the first application of paint (usually a translucent layer) that surrounds or sits behind a given character or element in the foreground. The background can help tie all the elements together, or it can ground them so they don't appear to be floating or simply stuck onto the wall.

Think in Layers

I like to think and work in layers. The first layer is usually the sky, the atmosphere or the painted background shape that will incorporate all of the elements. This stage is the time to lay in the composition and consider how all the elements interact with each other (preferably you have sketched something out on paper ahead of time).

Next, I begin to add the foreground by lightly sketching or painting in the elements. I work back and forth from foreground to background, integrating all the colors I'm using (see the sky in "Fairyland" on pages 50-52 for a good example of this).

One way to create the illusion of space is with color. Cooler colors, such as blues, greens and purples, can be used when you want an area to recede or appear more in the background. Warmer colors, such as yellows, reds and browns, can be used when you want something in the painting to come forward.

When painting a landscape, for instance, I use cooler tones in the background and warmer tones up front; I think of the background as a less defined and cooler silhouette to be laid in first. I then work in more detail toward the foreground. For the browns in my landscape, I consider the tones of the wood in the room (the wood-

work and the furniture) and incorporate those into the mural.

Often, I paint the main foreground characters and elements of my composition using a more opaque paint, which stands out against a lighter, more transparent background. In other words, the background, such as a landscape, is applied using thinner paint, and the characters that occupy it are painted with thicker, more opaque paint.

Standing Alone

If you are painting just one decorative element, such as a retro-style flower over a doorway, integrating it into a background other than the wall paint is not necessary. The flower can stand alone because it is not trying to achieve a place among a scene of flowers. A flower used in this way doesn't need a background finish to tie all of the flowers together or to ground them.

1

nature walk

My client, an expectant mother, felt it important that her baby's bedroom be happy, bright and playful. Shades of green and yellow and a frog motif were already established in the purchased bedding. She loved my signature turtle and felt strongly that he had to have a place within the scene I was going to paint.

The client made a list of soft, cartoon-style animals she would like, and a landscape was born from the simple fact that we needed to give the animals a place to interact.

Clearly, the primary focal point in the room would be the wall with a lovely arched window, and all the elements would create a natural frame around it.

Blue

Green-Brown

A willow tree in a corner frames the composition to the left in this unusual wall space. The willow tree is an important element for creating a calming, lazy-day tone in the room.

I incorporated the brown tones of the room's woodwork and furniture into the browns of the landscape.

willow tree
& stream

BRUSHES

no. 8 round
no. 8 flat
no. 12 flat
2- or 2½-inch (51mm or 64mm) chip brush

ADDITIONAL SUPPLIES

no. 2 pencil
white cotton rag

1 **Basecoat the Tree Trunk.** Depending on the layout of the room and your composition, decide where you want to paint the tree. Lightly sketch in the landscape, using your no. 2 pencil. Wash in the blue stream, using a soft cotton rag and blue paint. Still using the rag, dilute green-brown and wash in the distant bushes. Also lay in vertically hanging branches. Basecoat the trunk of the tree, using light tan and a 2- or 2½-inch (51mm or 64mm) chip brush. This brush creates good textural trunk markings. Keep this light, with smooth-flowing, vertical markings. Don't try to cover the wall color completely—allowing a little to show lends cohesiveness to the room.

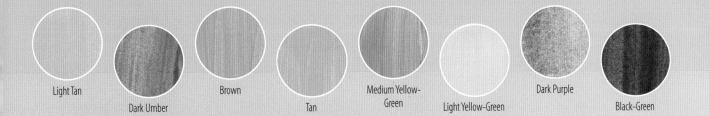

Light Tan

Dark Umber

Brown

Tan

Medium Yellow-Green

Light Yellow-Green

Dark Purple

Black-Green

Define the Stream and Bushes. Use a rag and diluted green-brown to define the stream area. Scumble some bushes around the edges of the stream. Then wipe back to create more tones and values in the bushes.

2

3 **Block In to Describe.** Still using the chip brush, add more bushes and grasses around the stream. Consider the scale of everything, making bushes and grasses larger in the foreground. Don't spend a lot of time on this—just block in to describe the background before putting in the foreground details of branches, leaves, etc. Don't worry if you get green on the tree trunk; you'll add more color to the trunk later. Visualize the look of water and bring more blue into the stream with horizontal strokes. Water markings in the foreground should be larger, because the movement of the water is more easily seen up close. Check for runs.

 **willow leaves**

Think about how willow leaves are shaped and how they grow. They have a feathery look to them and hang downward.

4 **Paint the Leaves.** Use a combination of no. 8 flat and round brushes with green-brown to add green tones on the leaves. Still thinking in general shapes rather than details, touch in the leaves on the tree, using loose strokes and the side of your brush. You can even wipe back with your rag a bit to create more values. By applying the paint liberally, you create a lot of tones. The lighter paint describes the background leaves and the darker tones describe the closer leaves. This is still the undefined undercoating.

5 **Begin to Define.** Using a no. 8 flat and a thin wash of dark umber, define the outside trunk edges. Blend softly, wiping back if needed with your rag. Clean up marks that you might have made on the trunk when painting the stream and bushes. If this thin wash doesn't cover, use a more opaque mixture (which you'll cover later with the lighter wash). Try to keep the freshness of the brushstrokes.

Using the same brush, add a little brown throughout the leaf area to define some thin willow branches. The brown helps unify the mural.

6 **Add More Color.** Using a no. 12 flat and tan, bring in warmer trunk tones and cover the pencil marks. Also apply tan lightly here and there throughout the mural. With the same brush and thinned medium yellow-green, add a little color to the leaves, keeping it evenly dispersed. This fairly transparent green creates depth in the leaves. Think of each stroke as describing a leaf or branch, and paint some leaves overlapping branches.

Step back to make sure you aren't adding too much color—it's easy to get carried away. Without cleaning the brush, add light yellow-green leaves. Light leaves over dark areas really pop!

7 **Finish Layering.** Step back again to see if any areas need more leaves or seem too open (the leaves should look clustered). Fill in the too-open areas with ragged-on green-brown. Use a no. 12 flat with green-brown over the ragged areas. As in the last step, use medium yellow-green and light yellow-green to finish the layered effect.

Keep in mind that you're striving for overall effect. Step back and look at the leaves as a whole to keep yourself from overworking the painting. Use a damp rag and thinned tan to lightly wash in some middle ground areas.

8 **Foreground and Background.** Using a rag, touch and dab a little dark purple into the background to better describe the bushes and the banks around the stream. This subtle effect helps push that area into the background, establishing more depth. Anytime the purple looks too dark, dab some of it off with a rag. Try not to go over the leaves, but if you do, you can always repaint them with an opaque application of leaf color.

Use a no. 8 flat and green-brown to add foreground grasses.

9 **Final Touches.** Add more green grasses with a no. 12 flat and green-brown. Use medium yellow-green and light yellow-green to scumble and loosely stroke in even more grasses. It's important to use tones that you've used elsewhere, so everything works together. Don't worry about cleaning the brush between the greens. You can now add as many or as few details as you want, such as flowers or cattails.

Use a small round brush with black-green to lightly outline. Be mindful of the leaves—you don't want to cover those in the foreground. Don't make the trunk edge perfectly straight—keep it varied to better reflect the texture. Lightly describe the bushes and the stream, keeping the edges light. Your fingers are great tools for smooshing, smudging or quickly removing paint from the foreground leaves.

Dark Lavender

Medium Green

Here you see a simple interaction of characters and elements rendered with a more opaque application of paint. By suggesting the cattails—not painting the entire stalk—you can fit the element anywhere as an accent.

BRUSHES
no. 2 round
no. 8 flat

ADDITIONAL SUPPLIES
no. 2 pencil

1 **Sketch and Basecoat.** Using a no. 2 pencil, lightly sketch in the shape of the fish. Basecoat the fish using a no. 8 flat with dark lavender, medium green and white.

fish & cattails

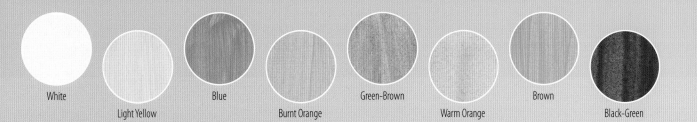

White

Light Yellow

Blue

Burnt Orange

Green-Brown

Warm Orange

Brown

Black-Green

2 Add a Second Coat.
Still using the no. 8 flat, add a second coat of the dark lavender and medium green to smooth out previous brushstrokes and make an opaque finish. While the second coat of green is still wet, use the same brush to add in some light yellow for a soft highlight.

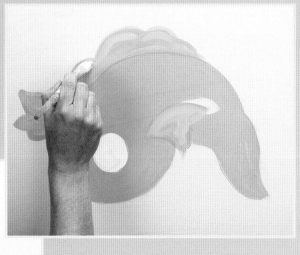

3 Add White and Correct the Shape.
Using the same brush, add a second coat of white to the fish's eyes. This is a good time to correct the shape if necessary. Add white highlights to indicate movement.

4 Paint the Water and Cattails.
At this point it's good to think about the motion of the fish. Using a no. 8 flat and thinned blue, paint water splashing off the fish's tail. Also add a little blue onto the fish body.

Decide where you want to place the cattails and sketch them in with your pencil. With the no. 8 flat, basecoat the cattail tops with burnt orange and the stems and leaves with green-brown.

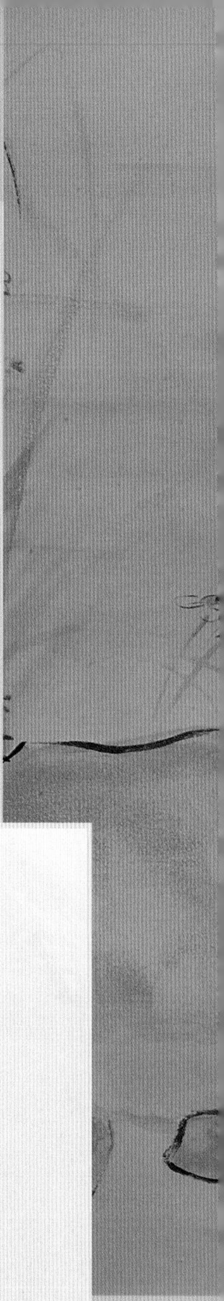

5 **Begin Adding Details.** Still using the no. 8 flat and medium green, paint a caterpillar onto one of the cattails. You can also add medium green to the stems. Add more light yellow to the fish's fins and a touch of the same color to the caterpillar.

✳ wiping back

Keep in mind that you can always wipe back if the paint is runny or heavy. Wiping back the water drops can make them look more transparent.

6

Finishing Touches. Paint the cattail tops with a mixture of burnt orange and warm orange. Use a no. 2 round to outline the cattails with brown. Use the same brush and black-green for the finishing outline. Return to the no. 8 flat to add orange wash to the cattail tops. Touch some of this color onto the fish. Step back and decide if you want to add a few more white highlights.

turtle

My signature turtle seems to have mass appeal. I even use him as a friendly opener on my sales brochure. I've also used him for quick demos in preschool and kindergarten classes. The kids love him! Now you can recreate him for some lucky child.

BRUSHES

no. 2 round
no. 8 flat
2-inch (51mm) chip brush

ADDITIONAL SUPPLIES

no. 2 pencil
white cotton rag

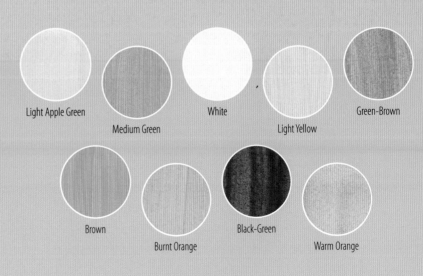

Light Apple Green

Medium Green

White

Light Yellow

Green-Brown

Brown

Burnt Orange

Black-Green

Warm Orange

✳ making changes

If you've sketched in your character and want to move a leg or change a gesture, use a wet rag or kneaded eraser to eliminate the pencil lines. Then, follow up with the basecoat colors.

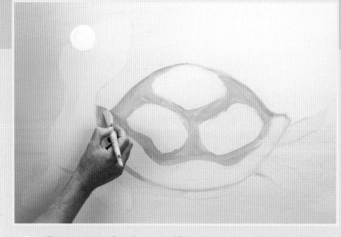

1 **Basecoat the Large Shapes.** Using a no. 2 pencil, lightly sketch in the basic shape of the turtle. You can move a leg or change a gesture if you want. With your no. 8 flat, basecoat the large shapes of the turtle in light apple green, medium green and white (for the eye). Begin with general shapes and work toward specific shapes.

✳ **create as you go**
Remember this is just paint. You can always go over it if you don't like what you see.

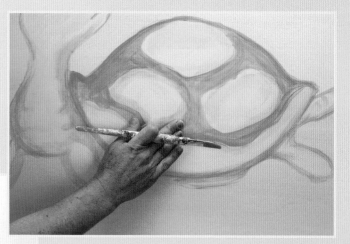

2 **Brighten and Tone Down.** Using a rag or 2-inch (51mm) chip brush, add a light yellow wash to brighten up or highlight the light green areas of the turtle. Tone down the medium green areas, using a no. 8 flat and transparent green-brown. This gives the turtle dimension and helps define the area. Also add a little green-brown around the edges of the light apple green. Smudge with your finger to blend the edges.

3 **Brighten and Highlight with White.** Brighten the eye, using the no. 8 flat with the same white you used for the basecoat. Then add white highlights on the turtle where you imagine light would fall on its humpy shell.

✳ **bringing up the color**
If you see something really dulling out, it usually needs a warm wash.

4 **Eliminate the Brushstrokes.** Chances are, the brushstrokes are too distinct, so go over the darkened areas of the turtle with a wash of brown. This also warms up the area.

✳ eliminating pencil lines

Remaining pencil lines can usually be covered with black outlining at the end. If outlining doesn't cover them, remove them with a wet rag.

5 **Add a Warm Wash.** Add a warm wash of burnt orange, using a no. 8 flat.

6 **Add Grass and Outline.** Use a no. 8 flat with green-brown to brush in some grass around the turtle. This integrates it into the surroundings. Outline using a no. 2 round and black-green.

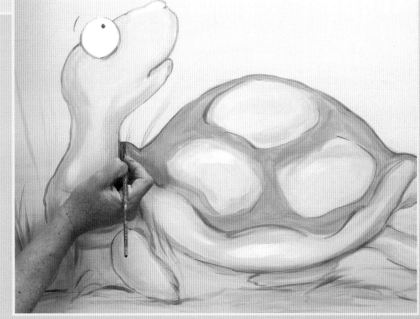

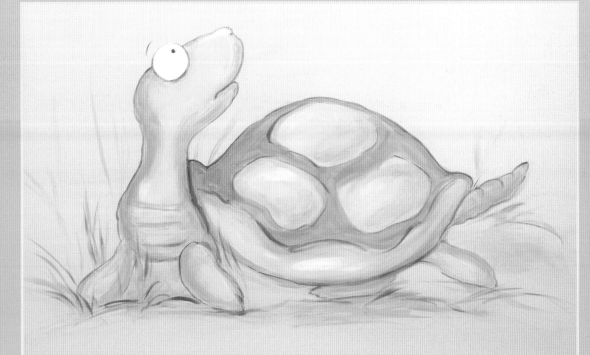

7 **Punch up the Color.** Use your no. 8 flat and punch up the color with a thin wash of warm orange.

frog & dragonfly

Medium Green

Green-Brown

Since first creating the frog and dragonfly for this mural, I've painted similar small scenes in other children's rooms. It's a charming vignette that can float merrily on a small piece of wall alongside a closet or under a light switch.

BRUSHES
  no. 2 round
  no. 8 flat

ADDITIONAL SUPPLIES
  no. 2 pencil

1 **Sketch and Basecoat.** Sketch in the frog and dragonfly using a no. 2 pencil. Then basecoat the frog with a no. 8 flat, using medium green and green-brown. In my mural, the length of the frog from "finger" to toe is about 12 inches (31cm), but you can make him whatever size works in your space.

White

Medium Yellow-Green

Light Yellow

Warm Orange

Melon Pink

Raspberry Red

Blue

Black-Green

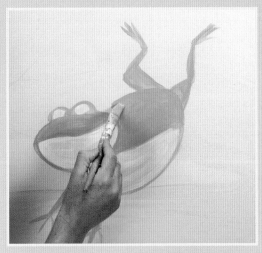

2 Paint Face, Define Shape. With a no. 8 flat, paint the bottom of the face area and the belly with a wash of white. Paint the eyes with full-strength white. Define the shape of the frog with medium yellow-green. This helps eliminate the brushstrokes while allowing some of the basecoat to show through. This is a good time to adjust and define edges.

3 Add Detail. With the same brush, add some light yellow over the medium yellow green. You can also touch some into the white area. Use warm orange on a no. 2 round to define the toes. Also add a few touches on the tops of the eyes and the nose. Use green-brown to define the toes and the edges.

4 Paint Tongue and Dragonfly. Paint the tongue with melon pink on a no. 2 round. While this is wet, touch in a little raspberry red and blend. With the same brush, paint the dragonfly body blue. Then, touch in a little medium yellow green. Paint the wings with white.

5 Add Finishing Details. Paint over the white eyes to brighten them. Also touch highlights on the characters' bodies. Add a little light yellow to the back of the bumps and then outline, using a no. 2 round and black-green.

2

for baby

A favorite theme for baby and toddler rooms is classic nursery rhymes or fables. You can combine as many or as few characters as you want, depending on the walls of the room.

I'm most inspired from the illustrations in children's books, both old and contemporary. I may like the gesture of an animal here, the face on a farmer there and the style of the landscape somewhere else. Usually a whole scene is created by combining parts from many sources, adding my own spin on the overall mural as well as the individual elements. I encourage you to try the same method.

Many people like the old-style Mother Goose. Here is a rendition you can easily reproduce. Keep in mind that a true saturated red is difficult to achieve with latex paint so you may need several paint layers to get the color you want. Also, feel free to adjust these colors to match the décor of the room you're painting.

BRUSHES

no. 2 round
no. 8 flat

ADDITIONAL SUPPLIES

no. 2 pencil

mother goose

HOME OF THE MCDONOUGH FAMILY

1 **Basecoat.** Lightly sketch the figure onto the wall, using your no. 2 pencil. With a no. 8 flat, basecoat the goose with butter yellow, the book with medium green, the hat with burnt orange, the shoes with tan, the cloak with blue, and the face and hand with fleshtone. Paint the body and hair white.

Butter Yellow

Medium Green

Burnt Orange

Tan

Add a Second Coat. Add a second coat to each of the colors, eliminating most of the pencil lines as well as brushstrokes. Use a wash of warm orange on the edge of the bristles of your no. 8 flat to define the feathers, beak, hat and the feet.

Paint the Face and Hands.

Using the no. 8 flat, add a wash of pure pink to the face and right hand. While painting this demonstration, I noticed at this point that I had forgotten to paint Mother Goose's hand holding the book. To correct this, I laid in a white basecoat for the hand to block out the undercolor of the book.

Highlight and Define. Still using the no. 8 flat, add some white highlights and some butter yellow to the area above the shoes. Also highlight the bow, scarf and goose legs with pure pink. Highlight and define some feathers with white. Paint the corrected hand with fleshtone and then define the hand with pure pink.

Blue

Fleshtone

White

Warm Orange

Pure Pink

Raspberry Red

Purple

Blue-Black

5 **Begin to Define and Outline.** Mother Goose's blouse has a red-and-blue-circle design. Paint the red dots with raspberry red and a no. 2 round brush. Using the same brush and color, define the pink lines on Mother Goose's leg. Add some raspberry red to her lips and define her nose, cheeks, hat and feet by outlining with the same color. Still using the no. 2 round, use blue to define her hair and add dots to her blouse.

6 **Continue to Define.** Using a no. 2 round brush, define Mother Goose's cloak, shoes and the flower in her hair with a wash of purple. Add a touch of the same color to her hair. Paint the ribbon with blue. If the blue has thickened, add a little water—you want the paint to flow easily.

7 **Add Final Details.** A few areas seem a little dull. To correct this, take a no. 2 round and add a warm orange wash to Mother Goose's hat and to the feet and beak of the goose. Then beginning at the top of the entire figure, outline with blue-black. When working on the goose, think about the lay of the feathers. Keep the lines light and airy.

Colors and patterns for Humpty Dumpty were selected to match existing bedding fabrics. The client also emphasized that the colors not be gender specific to afford flexibility for future little ones.

BRUSHES

no. 2 round
no. 8 flat
no. 12 flat

ADDITIONAL SUPPLIES

no. 2 pencil
white cotton rag

humpty dumpty

Sky Blue

Medium Green

Butter Yellow

Blue

Burnt Orange

White

Brown

Fleshtone

Raspberry Red

Blue-Black

1 **Begin by Basecoating.** Lightly sketch in the figure with a no. 2 pencil. Use a damp rag to wash in a very light background around Humpty Dumpty using a thinned wash of sky blue. Use your no. 8 flat to basecoat the arms with medium green, the "body" with butter yellow, the "egg pants" with blue, and the shoes and hair with burnt orange.

2 **Begin to Define Edges.** Use your no. 12 flat to scumble (see page 16) some white onto the face area. Use the no. 8 flat to scumble white onto the top of each leg. Using your no. 12 flat, add a second coat of blue on the pants, medium green on the arms and burnt orange on the shoes. Switch back to your no. 12 flat and use brown to define the edges of the shoes and the curls in the hair. Also paint the hands with fleshtone.

3 **Detail the Clothing and Hair.** With a no. 2 round brush and raspberry red, paint little dots in a circular fashion on Humpty's stockings. Touch in a little of the red to emphasize the hair curls. Also add some red shoelaces. Load the same brush with blue, and paint the dots on Humpty's stockings. Use white to paint stripes on each sleeve and to touch in hair highlights.

4 **Highlight and Define.** Use your no. 2 round brush and white to add highlights to Humpty's pants and the egg. With the same brush, highlight the shoes with butter yellow and add definition to the hair with burnt orange.

✳ **subtle color**

Whenever you want to paint something subtle, such as Humpty's pink cheeks, wipe back with a wet rag after applying the color.

5 **Final Touches.** Paint the cheeks using a no. 8 flat and watered-down raspberry red. Have a wet rag ready to wipe back, if needed. If the color dries too light, you can punch it up with a bit more raspberry red applied in a circular manner and then smudged in a circular manner with your finger. Using the same color on a no. 2 round brush, outline the hands. Remove any pencil lines and check for areas that need touching up. Then apply blue-black outlines on the rest of the figure, keeping them active and fun.

As I stepped back and looked at this painting, it occurred to me that Humpty's falling motion could be exaggerated by bringing his hair forward, so I added another curl. When you make changes like this, you may need to paint over the black outline a couple of times to cover it.

more ideas

fairyland

Softness is key in this baby girl's nursery. Layering washes of colors allows the wall color, yellow in this case, to come through, keeping the mural softly integrated with the room.

Building transparent layers also keeps the freshness of the painting and prevents overworking. Begin with the background sky and work forward to the foreground greenery.

The two demonstrations after this one give instructions for painting the bunny and the fairy.

sky

Sky Blue

Medium Yellow-Green

White

Dark Purple

BRUSHES

no. 2 round
no. 8 flat
no. 12 flat
2-inch (51mm) acrylic

ADDITIONAL SUPPLIES

no. 2 pencil
white cotton rag

1 Paint the Background and Moon. Using a no. 2 pencil, lightly sketch an oval approximately 3' x 4' (91cm x 122cm). Fill in the oval with a damp rag and a wash of sky blue. Then wash in diluted medium yellow-green on the left side (the blue doesn't need to be dry). Once the blue dries, sketch in the crescent moon and paint it white with a no. 12 flat brush.

✱ the perfect oval

If you feel uncertain about freehanding a symmetrical oval shape, you can cut a large shape from brown craft paper, tape it to the wall and trace around it. See "Creating a Template" on page 17.

2 **Paint the Stars.** Use a 2-inch (51mm) brush to add a second layer of the sky blue wash into the background. Keep this transparent; remember you want the wall color to show through. Use a no. 2 round brush and opaque white paint to dot in tiny stars throughout the sky. Vary the size of the stars, painting some with the very tip of the brush and others as larger white circles. Take this opportunity to place the stars over imperfections left from the ragging. Add another wash of white on the moon.

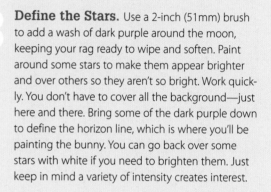

3 **Define the Stars.** Use a 2-inch (51mm) brush to add a wash of dark purple around the moon, keeping your rag ready to wipe and soften. Paint around some stars to make them appear brighter and over others so they aren't so bright. Work quickly. You don't have to cover all the background—just here and there. Bring some of the dark purple down to define the horizon line, which is where you'll be painting the bunny. You can go back over some stars with white if you need to brighten them. Just keep in mind a variety of intensity creates interest.

4 **Add the Greenery.** Using your no. 8 flat, no. 2 round and medium yellow-green, paint the greenery. Dull some of the leaves by adding just a touch of the dark purple wash to the medium yellow-green. You can go back in with a wash of sky blue if the sky begins to look too grayed out.

Tan   White   Light Tan   Dark Umber   Dark Lavender   Reddish Brown   Dark Purple   Medium Yellow-Green

bunny

As an artist, you are the visual storyteller. Strive to capture the gesture of the unmistakable floppiness of a stuffed animal just before it comes to life. Create your own story with this irresistible, lovable bunny as the main theme.

BRUSHES

no. 2 round
no. 8 flat
no. 12 flat

ADDITIONAL SUPPLIES

no. 2 pencil

1 Begin by Basecoating. Lightly sketch the design onto your surface with a no. 2 pencil. With your no. 8 flat, basecoat the body of the bunny with tan and the belly with white.

2 Define, Soften and Blend. Use the no. 12 flat and light tan to define the roundness of the bunny and to soften the brushstrokes. Then define the edges using the no. 8 flat and dark umber. Work wet-into-wet to keep the fur looking soft and blended. Bring the dark tone and medium tone together by working back and forth, adjusting and smoothing.

3 Continue to Blend and Define. Use a no. 8 flat to add a thin wash of dark lavender to the inside of the ear. Lightly touch a little of this color onto the floppy ear, the nose and the mouth areas. Soften and blend with light tan. Then dry-brush reddish brown here and there to warm up the bunny. Use your no. 2 round with dark umber to define the face, edges and creases.

4 Final Details. Define the eye, nose and mouth with dark purple and a no. 2 round. Paint the tail with white and a no. 8 flat. Then define the tail with a no. 2 round and a touch of dark umber. Still using the round, add tiny stitches of diluted dark purple. Touch a white dot into the eye. Step back to see if you need to add definition or highlighting. Then ground this fellow by adding grass with a no. 8 flat and medium yellow-green.

Fleshtone

White

Dark Umber

Pure Pink

Tan

Light Tan

Purple

Black

fairy

I wanted to customize the fairy for this nursery and the child who would occupy it. As was obvious from the wall hangings, fabrics and knickknacks, the color pink and an abundance of femininity were very important to the new mother. It just made sense to dress the fairy in pink. I also gave the fairy dark-toned skin and brown hair to resemble the little girl who would be sleeping below her.

BRUSHES

no. 2 round
no. 12 round
no. 8 flat

ADDITIONAL SUPPLIES

no. 2 pencil

1 **Begin by Basecoating.** Use a no. 2 pencil to lightly sketch the design onto your surface. With a no. 8 flat, basecoat the face with fleshtone, the dress and wings with white, the hair with dark umber, and the headdress with pure pink.

2 **Begin to Define the Face and Gown.**
Use pure pink and a no. 8 flat to outline and define the gown, keeping the effect super soft by working wet-into-wet. Remember to keep this really transparent because "fairies are always transparent you know." Take a little diluted tan on a no. 2 round and outline the face and hands. Then lighten the hair just a bit with light tan.

Dark Lavender

Sky Blue

3 **Define the Face, Hands and Hair.** Go in with a purple wash on a no. 2 round and define the facial features. It's easy to get too detailed on this small face, so keep it simple. Mix black and purple and, still with the no. 2 round, softly define the face and facial features. Keep this really, really light. Use the same color and brush to define the sleeves, making small touches rather than a continuous line. Also, define the thumb. If needed, use fleshtone to soften lines. Still using a no. 2 round, add thin purple wash shadows to the hair, on the sleeves and anywhere else you feel they're needed. Keep this light and minimal.

4 **Final Touches.** Using the no. 2 round, add dark lavender to further define the headdress and the dress. With the no. 8 flat, add white to the wings, dress and hair. Use a wet rag to remove any pencil marks. To help define the fairy's shape, add a background wash, using a soft no. 12 round and a wash of purple or sky blue (whichever you prefer).

✳ fairies are everywhere

A lot of fairy information is available online and in the marketplace. You can find inspiration to customize and embellish your own fairy from book illustrations, stationery, fabrics, and even home décor items.

3

trees

Often, I'm requested to paint a tree as the focal point of a room. Finding inspiration for this isn't difficult; I can look out the window of my home and see many varieties of trees, all with interesting textures and shapes.

While it's important to observe a tree up close, it's also helpful to observe the tree, and especially the leaves, from a distance. Note that you can see the sky through the leaves and that the leaves appear as clusters rather than individual shapes. Notice also the range of highlights and shadows that defines each leaf cluster.

THE CASTRUCCI HOME

When painting a tree, first make sure that the base of the trunk is substantial enough for the foliage you intend to paint. Also, borrow brown tones from the existing furniture and molding. In this demonstration, I adjusted the trunk's colors to tones appropriate for a cherry-colored crib.

BRUSHES

no. 8 flat
no. 12 flat
3-inch (76mm) chip brush

ADDITIONAL SUPPLIES

no. 2 pencil
white cotton rag

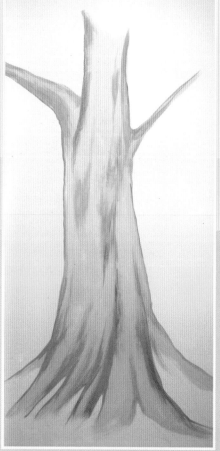

soft realistic tree

1 **Paint the Tree Trunk.** Use a no. 2 pencil to lightly sketch the design onto your surface. Then use a 3-inch (76mm) chip brush to basecoat the trunk with light tan, stroking vertically. Allow the wall color to show and let the strokes remain visible. These vertical brushstrokes help define the linear appearance of the trunk. With a no. 12 flat, add some reddish brown to the trunk, still letting the brushstrokes show. Use the darker color to help hide the pencil marks.

When you have a lot of pigment on your brush, define the darkest areas of the trunk. When you have less paint on the brush, define the soft ridges and lines. Make loose strokes, varying the length and width. You can create the look of even more texture by using short, horizontal strokes or by scrubbing with the bristles as the paint leaves the brush.

Light Tan   Reddish Brown   Green-Brown   Dark Sage   Sage Green   Olive Green   Dark Umber

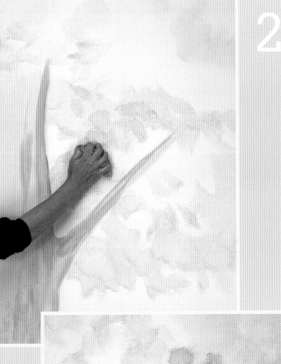

2 Add the Foliage.

Add the Foliage. Using a moist rag and diluted green-brown, create a basecoat for the foliage. As you paint, step back and look at the tree from a distance to make sure it's shaping up as you want. You can't tell whether you're creating believable foliage clusters if you stand too close. Rub the green-brown around but make sure the edges of your rag create a leaf-clump shape. Add a second layer of the same color. This helps further shape and define the leaves. This technique is similar to the faux painting method of ragging.

3 Create Dimension.

Create Dimension. Create leaf clusters of various sizes and shapes. Using your no. 12 flat, scumble dark sage, sage green and olive green, repeatedly going from one color to another. Keep a rag on hand to rub back so the paint won't get too heavy. You'll begin to see high-lights and shadowy depth in each cluster. Step back often to get a good look at the overall appearance. Strive to keep the effect light and soft. It's okay to keep some areas untouched.

4 Define the Tree Trunk.

Define the Tree Trunk. Use a no. 8 flat and dark umber to define the tree trunk a bit more, but keep a bal-ance in weight between the foliage and the tree trunk. If needed, add more olive green into the leaves.

Palm trees have unique characteristics, so unless you live in an area where they're found, I encourage you to use a lot of photos to better depict the way the palms grow, the direction they fall from the branches and the effect of the light source upon them.

BRUSHES

no. 8 round
no. 8 flat
no. 12 flat
2-inch (51mm) acrylic

ADDITIONAL SUPPLIES

no. 2 pencil
white cotton rag

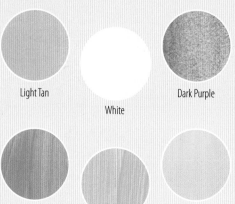

Light Tan

White

Dark Purple

Medium Yellow-Green

Sage Green

Light Yellow-Green

palm tree

✳ **more texture**

Add more texture to the trunk by loading a dry 2-inch (51mm) flat with white and pouncing the bristles here and there.

1

Basecoat Trunk and Add Markings.
Using a no. 2 pencil, lightly sketch in the tree trunk. Then load a 2-inch (51mm) brush with light tan to basecoat the trunk with vertical brushstrokes.

A palm has many horizontal markings and irregularities in the bark. Mix light tan with a little white and, with the flat bristles of a no. 12 flat, pull the paint across the trunk, creating wide markings. Make some thinner markings by pulling the paint across with the chisel edge of the bristles.

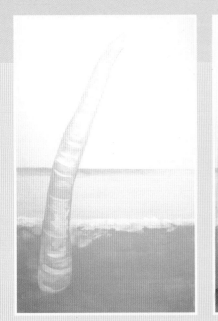

3 **Create Texture.** Using a no. 8 flat, define the trunk edges and bark irregularities and grooves. Start by applying a ½-inch (13mm) line of dark purple to the trunk edge. While this is still wet, quickly pull the paint toward the center, following the roundness of the trunk. Vary the amount of paint pulled in as you work up and down the trunk. The top of the trunk will go into the foliage so you don't have to worry too much about that area. Wipe off overly dark areas with a moist rag.

Use a 2-inch (51mm) brush and dark purple to create a shadow on the sand opposite of the light source.

2 **Add White Ridges.** Still using the no. 12 flat, add white ridges to the tree bark, working into the still-wet tan. Keep in mind the roundness of the trunk as you paint, and make irregular marks .

4 **Begin Painting the Leaves.** Mix medium yellow-green with dark purple. Then, switching between your no. 8 round and no. 8 flat, use long, loose strokes to paint the leaves, keeping in mind the direction they fall.

5 **Add the Darker Leaves.** Still using the no. 8 flat and no. 8 round brushes, add dark purple leaves (the color doesn't look as purple when it overlaps the green).

6

Add the Light Leaves. Using the same brushes and long, loose brush-strokes, add some light leaves using sage green. Add some even-lighter leaves with light yellow-green, placing them where the sun or light source would be hitting the strongest.

apple tree

For this room I changed the style or tone of a realistic apple tree by enhancing the color and creating an outline. Here, instead of striving for realism, strive for "happiness"!

Bright Tan

Burnt Orange

Apple Green

Raspberry Red

HOME OF THE MCDONOUGH FAMILY

BRUSHES

no. 2 round
no. 8 flat
no. 12 flat
1-inch (25mm) chip brush

ADDITIONAL SUPPLIES

no. 2 pencil
white cotton rag

2 Paint the Apples. Use a no. 8 flat to apply raspberry red to the apples. Add pure pink to each apple center to make them appear more rounded. Keep the strokes loose and fun.

1 Begin the Trunk and Foliage. Use a no. 2 pencil to lightly sketch in the tree. Then use a 1-inch (25mm) chip brush to basecoat the trunk with bright tan. Define the edges with burnt orange and a no. 8 flat. Using a moist rag in circular motions, apply an apple green basecoat for the leaves. This tree is bright and colorful. The foliage can be more intense than it would be in reality because it's in a fictional setting.

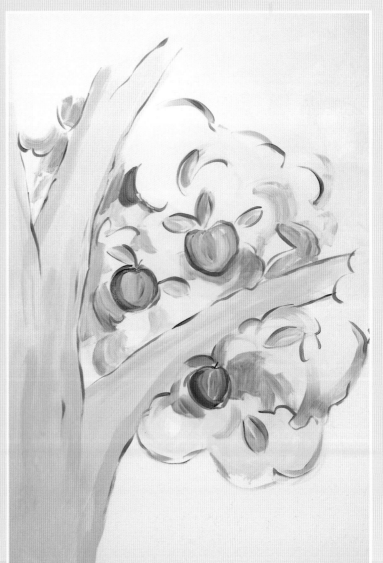

Pure Pink

Medium Green

Black-Green

3 Finish the Foliage and Outline. Using your no. 12 flat and medium green, add some leaves with loose strokes. This helps create depth and define the roundness of the foliage. Then outline with black-green and a no. 2 round. Keep the whimsy by making the lines loose and fun.

(LEFT) HOME OF JIM, WHITNEY, ALEXANDRA & SARA BISSANTZ; (RIGHT) HOME OF LUANNE, KENNY & LEAH KINMAN

4

animal friends

Customizing animals to the request of
a child or new mother is my favorite thing
to do in a child's room. Children played
an active part in the creative process for
many murals in this chapter, from one girl's
white kitty to the caricatures of a family's
playful dog and cat. When you can identify
and personalize the elements in a room
especially for a client or child, you create
something they'll treasure for years to come.

rabbit

Brown

Dark Umber

Reddish Brown

Light Tan

White

Black

I chunked up this rabbit a little to please my client. One of my main goals for this little guy was to capture the look of soft fur. To achieve this, work wet-on-wet without changing or cleaning your brushes between colors.

BRUSHES

no. 2 round
no. 8 flat
no.12 flat

ADDITIONAL SUPPLIES

no. 2 pencil
white cotton rag

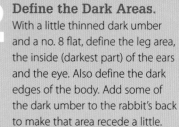

1 **Basecoat the Rabbit.** Use your no. 2 pencil to lightly sketch the design onto your surface. Basecoat the rabbit with a no. 12 flat and brown. Keep the strokes circular and soft, and wipe out the hind leg muscle, chest and cheek with a moist rag.

2 **Define the Dark Areas.** With a little thinned dark umber and a no. 8 flat, define the leg area, the inside (darkest part) of the ears and the eye. Also define the dark edges of the body. Add some of the dark umber to the rabbit's back to make that area recede a little.

Warm Orange

Medium
Yellow-Green

Light Yellow-Green

3 Unify the Shape. Using the no. 12 flat, unify the shape by scrubbing in thinned reddish brown with a circular motion. This will cover any wall color that is showing, but be careful not to make it too dark. With a no. 8 flat and light tan, add dimension to the rounded body areas by brushing on, then wiping and blending. With a no. 12 flat and reddish brown, make soft, little fur marks here and there. Use reddish brown on the corner of your no. 12 flat to define the edge of the ear, around the nose, the cheek and the round area below the nose.

4 Round Out the Shape. To round out the body shapes further, touch in some white with a no. 8 flat, rubbing back to soften. With the same brush, apply white to the front leg (to help bring it forward) and to the top of the head, the shoulder area and a bit on the ears. Once the rabbit begins to appear more rounded, switch to a no. 2 round and add a few individual hairs here and there. Using the same brush, define the eyes with white above the eye and around the rim of the nose. Also add white to the front of the chest and the top of the paws.

5 Begin to Define.
Use dark umber and a no. 2 round to define edges and add little hairs here and there.
Also define the eye a little more, as well as the nose area and the area between the legs. Step back and look at your mural to see if you need to add middle tones (brown, reddish brown and thinned dark umber) to reestablish the roundness of the body. Add a touch of black to the dark umber and further define the eye, the inside of the ear and the area between the legs. Use white to add a tiny curved highlight right above the eye and to touch in a few more hairs.

6 Finishing Touches. Once everything is dry, warm up the body with a very light wash of warm orange, using a no. 12 flat. (Don't worry if it looks rather intense when first applied.) Use a no. 8 flat with medium yellow-green and light yellow-green to add grass around the rabbit. Touch in a bit of thinned light yellow-green here and there on the rabbit's body to tie him in with the setting.

white cat

| White | Green-Brown | Blue | Pure Pink |

My goal for painting this little ball of white fur was to bring out the softness and fluffiness. To this end, the background became an important factor. Tucking the cat away in a darker field of wildflowers enhanced his shape and fluffy, white fur.

BRUSHES

no. 2 round
no. 8 flat
no. 12 flat

ADDITIONAL SUPPLIES

no. 2 pencil
white cotton rag

1 Sketch and Basecoat.

Lightly sketch the cat onto your surface with a no. 2 pencil. Begin with a white basecoat, applied with a no. 12 flat. Wash in a green-brown background. Paint in the eyes with a thin blue wash, using the edge of a no. 8 flat.

HOME OF THE THORNELL FAMILY

Dark Purple

Medium Yellow-Green

2 **Begin to Define.** Using a no. 12 flat, add another coat of white (the pencil lines will still show at this point). Continuing with white, define the muzzle and the chin a little more. Using a no. 2 round, add a touch of pure pink around the eyes, in the ears, and around the muzzle and nose. At this point, you might want to indicate flowers by touching a little of the pure pink into the background grass area.

3 **Shade and Define.** With this cat you are working with a small value range to keep the effects soft and subtle. Define the roundness with a wash of dark purple. Shape up the eyes by touching in a very thin, very subtle dark purple with a no. 2 round. Also add a tiny bit in the ears and a little around the head. Using a no. 8 flat, alternate dark purple with white, painting wet-on-wet to shape the body, limbs and head. To better define the cat's shape, darken the background with another layer of green-brown applied with a no. 12 flat. Paint this right against the cat's body and then rub it out a little with a moist rag. You can eliminate pencil lines now, if necessary. Lay in grass with a no. 8 flat and medium yellow-green. Add a thin layer of that color on all parts of the cat. Then rub it out.

4 **Add the Final Details.** Using a no. 8 flat, add a little more dark purple to define the legs or to slightly darken the edges of the body, head and muzzle. This makes them appear rounder and helps them recede. With the same brush, go back in with white to highlight and add fur. Think fluffy! Brush on the paint in the direction of the hair growth. Stand back and make sure the contrast is right—enough to define the cat while keeping the effect soft. If you want to add a collar, consider how the fur would come over it in places. Using your no. 2 round, very lightly paint the eye irises with dark purple circles. Then touch in a white highlight. Stroke in a few final foreground grasses, using medium yellow-green on a no. 8 flat.

bluebird

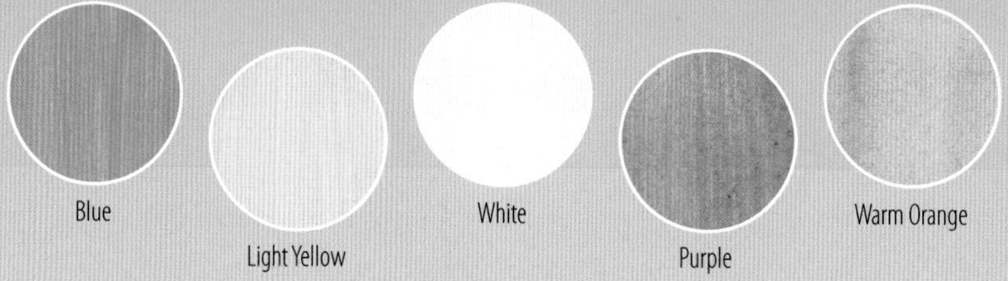

Blue
Light Yellow
White
Purple
Warm Orange

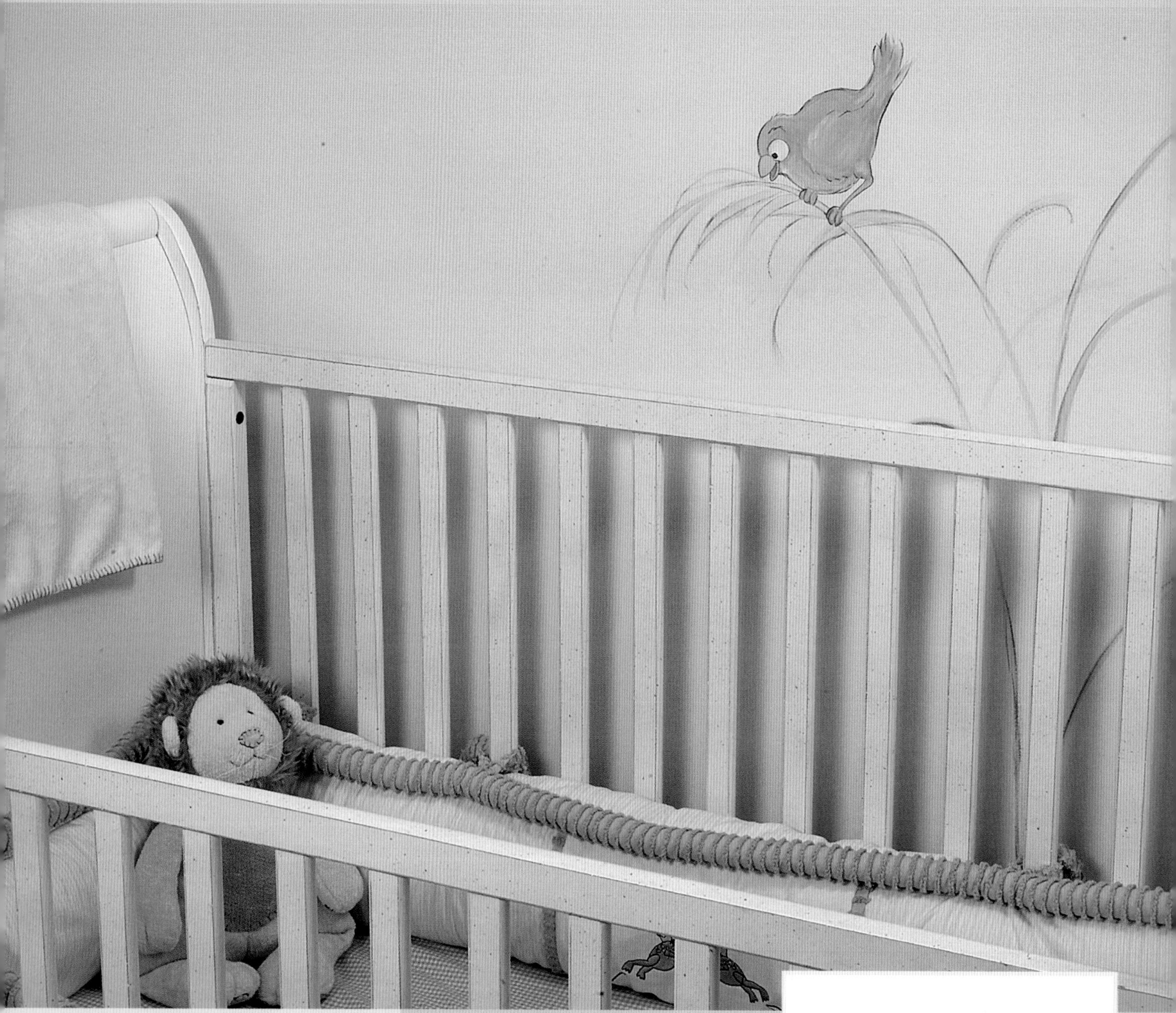

I designed this sweet, little bluebird to peek over a little one's crib. He's ideal for welcoming baby and for introducing little ones to an imaginative world created with paint. You'll be surprised how easy this bird is to paint.

HOME OF KORY & GRETCHEN LYONS

1 **Basecoat the Bird.** Use a no. 2 pencil to lightly sketch the shape of the bird onto your surface. With a no. 8 flat, define the bird's body shape and feathers with a blue basecoat (you don't need much). Using a no. 2 round, paint the beak and legs light yellow and the eyes white.

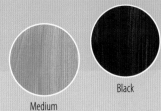

Medium
Yellow-Green

Black

BRUSHES

no. 2 round
no. 8 flat

ADDITIONAL SUPPLIES

no. 2 pencil

3

Add White.
While the blue is still wet, use your no. 8 flat to wash in thinned white on the wing, eyes and tail feathers. Then add highlights here and there on the body.

2

Fill in the Body. Fill in the rest of the body with thin blue on a no. 8 flat.

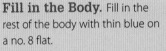

5

Outline and Highlight. Use a no. 2 round to wash the beak and legs with warm orange. Paint the branches with a no. 8 flat and medium yellow-green. Thin the green and add some tall grasses. Use a no. 2 round to add thinned black outlining and white highlighting. Wipe off any remaining pencil lines.

4

Add Color and Shading. Use a very thin wash of purple on the same brush to create a shadow along the edges. Go back in with blue if the paint underneath lifts. Just work back and forth until you achieve the color and shading you like.

cat & dog

Painting a nice portrait of your pet is pleasant—but you'll have a blast painting a caricature of your favorite canine or feline buddy that captures the total essence of its personality! I used a reference photo for the dog, but only loosely tried to reproduce the likeness. Keep your brushstrokes fun and lively so you won't loose the gesture of your frolicking friends!

BRUSHES

no. 2 round
no. 8 flat
no. 12 flat

ADDITIONAL SUPPLIES

no. 2 pencil

1 **Basecoat the Cat.** Lightly sketch in the pouncing gesture of a cat, using a no. 2 pencil. With a no. 12 flat, basecoat the body with black. Use a no. 8 flat and pure yellow to basecoat the ant, painting with a circular motion. Then paint the bow pure pink.

2 **Final Details.** Use your no. 8 flat to swipe a little red onto the edges of the bow and ribbon. With a no. 12 flat and black, reinforce the roundness of the cat's body and the pouncing gesture of its limbs. Use a no. 8 flat to add a little white on the paws and legs. Use a no. 2 round to add the red stripes on the ant. Finally, using a no. 2 round with black, loosely outline the ears, eyes, bow and ant.

Black Pure Yellow Pure Pink Red White Brown-Gold

1 Basecoat the Dog.

Lightly sketch the dog and Frisbee with a no. 2 pencil. In this view, the Frisbee is not a circle, but an ellipse. Use your no. 8 flat like a pencil to outline the dog with thin black, staying loose and gestural. You don't have to stick to the pencil lines! Loosely fill in the dog's head, back and legs with a no. 12 flat. Think in terms of drawing with paint rather than laying in thick layers. Let the wall color come through.

✳ Do Jumping Jacks!

Don't stress about anatomy! Just try to capture the fun of playing Frisbee with a dog. If you have to, stop painting and do jumping jacks to loosen up!

2 Add More Detail.
Loosely sketch in the brown fur with a no. 12 flat and a wash of brown-gold. Do the same with white for the white fur. Be loose in gesture, but commit once you have the anatomy correct. Use the same brush and red to paint the Frisbee and the collar.

3 Define and Keep it Fun.
Define the eye with a thicker black, a no. 2 round and two quick lines. Outline the darkest area around the face, the nose and the mouth. Define the collar with a quick line. Use a thicker line to define the Frisbee's inside edge. If needed, add definition to the dog's hindquarters and feet.

more ideas

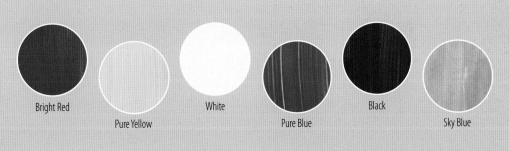

bright fish

A bright and colorful fish appeals to kids of all ages. What's especially great, though, is finding that special bit of whimsy that appeals to the personality of your child.

Bright Red

Pure Yellow

White

Pure Blue

Black

Sky Blue

BRUSHES

no. 2 round
no. 8 round
no. 8 flat
no. 12 flat

ADDITIONAL SUPPLIES

no. 2 pencil

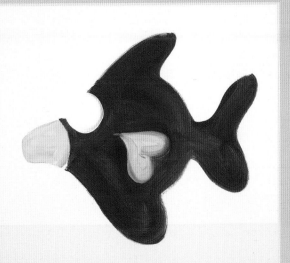

1 **Basecoat the Fish.** Use a no. 2 pencil to lightly sketch in the shape of the fish, marking off the eyes and snout. With a no. 12 flat, basecoat the fish with bright red and pure yellow as shown. Basecoat the eyes with a no. 8 flat and white.

(ABOVE) HOME OF TARI SASSER
FOR HER SON CONRAD

2 **Add More White.** After the paint dries, use a no. 8 flat to paint two white stripes around the body of the fish. These serve as a basecoat for the blue stripes, which wouldn't show if painted directly on the red. Also add a coat of white to the eyes.

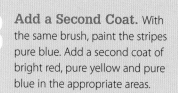

3 **Add a Second Coat.** With the same brush, paint the stripes pure blue. Add a second coat of bright red, pure yellow and pure blue in the appropriate areas.

4 **Highlight and Add Details.** Use a no. 2 round and a little pure yellow to highlight the red fins. Use a no. 8 round with bright red to highlight the yellow areas. Use a no. 8 flat to highlight the blue stripes with white. With a no. 2 round and black, add expressive eyebrows and a pupil. Paint bubbles and ripples around the fish with a no. 2 round and a wash of sky blue.

HOME OF TARI SASSER FOR HER SON CONRAD

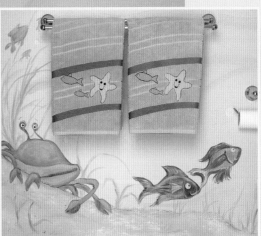

HOME OF THE
COLLINS FAMILY

5

action kids

Kids' activities and interests are many and ever-changing, making it difficult to pick just one theme for their bedrooms. In this chapter you'll find several general themes appropriate for an active child's room. You can change the colors or adapt the content to your liking. If you begin with a more general theme, you can later either widen or narrow the thematic scope as your child's interests develop or change.

puffy cloud

White

Dark Purple

Sky Blue

Puffy clouds are always popular and can be used as an interesting background for many themes, including the biplane in the following demonstration. This cloud, though simple, is very realistic and looks great in any type of room. Try it! You'll love how easy it is to paint!

BRUSHES

4-inch (102mm) chip brush

ADDITIONAL SUPPLIES

Sea sponge
White cotton rag

1 Create the Cloud Shape. Begin the cloud formation by applying white in a circular motion with a 4-inch (102mm) brush. There's no need to sketch first.

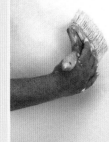

2 Add Shadows. Let the white paint dry thoroughly. Then add shadows to the cloud's underside with a damp rag and a wash of dark purple. Apply the color in a circular motion, defining the shape.

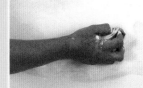

3 Add More Dimension. Before the dark purple completely dries, use another damp rag to blend and add in a wash of sky blue, still using the circular motion. This adds dimension, making the cloud look realistic.

4 **Adjust and Soften.** Using a 4-inch (102mm) brush and white, soften the edges by dabbing and wiping. Think about where the puffiest part of the cloud would be. If you don't like some of the brushstrokes that are showing, dab over them. Immerse a sea sponge in white and dab on a little more texture and dimension. Adjust and soften until you like the cloud shape.

biplane

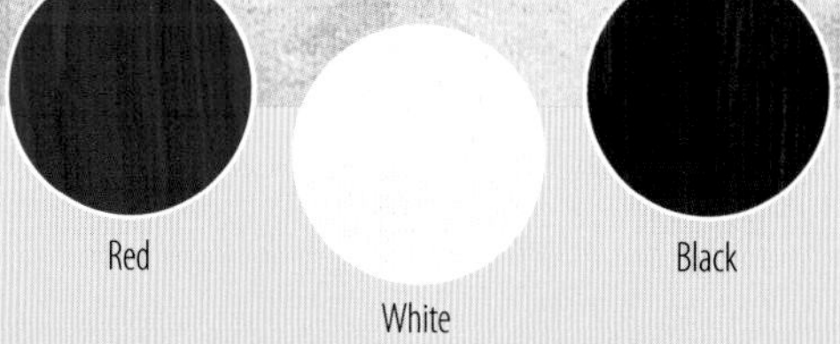

Red

White

Black

When executing a mechanical element such as an airplane, the eye needs to see total symmetry and clean edges, or your painting will look amateurish. For this biplane, first determine the center point. Measure to the left and the right for the wings and above and below for the plane's height. Make a center axis line.

BRUSHES

no. 2 round
no. 8 flat
no. 12 flat
2-inch (51mm) chip brush

ADDITIONAL SUPPLIES

measuring tape
no. 2 pencil
blue painter's tape
sea sponge (optional)

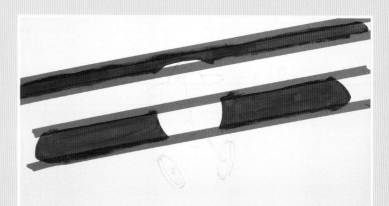

Paint the Wings. With a no. 2 pencil, lightly sketch the airplane onto your surface (see demo introduction). Tape off around the wing area with blue painter's tape. Paint the wings with red and a no. 12 flat. Allow to dry.

2 **Add More Red.** Add a second coat of red to the wings. Then remove the tape and paint the curved parts of the plane, using red and a no. 8 flat. Using a no. 2 round with red, add the vertical lines that attach the wings to each other (you may want to tape these as well if you feel uncertain about painting a straight line).

3 **Begin to Define.** Paint the white "starburst" propeller area using a no. 8 flat and white. Load the brush with black and paint the window, tires and inner nose area. Thin the black and add the shadow on the left side of the plane body. Use the same color and a no. 2 round to outline the front rims of the wings. Then add the crossed wires between the wings. Use white on the no. 2 round to highlight areas on which the sun would shine, such as wing edges, window, tires and nose, including the rounded trim. Clean up rough edges with wall color paint.

4 **Cloud and Final Touches.** See "Puffy Cloud" on pages 82–83 for directions for painting the cloud. Then using a 2-inch (51mm) chip brush and a little white, drybrush a light circle around the biplane body to suggest a propeller in motion. Begin the circle within the cloud area and work the motion lines outward from there. You may want to use a natural sea sponge to soften the edge or to hide blemishes.

✳ **the nature of red**

To achieve a saturated or opaque red, you must apply more than one coat.

soccer ball

When painting something round, such as a soccer ball, make sure you're painting on the same level as the ball—even if it's low—otherwise, the ball could look misshapen. If you're not comfortable freehanding, you can use a compass or trace a round object.

BRUSHES

no. 2 round
no. 8 flat
no. 12 flat

ADDITIONAL SUPPLIES

no. 2 pencil
compass or round object
   (optional—see demo
   introduction)
white cotton rag

✳ a simple fix

If you paint the ball too large, remember this simple fix: Wipe back into the shape and add a darker background of sky and grass.

White

Sky Blue

Navy

Blue-Black

Green-Brown

Medium
Yellow-Green

1 **Basecoat the Ball.** Use a no. 2 pencil to lightly sketch the ball onto your surface (see demo introduction). Basecoat the ball with white, using a no. 8 flat to outline and a no. 12 flat to fill in. With a damp rag, wipe in a wash of sky blue for the sky.

2 **Add the Shapes.** Add a second coat of white and let dry. Then use your pencil to lightly draw in the pentagonal (five-sided) shapes. Find a real soccer ball or a picture of one to help you with placement. Begin the first pentagon in the upper center of the ball. Before painting, you might want to dot the corners with a pencil. The pentagons on this ball are navy because of the colors in the room, but you can paint them black if you prefer. Each white shape that surrounds the navy shape has six sides. Block these in by painting lines straight out from each pentagon point with a no. 2 round and blue-black.

3 **Add Background.** To better define the outside edge of the ball, mix a little of the blue-black with sky blue and swipe around the ball with a damp rag. Rag in the grassy area using a green-brown wash, stroking upward to indicate grass.

4 **Finishing Touches.** When adding the shadows, keep your light source in mind and work quickly to avoid stroke marks. Using a no. 12 flat with very thin navy and a little blue-black, follow the whole circle, making the shadow wider at the bottom. Use a bit of the same wash on a no. 2 round to outline the whole ball very, very lightly. Rub out visible pencil lines. Using a no. 8 flat and white, go back in to brighten the white areas where the light would be hitting strongest. Also clean up the edges. Use a no. 8 flat and medium yellow-green to add grass.

ball, bat & glove

Green-Brown

Navy

Gray

Brown-Gold

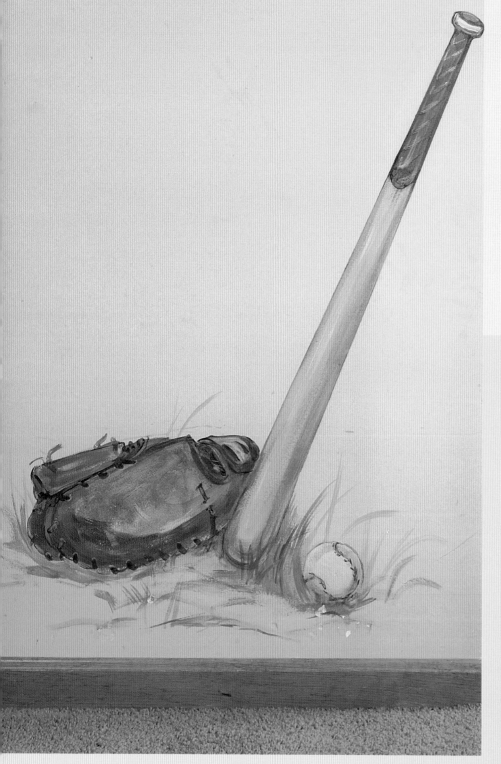

HOME OF PAUL, AMY, LOGAN AND BRADY LUCK

The glove in this mural was based on a wonderful old glove that belonged to my client's father. You can pack sentimentality into your work by depicting objects meaningful to you.

BRUSHES

no. 2 round
no. 8 flat
no. 12 flat

ADDITIONAL SUPPLIES

no. 2 pencil
blue painter's tape
white cotton rag

1 **Basecoat Loosely.** Use a no. 2 pencil to lightly sketch the bat, ball and glove. Block in the grassy area with green-brown and a damp rag. Mask off the bat with blue painter's tape on either side and around the handle. Using a no.12 flat, basecoat the bat grip with navy, the wood with gray, the glove with thin brown-gold and the ball with white.

White

Pure Blue

Black

Reddish Brown

Dark Umber

Pure Yellow

Bright Red

Medium Yellow-Green

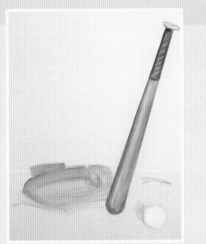

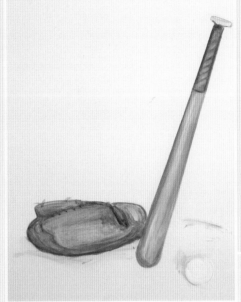

2 Paint the Bat.
Still using a no. 12 flat, add a second coat of gray to the bat. Then, working wet-into-wet, add a white highlight with a no. 8 flat. With the same brush, add a second coat of navy to the handle. Make the handle appear more rounded by painting pure blue down the center with a no. 2 round. While the blue is still wet, use a no. 8 flat to add white highlights, placing them at an angle to simulate a taped handle. Add thinned black to deepen the sides of the bat, working back and forth and keeping the paint as wet as possible for blending and smoothing. Let dry and remove the the tape.

3 Paint the Glove and Ball.
Give the ball another layer of white with a no. 8 flat. While wet, define the ball edges and stitching line with a bit of gray. Use a no. 12 flat to wash the glove with reddish brown. Define the glove edges, finger pockets and underside with a no. 8 flat and thinned dark umber. Using a no. 2 round and thinned black, lightly define the edges and stitching. This will take on a brown-black cast from the surrounding paint.

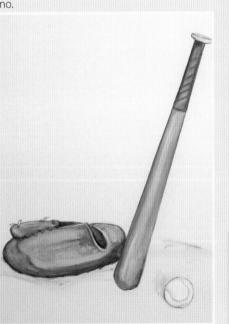

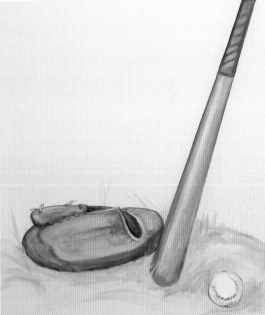

4 Highlight and Define.
While the glove is still wet, use a no. 12 flat and a wash of pure yellow to highlight the most rounded areas of the finger pockets. Use a no. 2 round with a mixture of dark umber and black to outline the dark pocket and around any other areas that need more definition. Use thinned black and a no. 2 round to outline the bat and define the roundness at the end of the bat handle and on the tape. Keep a fluid line all the way down each side of the bat. Also define the edge of the ball and the stitching.

5 Final Touches.
Paint the ball's stitches with the no. 2 round and bright red. Then go back in with white and highlight the ball wherever it needs definition. Add grass with a damp rag and medium yellow-green. With a no. 8 flat, take that color right up to each item and add some blades of grass.

more ideas

HOME OF PAUL, AMY, LOGAN & BRADY LUCK

6

storybook land

Okay, I admit I'm a sucker for the princess theme, even though (or maybe because) it has no basis in reality! With this mural I had an opportunity to pull out all the stops on feminine charm and frill—the hair, the dress, the shoes, the jewelry, even the landscape—all with plenty of pink and purple. You can personalize any of these items for the lucky princess who receives your painting!

castle & road

Sky Blue

Green-Brown

Dark Purple

Layering and working background to foreground is the best way to create the depth you need for this landscape composition. Remember to build cohesiveness by incorporating room colors into the mural.

BRUSHES

no. 2 round
no. 8 flat
2-inch (51mm) chip brush

ADDITIONAL SUPPLIES

white cotton rag
no. 2 pencil

1 Basecoat the Background. Throughout this step, think in terms of light washes and keep the edges soft. Use sky blue and a damp rag to wash in the sky. Still using a damp rag, basecoat the landscape with thinned green-brown and the mountains with dark purple. Use your finger to give the mountains smooth tops. Let these colors dry, and then lightly sketch the castle with a no. 2 pencil, being mindful of where you'll place the road. Use a no. 8 flat and a no. 2 round to basecoat the rooftops with brick red. Use a no. 8 flat to basecoat the castle walls with burnt orange. Keep the castle and mountains fairly light to create the illusion of distance.

2 Begin to Define. Clean up the castle edges by lifting paint with a moist rag or by using a no. 8 flat with a wash of sky blue or white. Straighten rooftops (cover an area with a cloud, if needed). With your no. 8 flat, add green-brown around the castle, creating more horizon line and indicating trees and bushes. Use a 2-inch (51mm) chip brush with olive green to wash in greener areas in front of the castle. Use light tan on a damp rag to rub in the walkway—keep this loose so the wall color shows through. Using your no. 8 flat and brown, add depth in the walkway and define the separate castle walls. With the same brush, add a little white to the light tan and further differentiate the walls. Then lightly drag a little of this color onto the roofs.

Brick Red Burnt-Orange White Olive Green Light Tan Apple Green Black

3 **Add a Dark Purple Wash.** Use a no. 8 flat with a wash of dark purple to add detail to the walls and roof and to create shadows here and there. With the same color and brush, touch in windows—don't get too detailed. Create an over-all cohesive look to the landscape by adding dark purple touches here and there in the foreground, on the mountains and into the background area. Keep this very light; it will dry darker.

4 **Bring in More Color.** Using your no. 8 flat and a wash of white, scrub in clouds around the castle. You can use this to cover messy wash marks. Use a no. 2 round to paint the flags, incorporating colors from the room (this room had a lot of pink and purple in it). With a no. 8 flat add bushes, using mixtures of all the browns and greens used so far. Go back and forth among colors without cleaning the brush, taking advantage of the resulting variations. Add touches of apple green here and there and smudge with your fingers.

5 **Final Touches.** Add a touch of dark purple to thinned black and outline lightly throughout with a no. 2 round. This should be fairly transparent, just enough to define a bit. Add light details to the door and windows. The castle is now ready for its princess!

princess

White

Dark Lavender

Melon Pink

When painting a figure, ask a friend to "strike a pose." You can also use reference photos for the braids, horse, etc. For clothing you can drape fabric and study how the light falls on the folds. This extra effort will pay off with a more realistic painting.

BRUSHES

no. 2 round
no. 8 flat
no. 12 flat

ADDITIONAL SUPPLIES

no. 2 pencil

1 **Sketch and Basecoat.** Use a no. 2 pencil to lightly sketch the princess and horse. With a no. 12 flat, basecoat the horse white, the princess' sleeves and vest dark lavender, the skirt and puffs melon pink, the hair reddish brown, the hands and face fleshtone and the horse's headdress and saddle-cloth blue. Define the vest, sleeves and curve of the skirt with a light wash of dark lavender.

Reddish Brown | Fleshtone | Blue | Brown-Gold | Dark Umber | Purple | Dark Purple | Mustard Brown

2 **Define the Curves.** Paint the princess' crown with a no. 8 flat and brown-gold. Then block in the bridle and chest plate. Define the hair and braid with dark umber. Define the hair flow and arm position with dark lavender (more saturated than color in step 1). Define the fall of the fabric with a wash of purple on a no. 12 flat. Elements in this mural are curved and feminine, so let your strokes flow.

3 **Highlight and Brighten.** Redefine the curves in the dress with a no. 12 flat and melon pink, stroking in the direction of the fabric's flow. Also touch melon pink into the white of the horse. While this color is still wet, define the billowiness of the fabric by working in a little white. Simply drag the brush over different areas to highlight and brighten.

4 **Define.** Load the no. 12 flat with dark lavender to further brighten and define. Add a bit of this color into all areas to keep the mural cohesive. Use a no. 8 flat with dark purple to add depth and shadows where you feel the painting needs more dimension or curve.

5 **Add Final Details.** With a no. 2 round and dark purple, add eyelashes and other details to the princess' face and the horse's eye, mane and plume. Continue defining the braid, using a no. 8 flat with brown-gold and mustard brown. Using the same brush and mustard brown, finish the bridle details. When the bridle dries, drag brown-gold over the top.

Use the no. 8 and no. 12 flats with thinned colors to unify the mural, adding colors from the horse onto the dress and the colors from the dress onto the horse. Touch in any other fine details with a no. 2 round and a wash of purple.

Although I designed this scroll border to frame the "Storybook Land" mural, you can resize it to fit any composition you please. This border has a nice symmetrical and feminine scroll in the corners.

For added interest, you can let your design flow on top of the border or even outside of it. Consider the size of your planned composition and measure for the border first.

BRUSHES

no. 2 round
no. 8 flat
no. 12 flat

ADDITIONAL SUPPLIES

corner stencil (see page 17)
level
measuring tape
no. 2 pencil
blue painter's tape

✳ Border Ideas

- Look in vintage children's books for more border design ideas.

- If you're insecure about free-handing, simply enlarge the design with a copier until it's the size you need.

- To help repeat the scroll shape on all four corners, make a stencil (see page 17).

scroll border

Mustard Brown

Brown-Gold

Light Tan

White

Dark Umber

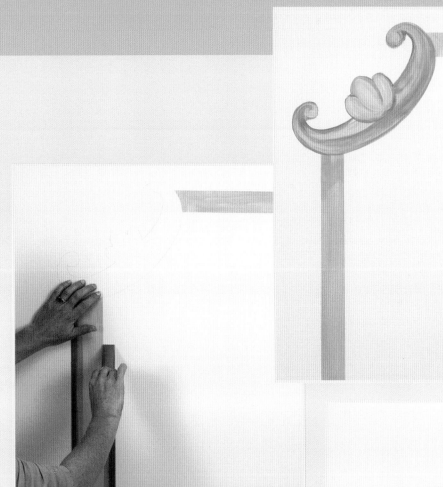

2

Paint the Scrolls. Using the same brush, paint the scrolls mustard brown. While the scrolls are still wet, use a no. 2 round and a darker tone of brown-gold to outline the edges. Keep the paint transparent—you just want to give the design dimension. Use brown-gold on a no. 8 flat to lay in a shadow on the curve. While these colors are still wet, mix light tan with a little white and, with the same brush, add a little highlighting to the scroll curves and center embellishment.

1

Paint the Border. Create a corner stencil as explained on page 17. With the help of a level, measure an area for the border and then use the stencil to lightly trace the corners with a no. 2 pencil. Tape off each side of the border with blue painter's tape. Paint the border with mustard brown using a no. 12 flat (mustard brown will be the medium tone). Remove the tape. If you find bleed-through, use your wall color to touch up.

3

Continue to Define.
Add a touch more white to the previous mixture and further highlight the scroll curves and center embellishment. Use a no. 8 flat to carefully stroke thinned dark umber down the inside and outside edges of the straight sides. Then use the light tan and white mixture to highlight down the center. With a no. 2 round and a touch of dark umber, outline the curled edges of the scroll and the center embellishment. Then lightly outline the straight sides of the border.

flying swan

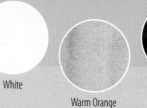

White

Warm Orange

Black

Dark Purple

When you paint a white object, such as this swan, you must consider the wall or background color. You may have to adjust values (range of dark colors to light colors) within the swan to make it stand out more or to bring it forward from its background.

BRUSHES

no. 2 round
no. 8 flat
no. 12 flat

ADDITIONAL SUPPLIES

no. 2 pencil

1 Basecoat the Swan. Using a no. 2 pencil, lightly sketch the swan onto your surface. Then use a no. 12 flat to paint a white basecoat. Pull the strokes on the wing outward in the direction of the feathers.

2 **Add Shadows and Definition.** Paint the beak with a no. 8 flat and warm orange. Sketch in the dark areas around the beak with a no. 2 round and black. Use a dark purple wash and the no. 8 and no. 12 flats to add shadows to the body and tail and to shape the wings.

3 **Blend and Soften.** Using white on a no. 12 flat, subtly define the body. Paint the wings with a no. 8 flat and white, brushing in the direction of feather growth. To achieve a smooth and blended look, while the white is still wet, take the no. 8 flat with white still on it and dip it into dark purple. Then further soften and blend all edges, including the wings and body. Just keep working back and forth while the paint is wet.

4 **Add More Color and Definition.** Add a little more warm orange to the beak with a no. 8 flat. Then thin the orange and drag a little here and there on the body to warm it up. Use a no. 2 round and black to add just a little more outline around the face, eye and beak. Use a no. 2 round with dark purple to lightly define the edges of the feathers just a little more. Load the same brush with white and add a tiny eye highlight. Also add a highlighting stroke to the beak and the feet.

more ideas

(LEFT) HOME OF BROOKE MICHAEL MURPHY; (ABOVE) HOME OF THE THORNELL FAMILY

7

flowers

Whether painting a baby's or a teenager's room, flowers can be a colorful addition to the overall design. They can be depicted in many ways, from childlike and fun to realistic and serene. The personality and colors of the room, as well as your personal style, should help you decide what direction to go.

Everyone has a personal style; don't be afraid to work with yours. You can borrow ideas or get inspiration from other painters, but if you allow your own style to show through, you'll have the satisfaction of a floral design that's uniquely yours!

trellis

For this project, think simple, soft and impressionistic. You can use reference photos to help you with growth direction and overall shape, but don't get bogged down in details. Consider the way flowers look from a distance; you don't see all the details, but they're still beautiful. Whenever you're painting a mural, you must think about the overall effect—how it looks from a distance as part of the design in the room.

BRUSHES

no. 2 round
no. 8 round
no. 8 flat or filbert
no. 12 flat

ADDITIONAL SUPPLIES

blue painter's tape
no. 2 pencil
white cotton rag

✳ a brush option

When painting the curves of the trellis, you may want to try a filbert brush instead of a flat. The bristles on a filbert are curved, which I find makes painting curves easier.

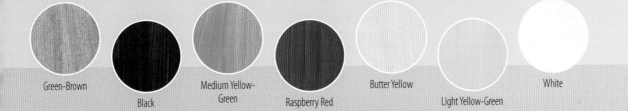

Green-Brown	Black	Medium Yellow-Green	Raspberry Red	Butter Yellow	Light Yellow-Green	White

1 **Pencil in the Scroll, Paint the Background.** Use blue painter's tape to tape off the area you want to protect. Then use a no. 2 pencil to lightly sketch the curves of the trellis. It's important to get the shape the way that you want it. Use a damp rag to wash in the background foliage with green-brown. Imagine the overall shape of a clinging clematis as it flows around the arched window (or other area you're painting). Paint the scroll with a no. 8 flat or filbert and a very fluid wash of black. Also paint the bottom posts of the gate.

2 **Begin to Layer.** Still using the no. 8 flat and black, add the wrought iron leaf shapes to the curves. Using a no. 12 flat and green-brown, paint leaves randomly over the green background. Also touch in some soft leaves with the same color on the edge of a damp rag. Turn the rag as you touch to simulate multidirectional leaf shapes. Don't layer too fast, and keep it subtle. Allow the wall color to show through.

At this point, define and fix black scroll areas that need work. Step back and look at the leaves; the transparent washes give them dimension. Make adjustments, darkening or wiping back. Don't overwork this; keep it light and airy.

Using your rag, add some medium yellow-green into the background. This should be a little thicker than the green-brown wash. The thickness of the paint and lightness of the value add brightness and dimension, bringing the color to the foreground.

 correct the shapes

If you want the curves to work, you have to keep the paint really wet and fluid. If the shapes aren't correct, go back into the curves with your rag and buff the shapes out—at this stage you can still fix things.

3 **Paint the Flowers.** Using a no. 8 round and raspberry red, paint the flowers. If you have reference photos, check them for the growth direction and the overall shapes of the flowers and their clusters. Remember to paint buds, creating interesting areas throughout the trellis. Use butter yellow and a no. 2 round to dab in soft yellow centers.

4 **Break up the Background.** Use a no. 12 flat to touch in light yellow-green to brighten up areas here and there. This color is a little more opaque, so you can cover up imperfect areas on the scroll. Vary the shapes but keep the effect light and airy. You can also use this color to break up any background areas that are too dark. Use the unwashed brush to touch in more leaves with green-brown.

5 **Add Dimension and Unify.** Add more dimension to the flower petals, using a no. 8 round brush and a little thicker mixture of raspberry red. Go back in with medium yellow-green and add a few leaves right around each flower. You can also drag a bit of this green wherever you think the design needs more dimension or unification of shapes.

6 Final Details. Using a no. 2 round and green-brown, outline and define some leaf clusters. Keep this light—very loose and minimal. You may even need to go back and soften some of these outlines with your finger or a rag. You can also define the spaces between leaves and around the yellow flower centers. Add just a few tiny dots on the open flower centers. With the same brush, also dot white into the centers and add a light butter yellow highlight to the scroll. Keep it soft by smoothing with your finger or a rag.

ribbon & bow

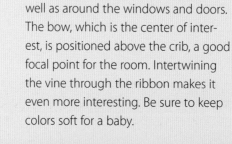

White

Green-Brown

Dark Purple

Raspberry Red

Melon Pink

BRUSHES

no. 2 round
no. 8 flat
no. 12 flat

ADDITIONAL SUPPLIES

no. 2 pencil
white cotton rag

The drama of this ribbon is in the fact that it encompasses the whole room from ceiling to floor molding, as well as around the windows and doors. The bow, which is the center of interest, is positioned above the crib, a good focal point for the room. Intertwining the vine through the ribbon makes it even more interesting. Be sure to keep colors soft for a baby.

✳ study a bow

You might find it helpful to tie a bow so you can see how the creases look and the ribbon flows.

2 Add Dimension. Use a no. 8 flat and a dark purple wash to add dimension to the bow. Keep the paint wet and work quickly with your rag ready to wipe off runs. Make this soft and light. If you ever feel the color is becoming too dark, go back in with white to brighten it back up. Alternate between the dark purple and white.

1 Sketch the Bow and Vine. Using a no. 2 pencil, lightly sketch the bow onto the surface. Using a no. 12 flat, paint the bow with white. Sketch in the vine with a no. 2 round and green-brown.

3 Paint the Flower Buds. Dab flower buds onto the vine with raspberry red on a no. 2 round and your fingertips. Keep this light, and vary the spacing between the buds. Because the red is so transparent, you'll get a whole range of values just by dabbing. With the same brush and color, create a decorative red edge on the ribbon, varying the intensity of the red pigment. Cover any pencil lines in the process.

4 Add Flower Centers. With your fingertips, dab dots of white and melon pink here and there throughout the buds. Use a no. 2 round to add tiny dots into the flower centers.

This flower border is simple and fun, and you can adjust the colors to match your own décor. This border should be lively—stay loose and keep the gesture!

This border can also be teamed up with a striped design such as the one shown on page 122.

BRUSHES

no. 2 round
no. 8 round
no. 8 flat

ADDITIONAL SUPPLIES

tape measure
4-inch (102mm) roller
no. 2 pencil

wavy flower border

White

Raspberry Red

1 Paint a Wavy Border. Measure 4 inches (10cm) and 10 inches (25cm) from the ceiling, making light marks with a no. 2 pencil every couple of feet. This provides upper and lower boundaries for your wavy border. Over a pink wall color, use a 4-inch (102mm) roller to roll an opaque white hill-and-valley wave around all four walls.

Use raspberry red and a no. 8 flat to paint simple, straight flower petals. Keep them fun—they don't have to be perfect. Use melon pink and a no. 8 round to paint swirls. Use a no. 8 flat and bright celery to paint leaves. Use blue and a no. 2 round to add dots.

HOME OF THE BINFORD FAMILY

Melon Pink

Bright Celery

Blue

Butter Yellow

Bright Yellow-Green

Purple

2 **Add Flowers Centers and Outline.** Paint the butter yellow flower centers, using a no. 2 round. Use the same brush and bright yellow-green to outline the leaves. For more interest, offset the outline rather than following the exact shapes. Also paint little leaf shapes around the swirls and add a little of the same green into the yellow flower centers. Still using a no. 2 round, add some raspberry red lines to the swirls and add purple dots into the center of the blue dots. You don't have to adhere to a strict, repeated pattern or even the same colors. Get crazy! Have fun! Make it yours!

more ideas

HOME OF JIM, WHITNEY, ALEXANDRA & SARA BISSANTZ; BACKGROUND GRID PATTERN PAINTED BY RONALD SCHMIDT

8

easy designs

Following are several fun and simple ideas. These good, basic designs can be manipulated in size and color to match any theme or color scheme. And they're super easy. Even if you're a novice at painting, you can pick up a brush and create a fun room for a favorite little one. You and that special child will be glad you did!

Don't hesitate to add your own twist here—or anywhere else in this book. Everyone is creative. Just trust your instincts and go for it!

Placing the Diamonds

The size of the diamonds for this border was decided by what we could afford—spatially, that is. I determined that a height of 30 inches (76cm) would work well in the area below the chair rail. A width of 18 inches (46cm) fit the length of the wall, allowing room for adjustment if needed.

Once I determined the size, I made a diamond-shaped template. You can easily make such a template using the oval template instructions (see page 17)—just substitute a concave cut for the convex curve. I started with a 22" x 30" (56cm x 76cm) piece of posterboard, marked the desired height and width of my diamond, and then folded the board into quarters. I then cut a concave arch from mark to mark. When I unfolded the posterboard, I had my diamond template.

I lined up the straight, outside edges of the template (as shown in step one) and, before actually tracing the shape onto the wall, I lightly marked the diamonds' widths across the wall, adjusting when necessary.

diamonds

Use your own colors to paint this border for your child. Keep it simple and fun. The "Diamonds" and the "Swirls" (page 121) borders are demonstrated separately in this book, but originally were done as a set. The child asked that her room include a poodle, the color blue and a French café feel. I picked up the swirl design from the bed's backboard and the fabric-covered cornice boards.

Dark French Pink

White

French Pink

Sage Green

Blue

Black

BRUSHES

no. 2 round
no. 8 round
no. 12 flat
2-inch (51mm) chip brush
3-inch (76mm) chip brush

ADDITIONAL SUPPLIES

no. 2 pencil
level
tape measure
diamond template (see "Placing
    the Diamonds," page 118)
4-inch (102mm) roller
white cotton rag

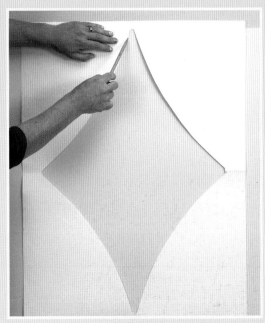

1

Measure, Tape and Trace With the help of a level, use blue painter's tape to mask off the wall at chair rail height. Then measure down about 2 inches (5cm) and tape off again. Use a 2-inch (51mm) chip brush to paint a band of dark French pink. You'll need two coats for fully saturated color. Remove the bottom tape carefully. Once you've established where each diamond should be located (see "Placing the Diamonds," page 118), tape your template to the wall, aligning the top of the diamond with the bottom of the pink band. Then lightly trace the inside of the diamond shape, using a no. 2 pencil. Repeat this along the length of the wall.

2 Underpainting.

Underpaint with white and a 4-inch (102mm) roller. Paint over the pencil marks with the edge made by the roller. Don't clean up the ragged edge—it creates interest (sponge rollers are good for this also).

3 Paint Around the Diamond.

Using a 3-inch (76mm) chip brush and French pink, wash loosely around the diamond shape. This is a dry-brushed effect—the paint shouldn't be too wet. If you need to wipe back with a rag, maintain brushstroke direction. Vary the amount of pigment for interest. This is one time when you want brushstrokes to show and be part of the overall effect.

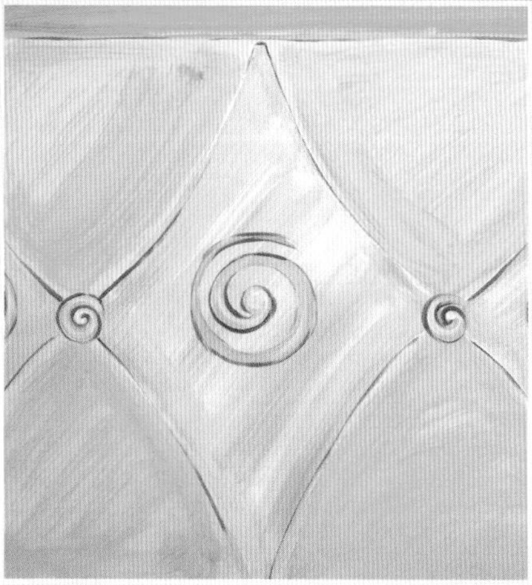

try a french curve

If you are uncomfortable making the curves, you can use a manufactured French curve as a guide.

Paint the Diamond. Using the same brush and technique, wash sage green into the diamond. Paint the swirl with a no. 8 round and a thicker mixture of sage green. Use a no. 12 flat with blue to paint the small swirls between each diamond.

Remove the Tape and Outline. Use a 2-inch (51mm) chip brush to add a wash of French pink across the upper pink band to brighten it up a little. Remove the tape and loosely outline all the elements with a no. 2 round and a thinned fluid mixture of black. Use the same brush to add a touch of white onto the swirls, giving them more dimension.

White

French Pink

Black

swirls

Taping for the Border

This border design has a top and bottom band. When taping a border near or on the ceiling, I recommend using KleenEdge tape. Blue painter's tape is a little stickier and sometimes lifts the ceiling paint. Tape off a 1- or 2-inch (25mm or 51mm) band at the top. After taping, measure for the depth of your border and tape off the bottom with blue painter's tape.

1 **Freehand the Swirls**. Follow directions in "Taping for the Border," (left). Using a no. 12 flat and white, freehand the swirls. Define the outside edge of each swirl a bit with a wash of French pink. Continue to fill in between the swirls, keeping the dry-brush strokes interesting and visible.

2 **Add Interest and Dimension.** Use a no. 12 flat to add a second wash of French pink here and there—it doesn't have to cover the previous wash completely. This adds interest and dimension. In some places use the flat bristles of the brush and in other places turn the bristles and create more linear strokes with the chisel edge of the bristles.

BRUSHES

no. 2 round
no. 12 flat

ADDITIONAL SUPPLIES

tape measure
KleenEdge tape
blue painter's tape

3 **Paint the Stripes.** When the paint is thoroughly dry, remove the tape and retape about 1 inch or 1½ inches (25mm or 38mm) above and below the bands. Use white and a no. 12 flat to paint the stripes. You may want to go back and punch up the white on some of your swirls. With a thin and fluid mixture of black on a no. 2 round, add outlining here and there above and below the border as well as throughout the swirls.

masked stripes

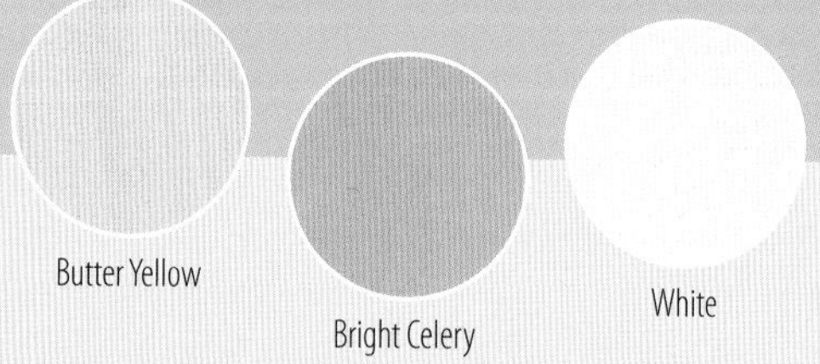

Butter Yellow

Bright Celery

White

I wanted to keep this design funky and fun for two cute and spunky twin girls, so I varied the width and color of the stripes and alternated between straight and loose edges. It's all randomly applied, but I did keep a balance of colors and stripe widths. The twins' mom was concerned about unifying this large room, so the bedding colors—raspberry red, pink and lime green—set the color scheme for the walls. (See pages 112-113 for the "Wavy Flower Border" demonstration.)

HOME OF THE BINFORD FAMILY

BRUSHES

no. 2 round
no. 12 flat
2-inch (51mm) chip brush
4-inch (102mm) chip brush

ADDITIONAL SUPPLIES

no. 2 pencil
level
blue painter's tape
4-inch (102mm) roller
   (can use sponge roller)
9-inch (229mm) roller

1 Choose Colors, Measure and Tape Off.

Measure where your largest stripes will be and mark with a no. 2 pencil every few feet. Use the side walls and window edges to guide the design. Check for straightness with a level.

Tape stripes that will have clean edges and roll on the colors—butter yellow, bright celery and white. For loose stripes use brushes. I used a no. 2 round for blue thin stripes here and there, a no. 12 flat for a melon pink stripe over a butter yellow stripe, a 2-inch (51mm) chip brush for a dry-brushed melon pink stripe and a 4-inch (102mm) chip brush for a dry-brushed raspberry red stripe. Keep the brush-stripe edges rough.

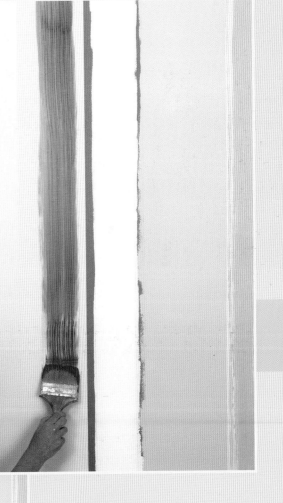

Blue

Melon Pink

Raspberry Red

2 Remove the Tape. Remove the tape carefully, lifting close to the wall.

numbers & letters

"Keep it simple" is my mantra. These quick and easy letters and numbers are a case in point. Capture a childlike simplicity by dropping any fancy serifs. Use primary colors and place the figures askew for a carefree look.

These colors are pure, opaque and bright. The paint should be saturated but thin enough to flow. Having the right paint consistency and stroking intentionally is important. You might find it helpful to practice on a board.

BRUSHES

no. 2 round
no. 12 flat
1¼-inch (32mm) acrylic
brush

ADDITIONAL SUPPLIES

no. 2 pencil

White

Pure Orange

HOME OF HAROLD POORE & LAURA MATIMORE

1 Paint the Letters and Numbers.
Lightly sketch the numbers and letters onto your surface using a no. 2 pencil. Then paint them with a 1¼-inch (32mm) brush and the bright colors listed in the palette.

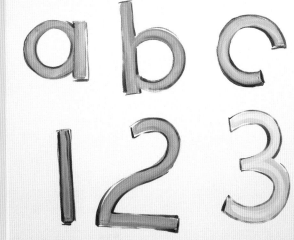

2 Highlight with White.
Using a no. 12 flat, add a little white to each color to slightly subdue and highlight. Just drag the brush over each letter and number quickly for a dry-brush mark.

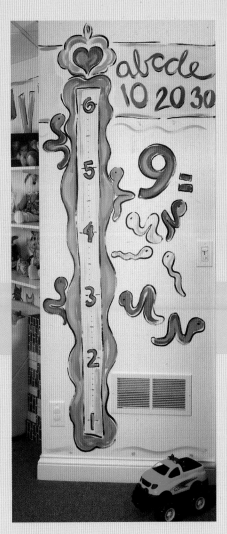

3 Add the Outlining.
Use a no. 2 round and black to loosely outline each letter and number. Keep this loose and fun, varying the line quality. A little dry-brush look just makes this more interesting.

Pure Purple

Pure Blue

Pure Yellow

Medium Green

Bright Red

Black

✳ versatility plus!
Letters and numbers have so many design possibilities! Use them simply in a basic border or as a part a more involved design. You see both applications here.

Cafe Regan

Menu
tea   25¢
cookies 10¢

Ooo lala!

très jolie

HOME OF THE COLLINS FAMILY

index

The best in ho~~me~~ ~~decoration~~ and inspiration is from North Light Books!

Painting Borders for Your Home with Donna Dewberry

Donna shows you how to use her renowned one-stroke method to create colorful borders that give character and style to every room in your home. Coordinating borders accompany each project, so you can make perfect accessories. With photos showing the borders in actual homes, you'll find the inspiration you need to create masterpieces for walls and furniture throughout the house.
ISBN-13: 978-1-58180-600-7, ISBN-10: 1-58180-600-0, paperback, 128 pages, #33125

Painted Illusions: Create Stunning Trompe L'oeil Effects with Stencils

Add incredible beauty and elegance to your home with *Painted Illusions*. Even if you've never painted before, you can achieve professional-quality results with these simple stencil techniques and Melanie Royals' easy-to-follow directions. In 19 step-by-step projects, you'll learn to create beautiful wall finishes that mimic fabrics such as linen, silk and damask as well as trompe l'oeil effects such as leather, porcelain, oak paneling, granite, carved stone, and more.
ISBN-13: 978-1-58180-548-2, ISBN-10: 1-58180-548-9, paperback, 128 pages, #32899

Fantastic Floorcloths You Can Paint in a Day

Want to refresh your home décor without the time and expense of extensive redecorating? Then painting canvas floorcloths is for you! Choose from 23 projects simple enough to create in a few hours. Designs range from florals to graphic patterns to holiday motifs, including some especially appropriate for kids' rooms. 12 accessory ideas inspire you to create a coordinated look. *Fantastic Floorcloths You Can Paint in a Day* makes adding creative touches to the home as easy as picking up a paintbrush.
ISBN-13: 978-1-58180-603-8, ISBN-10: 1-58180-603-5, paperback, 128 pages, #33161

Spectacular Walls! Creative Effects Using Texture, Embellishment and Paint

Create one-of-a kind rooms with wall texture and embellishments. Step by easy step, Jeannine Dostal shows you how to apply 38 unique finishes, featuring fresco-style glazing, sand-enhanced texture, embedded jewels, dimensional roses and much more. Styles range from whimsical to elegant, but one word describes them all--Spectacular!
ISBN-13: 978-1-58180-727-1, ISBN-10: 1-58180-727-9, paperback, 128 pages, #33399

❋ These books and other fine North Light titles are available at your local arts & crafts retailer, bookstore, or from online suppliers.

sixcolorworld

COLOR · CLOTH · QUILTS & WEARABLES

C&T PUBLISHING

Edited by Lee M. Jonsson
Technical information edited by Joyce Engels Lytle
Copyedited by Judith M. Moretz
Front cover design concept by Diane Pedersen
Cover production by John M. Cram and Kathy Lee
Book design by Lesley Gasparetti
Graphic illustrations by Lina Liu
Hand-drawn illustrations by Yvonne Porcella
Photography by Sharon Risedorph
Author photo by Elaine Faris Keenan

Library of Congress Cataloging-in-Publication Data
Porcella, Yvonne.
  Six color world : color, cloth, quilts, & wearables / Yvonne Porcella.
       p.   cm.
  Includes bibliographical references and index.
  ISBN 1-57120-035-5 (pbk.)
  1. Textile painting. I. Title.
TT851.P674 1997
746.6—DC21   97-3062
                                      CIP

Published by C&T Publishing, Inc.
P.O. Box 1456
Lafayette, California 94549

Printed in China
10   9   8   7   6   5   4   3   2   1

table of contents

acknowledgments

As I began to write this seventh book I could not help but reflect on the past twenty years and what has transpired. It was in 1977 that I made a trip to New York to visit the Metropolitan Museum of Art on the occasion of the Costume Department's exhibition of Chinese costumes. Maggie Brosnan, a special friend, went with me on this great adventure to the Big Apple. Although I had been there many years before when my grandmother gifted me with a high school graduation tour of the east coast, the 1977 trip was without an experienced tour guide. What resulted from the trip with Maggie were lasting memories, a reinforcement of my love for decorative costumes, and the birth of my career as an author of books featuring clothing patterns.

The idea to write a small book featuring my clothing patterns developed during the trip, and the plane ride home offered the time to set down the concept. It would be a small book containing five patterns. The last pattern was really the reason for writing the book, but I wanted to show the reader how I arrived at the

COVER OF *FIVE ETHNIC PATTERNS*, 1977

RIGHT: VEST HAS CENTER FRONT AND BACK PANELS, SIDE PANELS, SHAPED LOWER EDGE, AND SHOULDER BANDS.

design for my Samurai Vest pattern. The book featured first the Woman's Dress, then the Nomad Dress, the Pullover Shirt, the Long Vest, and finally the Samurai Vest with wings on the shoulders.

That early beginning led to this latest book which offers techniques as well as patterns for wonderful quilts and wearables, and continues experimentation with the process of fabric painting and working with color. The original pattern for the Samurai Vest has evolved into the Vest with Shoulder Bands.

Through the years my life has been full of learning experiences and, thankfully, successes. The friends who helped me along the way and certainly the great number of wonderful students who experienced my classes all influenced me in ways I cannot describe. Support, encouragement, interest, and excitement from those who touched my life gave me the courage to initiate many creative ideas and turn them into projects.

While I formulated the ideas for this book, the staff of C&T Publishing made being an author an easy task. My editor Lee Jonsson listened to me patiently and gently suggested solutions. Technical editor Joyce Lytle asked many questions and corrected any errors. I am grateful to her for such meticulous attention to details. Todd Hensley and staff are both supportive and encouraging to the artist who becomes an author.

For thirty-eight years my husband Bob has lived patiently through creative crises and with less than perfect meals. He is proud of my art as well as my other accomplishments. Also, I appreciate his help with the computer during the writing of this book. Our four children, Steve, Suzanne, Greg, and Don, are well on their way to their personal and very creative journeys, but they still find time to enjoy my success. Now we are experiencing the lively pursuits of ten wonderful grandchildren: Nick, Vince, Eric, Mikey, Mimi, Tori, Sarina, Elizabeth, Robbie, and Angelo. They are very special to me, and I have enjoyed making a quilt for each of them, specifically one reflecting the development of my quilt style over a seventeen-year period. Look for Robbie's quilt on page 85.

I also want to thank the many people who have graciously contributed to the realization of this book. Holley Junker gave me a book by Cennini, the perfect birthday present at the most opportune time. Chris Reed is a very talented interior designer, and I am grateful that she shared her time, home, and office with me. Thank you to Dr. and Mrs. Jerry Jones for lending their home, and to Mr. and Mrs. A. E. Buzz Carrade for lending their quilt. Sharon Risedorph has been photographing my work for over ten years, and she amazes me with her perfection. Cathie I. Hoover made a sample for the book featuring the Peplum Jacket, my 1982 jacket pattern, using my hand-painted fabric, so I could work on other projects. Steve Kalar shared my early days of fabric painting where we explored creativity. Kay Elson, Janice Rhea, and Marilyn Wright have been friends so long and are so full of enthusiasm for my work; they are the epitome of friendship. My sister Marilou always offers moral support. Grandsons Nick and Vince were the perfect helpers on photography days.

introduction

"The basis of the profession, the very beginning of all these manual operations, is drawing and painting. These two sections call for a knowledge of the following: how to work up or grind, how to apply size, to put on cloth, to gesso, to scrape the gessos and smooth them down, to model with gesso, to lay bole, to gild, to burnish; to temper, to lay in; to pounce, to scrape through, to stamp or punch; to mark out, to paint, to embellish, and to varnish, on panel or ancona [a panel with molding]."[1]

Marble Fudge ice cream, slightly melted and stirred—that's the color and pattern I wanted on fabric, and it became the reason I began to experiment with textile paints.

Fabric dying with chemicals never really appealed to me. In 1980 the choices for products to color fabrics were limited, and each required extensive steps to make the color permanent. Basically, I was too impatient to strap my fabric down to a frame and rinse thoroughly or steam set. I didn't care to make realistic images outlined with a resist which then had to be removed after the fabric was dyed. Also, some of the chemicals were offensive to my sensitivities, and since I had recently retired from nursing, I was not interested in acid and base reactions or precise measurement of components.

I was introduced to textile paint by a shop owner who inquired whether I would like to test a new product in her inventory. I invited two artist friends over to my studio and we tested, tested, and tested until suddenly eighty yards of fabric had been colored! By then the "dye was cast"—actually thrown away —so to speak, and fabric painting became my medium of choice. And when you become comfortable with something, it is difficult to change.

In the last few years many new products have appeared on the market and the paint industry has made coloring fabric easier. Products have become safer to use; there are no messy powders to mix, and setting the colors is done by ironing. The color choices have also been expanded, and fabric dyes have been formulated so they too are easier to use. The results are as exciting as the creative individuals who take the time to experiment.

SHADES OF CHOCOLATE
RIPPLE ACROSS MUSLIN
FABRIC, AND GOLD IS
ADDED FOR A FROSTY
SPARKLE.

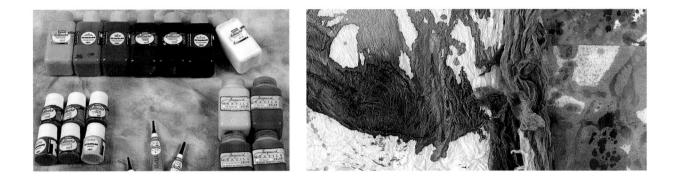

I still prefer the textile paints, and I will explain my techniques and discuss pitfalls in the following chapters. It is very easy to design your own unique fabric and have it available to use as soon as the paint dries on the fabric. Sometimes I forget that in the past it was much more complex and unpredictable.

Just before I began to write this book, a very special friend gave me a 1960 Dover Publications copy of *The Craftsman's Handbook*, which was originally copyrighted in 1933 by The Yale University Press. Translated by Daniel V. Thompson, Jr., in 1933, the Italian "*Il Libro dell' Arte*" is the extraordinary work of Cennino d'Andrea Cennini of Colle, who wrote it in the year 1437 "for the use and good and profit of anyone who wants to enter this [artist, craftsman, painter] profession."[2]

I have enjoyed reading this book, and perhaps it was put into my hands for a reason: to contrast for you some of the painstaking methods required of artists and craftsmen in the fifteenth century who mastered the art of painting not only on canvas and walls, but also on fabric.

In today's world, with products a simple "1-800" phone call away, it is impossible to comprehend selecting earthen minerals, grinding your own colors, or cooking your own sizing.

When you begin reading this book and trying the projects I hope you bear in mind that part of the joy of designing your own fabric is allowing yourself to be spontaneous and creative. Since most of us are going to use the hand-painted fabric in a quilt or garment, it is not necessary for each painted piece to be perfect or viewed as fabulous art by itself. The fun of fabric painting is returning to a youthful exuberance for the pleasure of making it yourself. Remember that experimentation can lead to powerful and innovative work.

supplies

Supplies found
AROUND THE HOME

A variety of glass or plastic containers with lids in all sizes

Large plastic basin or storage box

Empty plastic 64-oz. jar with the narrow top cut off for cleaning brushes

CHAPTER ONE

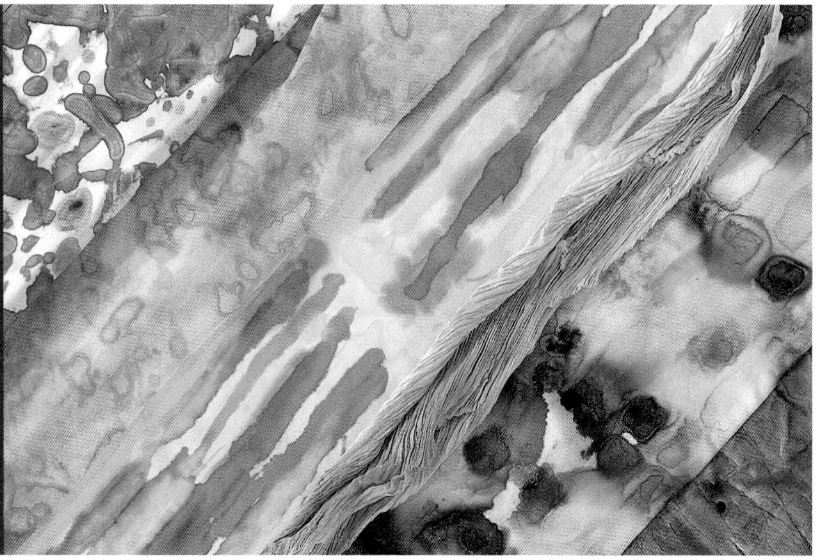

SELECTION OF PAINTED SILK FABRICS

Aluminum disposable pie pan

Dishwashing soap for cleanup

Spray bottle for water

Old towel for cleanup

Paper towels

New kitchen sponges to use for stamping projects

Old apron or painting type clothes

Rubber gloves to wear if you have a manicure or acrylic nails (Paint will stain nail polish.)

Popsicle sticks or tongue blades

Iron

Hair comb with large teeth

Scissors

Glue stick

Rock, kosher, or table salt

White tissue paper

Old newspapers

Supplies from the
HARDWARE STORE

Clear, smooth (not embossed), plastic drop cloth: 1 mil. thick, 9' x 12'

Bristle paint brushes in a variety of widths: 1", 1 1/2", 2" with 1/4"-thick bristles

Sponge brushes: 1" and 2" wide

Assorted plastic putty knives

Squeegee: 4" or 3" wide

Masking tape: 1/4" and 3/4" wide

Acrylic or glass: 16" x 20" x 1/8" thick

Supplies from the
ART SUPPLY STORE

Brushes for acrylic paint (pointed rounds): size 8 (about the size of the tip of your fifth finger), size 4 or 6 (to use for fine line work), and size 2, bright flat

Palette knife

Stencil brush: $1/2$" wide tip

Permanent black ink marking pens
with various tips (nibs), ultra fine to
broad

Fabric marking pens in a variety of
colors

Blank stamp pad

Rubber stamps

X-acto® knife with #11 blade

Watercolor pad: 11" x 15" (optional)

Additional Paints and Supplies for
SPECIFIC PROJECTS

Plastic painting syringe

Pearlescent Liquid Acrylic

**Liquitex® acrylic gesso, Liquitex
acrylic colored gesso permanent:**
alizarine crimson hue

Bob Ross® black gesso

Liquitex Iridescent gold and **Iridescent
white**

Liquitex gloss medium & varnish

**Turpentine distributed by
Grumbacher®**

Color Mist™

Pearl Ex Pigments®

Composition gold leaf sheets:
$5^1/2$" x $5^1/2$"

Gold leaf liquid quick sizing

SELECTION OF PAINTED
COTTON FABRICS.

FABRIC: COTTONS AND SILKS

Any good quality white fabrics in cotton or silk. See reference about fabrics in Why I Use Fabric Paint on page 11.

Silk fabrics: pongee, spun, twill, charmeuse, crepe, chiffon, and organza (See silk fabrics on page 8.)

Muslin: very inexpensive type at discount store (See wrinkled fabric upper left.)

Quilters muslin: bleached or unbleached

Dyer's cloth (top and bottom right, lower left)

Polished cotton (Deco Glaze) (horizontal over wrinkled muslin fabric)

Cotton flannel (cobalt blue color)

Cheesecloth (middle)

Dritz Shape Maker® woven fusible black interfacing

Pellon® Wonder Under® transfer web and **Sof-Shape® fusible nonwoven interfacing**

FABRIC PAINT AND FABRIC DYE

Setacolor® Transparent and **titanium white Opaque**

Setasilk®

Gutta® colorless and **colors**

Jacquard Textile Color® and **white Opaque**

Jacquard Pearl Ex Pigment

Dye-na-Flow® by Jacquard

Color Mist

FABRIC PAINTS AND
FABRIC DYES USED IN
THIS BOOK.

Today there are many new products on the market for coloring fabric. The decision to use one product over another should be based on personal needs. My preference is to use a fabric paint that becomes permanent, light, and colorfast on the fabric by heat setting with an iron. This is commonly referred to as "setting the color." Recent developments in the industry have resulted in fabric dyes that act like paints, which can be brushed onto fabric and are also heat set by ironing. When considering which product to use, there are a few things to understand. Basically, a fabric paint (or textile pigment) colors the fabric by coating the fibers with color. These paints can be applied in many different ways. A fabric dye chemically bonds to the structure of the fiber in the coloring process. Some dyes require steam setting for a period of time, some require the use of a fixative solution, and some can be set simply by ironing.

WHY I USE FABRIC PAINT   I like mixing my own colors and the ease of painting the color on fabric. Once the fabric is dry and heat set, it is ready to use in a project. You can also create colors and patterns not available in commercial fabrics. In a sense, you are creating your own specialty fabric.

I USED BOTH COTTON AND SILK FABRICS IN *THE FLOWERS THAT BLOOM IN THE SPRING.*

When using fabric paint you should understand that coating the fibers with color also adds acrylic resin to the fabric's surface. Too much paint can make the fabric stiff or, worse yet, leave lumps of pigment on top of the fabric. In 1982 when I began to use paint rather than fabric dye, my response to the build up of excess paint was to thin the paint with water. This resulted in a light pastel or watercolor effect on the fabrics, which was the subject of *Colors Changing Hue*, my 1994 fabric painting book. Because I was using silk fabrics I wanted these fabrics to retain their "silky" quality.

This book includes techniques which enable you to obtain darker colors, and more projects feature cotton fabrics. I still prefer using silk; however many of my completed projects are made using both silk and cotton together, or hand-painted fabrics mixed with purchased commercially-dyed fabric. See *Hearts for Robbie* on page 85.

Use caution when painting cotton with full-strength fabric paint. If the fabric has been layered on a plastic drop cloth and painted with thick paint, some of the resin from the paint may deposit on the back side of the fabric, creating a slick surface. Avoid this by diluting the paint and using a good quality fabric—not a lightweight or loosely-woven fabric. The slick resin can be removed if the fabric is first heat set by ironing the top surface of the fabric with a press cloth. Wash the fabric, rubbing the back side to remove the resin. Iron the fabric again after it dries.

Tumbling hand-painted fabric in the dryer removes some of the color. This loss of color is usually the result of fabric abrasion and not because the color has been set improperly. The tumbling action causes tiny fibers to loosen from fabrics. (This is where dryer lint comes from.) That is why I always hand wash, line dry, and then iron my painted fabric.

PRODUCTS USED IN THIS BOOK   Most of the samples in this book feature Setacolor Transparent and Opaque, Jacquard Textile Color, Jacquard Dye-na-Flow, and Setasilk. Although I have used these products for this book, I am not deliberately excluding any other products or brand names. Please feel free to try the techniques and projects in this book using any textile paint or fabric dye you are comfortable working with.

What you will encounter working with people who paint or color their own fabric is that each artist has a very personal reason for being faithful to a product. The reason for this is simple. Each manufacturer has a unique formula for the amount of pigment and the chemical components they use in their product. Therefore, the "same" color can vary between companies: one company may have a red violet and another a blue violet. The choice of which to buy becomes a matter of product availability, familiarity, or introduction by a teacher or friend. You should use what works for you because testing each new product can be a substantial financial expense.

Textile paints are usually compatible and I often mix brands together. However, you should always test the mixed products first on a scrap of fabric, allow it to dry, heat set it, and see how the colors mix. Then feel the fabric to test if the mixed products change the hand of the fabric.

On Dwight Way,
34" x 53"; THIS QUILT
SHOWS A WATERCOLOR
EFFECT ON SILK FABRIC.

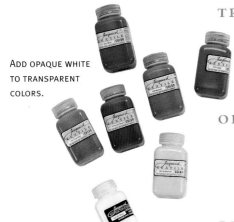

ADD OPAQUE WHITE
TO TRANSPARENT
COLORS.

TRANSPARENT PAINT Transparent paint must be used on light or white fabric. It can be thinned with water or with extender, which thins the paint without lightening the color value. Transparent paints are what I use most often in my work. Refer to Why I Use Fabric Paint on page 11.

OPAQUE PAINT Opaque paint can be used on dark fabrics. Some opaque paints are stiffer than transparent paints due to the opacity of the medium. You can buy opaque colors, or make your own by blending transparent paint colors with white opaque. See the *Opaque Hearts* wallhanging on page 92.

DYE USED AS PAINT Jacquard Dye-na-Flow and Setasilk are dyes which can be used as paints. They are heat set by ironing the wrong side of the fabric after painting. The colors are vibrant and the paints are usable on cottons as well as silks. Some techniques may require lifting the fabric off the table surface and suspending the fabric by pinning it on a stretcher bar frame. Notice the fabric is pinned on a wooden frame. Setasilk colors can be applied in an abstract pattern without a resist on silk.

Color Mist is available at most craft stores in the silk flower department. This product is color in a spray bottle and can be applied to silk flowers, fabrics, wood, ceramic, or paper. See the heart box on the bed on page 69. Try spraying through a piece of lace, a technique shown to me by Joyce Bennett, who works as a designer for Delta Technical Products. See the gold spray on page 65.

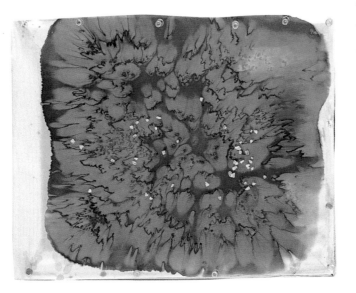

SILK SECURED TO A
WOODEN FRAME
WITH PINS

RIGHT: SETASILK
COLORS WITHOUT A
RESIST

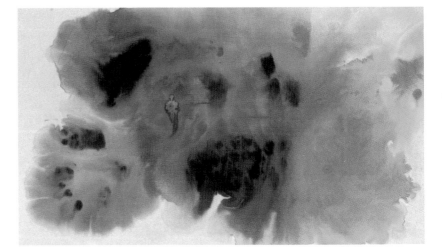

"Then take some gesso grosso, that is, plaster of Paris [gypsum], which has been purified and sifted like flour. . . . gesso sottile and it is some of this same gesso, but it is purified for a whole month by being soaked in a bucket. Stir up the water every day, so that it practically rots away, and every ray of heat goes out of it, and it will come out as soft as silk. Then the water is poured off, and it is made up into loaves, and allowed to dry; and then the gesso is sold to us painters by the apothecaries."[3]

ARTISTS' PRODUCTS   Liquitex Acrylic Iridescent paints (gold, copper, white, silver) are artists' products I use to accent my fabric painting. See *Violet Maud, Rapture, and Tea* black background fabric on pages 26 and 66.

I also want to acquaint you with some old standby products which are very familiar to painters but not frequently used by those who work with fabric. One of these products is gesso.

Gesso, an artist's material made from glue and white chalk, is commonly used as an underpainting medium. It is what artists use to size canvas. Gesso provides a white opaque surface which seals the canvas. Gesso can be applied thickly or thinly, with either a smooth or a textured surface. Since gesso is very thick, it will cover just about anything. It can be used to prime a wooden picture frame, and can be sanded after it is dry. See the small painted sewing chair and side table on page 69 and The Jacket Setup on page 75.

For the contemporary artist, gesso now comes in colors. Black gesso can transform white fabric into a solid black background. It can also be applied as a fine line when forced through a syringe. See the celebration banners on pages 135 and 138, and the Athlete on page 96.

TURPENTINE, GLOSS MEDIUM & VARNISH   These two artists' products can be used to transfer images to fabric. I use turpentine to release a carbon-based copied image onto fabric. Turpentine is a colorless, volatile solvent used to thin and manipulate oil paints. Pure gum spirits of turpentine is produced by distilling balsam from tapped pine trees. The more refined product is available at art supply stores. See photograph on page 9.

Gloss medium & varnish is a transparent acrylic which dries as a glossy film and is used by artists to protect a painted surface. It can also be used to secure an image which is copied on paper or fabric to another surface. See *So Special* banner on page 138.

GESSO APPLIED WITH A SQUEEGEE OR PUTTY KNIFE

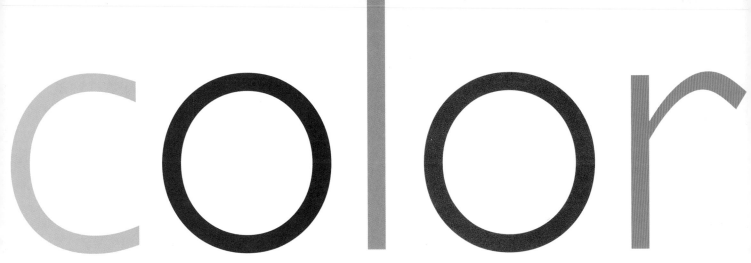

color

[In Renaissance times artists ground their own colors.] "To work it [the color] up properly, take a slab of red porphyry, which is a strong and solid stone; for there are various kinds of slabs for grinding colors, such as porphyry, serpentine, and marble. Serpentine is a soft stone and is not good; marble is still worse, for it is too soft.

CHAPTER TWO

But porphyry is best of all; and it will be better if you get one of those which are not so very much polished, and a foot or more in width, and square. Then get a stone to hold in your hand, also of porphyry, flat underneath, and rounded on top in the shape of a porringer, and smaller than a porringer, shaped so that your hand may be able to guide it readily, and to move it this way and that, at will. Then take a portion of this black, or of any color, the size of a nut; and put it on this stone, and with the one which you hold in your hand crush this black up thoroughly. Then take some clear river or fountain or well water, and grind this black for the space of half an hour, or an hour, or as long as you like; but know that if you were to work it up for a year it would be so much the blacker and better a color."[4]

FABRIC REQUIREMENTS

White cotton fabric: five 12" x 15" pieces and one 18" x 44" piece for cleanup. Sizes are approximate. (I always clean my brushes on a piece of muslin which I might use in a future project.)

PAINT AND OTHER SUPPLIES

Setacolor Transparent: cardinal red, cobalt, buttercup, parma violet, emerald, bright orange, bengal rose, black lake, pearl white

Setacolor Opaque: white

Plastic drop cloth: 9' x 12'

Brush: acrylic size 8 round

64-oz. plastic water bottle to clean brushes

Permanent marking pen: black, fine nib to mark color names on fabric

Iron to heat set sample

Watercolor paper pad: 11" x 15" (optional) (Use this for your color sample in place of fabric, or clean your brushes on the paper for an added bonus of painted paper.)

Most of the sample fabrics in this book use six colors: red, orange, yellow, green, blue, and violet. By mixing these with black or white or by mixing them together in selected combinations, you can achieve a vast collection of personalized colors.

THE THREE PRIMARY COLORS   Blue, red, and yellow are known as the primary colors. Blue has many different hues and names: ultramarine, cobalt, slate blue, cornflower blue, navy, cerulean, manganese, prussian, and turquoise, to name a few. Red can be alizarine crimson, naphthol red, cadmium red, cardinal, rose, vermilion, and chinese red. Yellow can range from lemon to buttercup to gold, cadmium yellow, naples yellow, turner's yellow, yellow/green, and ochre. Each of these named hues represents different colors. Some color theorists say that with the three primary colors you can mix all of the colors. My favorite color names are cobalt, crimson, and chartreuse. To me, just the words conjure up specific hues.

For the many years that I have used the French product Setacolor, one pigment, ochre rouge, seemed a contrast in concept. Ochre is often a synonym for yellow ochre used by artists, and rouge is French for red. How then red ochre? On a recent trip to the Vaucluse area of France we stopped to view the village of Roussillon. The area is the main mining and treatment area in France for ochre. The sudden outcropping of hills composed of richly colored ochre rises sharply out of the rocky Vaucluse terrain.

RED OCHRE

RED, YELLOW, BLUE

"Natural blue is a natural color which exists in and around the vein of silver . . ." "When you want to refine azurite (*l' açurro de la Magna*), take three ounces of honey, as light as you can get, and cut it with a little hot lye, not too strong. And then put in a pound of blue, and mix it up. Get it tempered so that you can grind it. Then take a little of this blue; put it on the porphyry, and grind it well. And put all the ground part into a glazed porringer by itself, and put into it some lye as hot as your hand can bear. And get the blue well spread through it, and mix it and stir it up thoroughly with your hand. Then let it settle until all the blue goes to the bottom. Then draw off all the water; and if you find that the water is charged with blue, put it into another porringer, and let it settle thoroughly. And then take some hot water and put it on to the blue, mixing it up with your hand as described above so as to get all the honey out of it. And then divide it up this way . . ."[5]

"A color known as vermilion is red; and this color is made by alchemy, prepared in a retort . . ." "But I advise you rather to get some of that which you find at the druggists' for your money, so as not to lose time in the many variations of procedure, and I will teach you how to buy it, and to recognize the good vermilion. Always buy vermilion unbroken, and not pounded or ground. The reason? Because it is generally adulterated, either with red lead or with pounded brick."[6]

"A natural color known as ocher is yellow. This color is found in the earth in the mountains, where there are found certain seams resembling sulphur; and where these seams are, there is found sinoper, and terre-verte and other kinds of color. I found this when I was guided one day by Andrea Cennini, my father, who led me though the territory of Colle di Val d'Elsa, close to the borders of Casole, at the beginning of the forest of the commune of Colle, above a township called Dometaria. And upon reaching a little valley, a very wide steep place, scraping the steep with a spade, I beheld seams of many kinds of color: ocher, dark and light sinoper, blue and white; and this I held the greatest wonder in the world—that white could exist in a seam of earth; advising you that I made a trial of this white and found it fat, unfit for flesh color. In this place there was also a seam of black color. And these colors showed up in this earth just the way a wrinkle shows in the face of a man or woman. To go back to the ocher color, I picked out the "wrinkle" of this color with a penknife; and I do assure you that I never tried a handsomer, more perfect ocher color. It did not come out so light as giallorino; a little bit darker; but for hair, and for costumes, as I shall teach you later, I never found a better color than this."[7]

Ochre in its natural state is a mixture of argellaceous sand and iron oxide. The region produces 3,000 metric tons annually. After washing and drying the mineral, some is baked in ovens to darken the pigmentation to obtain a reddish-orange color. The houses in the small village of Roussillon are painted with the sixteen to seventeen different shades of ochre yellow to red pigments, making quite a colorful statement on the landscape.

THE THREE SECONDARY COLORS   Green, violet, and orange are considered the secondary colors. It is possible to mix these colors by blending the correct combination of the primaries together. Yellow with blue makes green; red with blue makes violet; red with yellow makes orange. However, most painters prefer to buy the secondary colors already mixed to guarantee predictable color mixing. Green has many different hues and names such as: viridian, verdigris, verona, cadmium green, and hooker's green. Emerald is my choice but even this hue differs with each manufacturer. Violet can be ultramarine, madder-lake, mars, cobalt, and manganese. All are identified as violet but each has a different amount of red and blue. Names for orange hues are vivid red orange, cadmium orange, and brilliant orange.

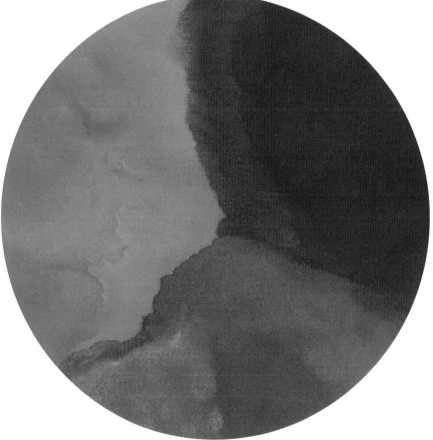

Green, violet, orange

"A half natural color is green; and this is produced artificially, for it is formed out of azurite; and it is

called malachite. I will not tell you how it is produced, but buy it ready-made."[8]

"A color which is made of azurite and giallorino is green." ". . . A color which

is made of ultramarine blue and orpiment is green. You must combine these

colors prudently." ". . . A color known as verdigris is green. It is very green

by itself. And it is manufactured by alchemy, from copper and vinegar."[9]

"If you wish to make a pretty violet color, take fine lac and ultramarine blue, in equal parts. Then, when it

is tempered, take three dishes as before; and leave some of this violet color

in its little dish, for touching up the darks. Then, with what you take out of

it, make up three values of color for laying in the drapery, each stepped up

lighter than the others. . . If you want to make a violet for use in fresco, take

indigo and hematite, and make a mixture like the previous one, without the

tempera, and make four values of it in all."[10]

Although Cennino has no specific words about mixing orange, it can be a slightly yellowish-vermilion.

Cennino offers a formula for fresco flesh paint: raw sienna tinted with white.

Terra di Siena is still mined in Tuscany for artist pigments. Today, cadmium

orange is the most often used orange hue.

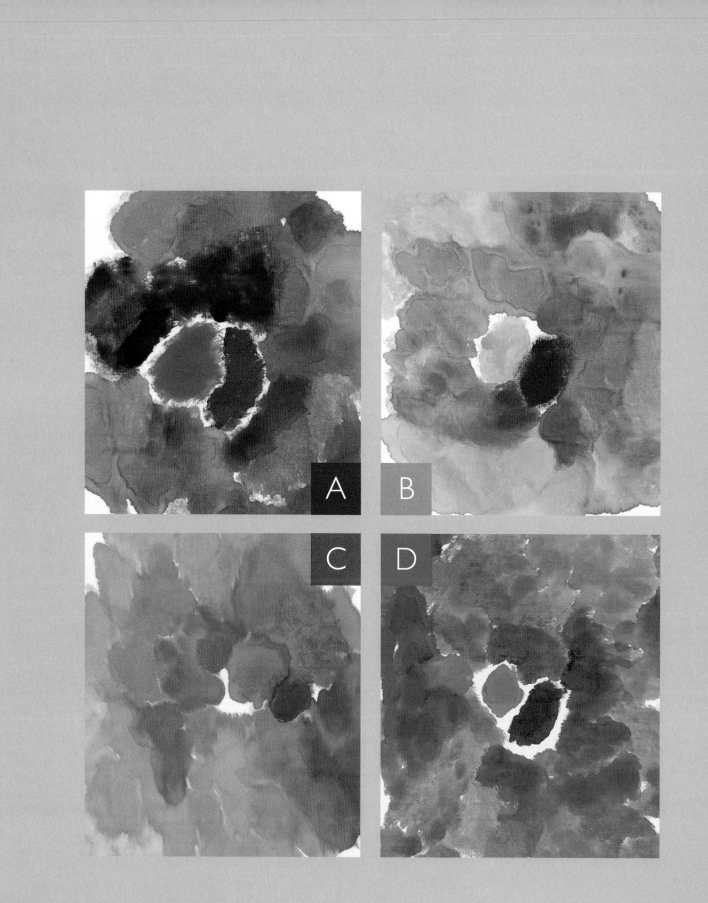

THE MUD FACTOR   Yes, it is easy to make mud. This usually results from mixing color combinations which when joined together form a neutral, and to the untrained eye, this color looks like mud. It could be brown mud or gray mud. To the trained eye it can look beautiful, since "mud" can be transformed into a wonderful color by adding small amounts of a primary or secondary color to the mixture. For example, red, when mixed with its complement, green, makes a wonderful neutral gray. Buttercup mixed with violet makes a rich brown. Cobalt blue mixed with orange makes a blue-gray; but if more orange is added, the result is a rich brown. These mud colors depend on the specific hues of the two colors which are mixed together. For instance, a rose red with an emerald green may give you a mauve or blue-gray color because of the additional blue which has been added to this red and this green. For this reason you should know your paint product and understand just how the colors mix. A word of caution: inexpensive or school-grade paints may not give you the colors you want. Investing in quality products guarantees good results.

A. COMPLEMENTS RED AND EMERALD WHEN MIXED MAKE A NEUTRAL GRAY.

B. COMPLEMENTS BUTTERCUP AND VIOLET WHEN MIXED MAKE A RICH BROWN.

C. COMPLEMENTS COBALT AND ORANGE WHEN MIXED MAKE A BLUE GRAY.

D. ROSE MIXED WITH EMERALD.

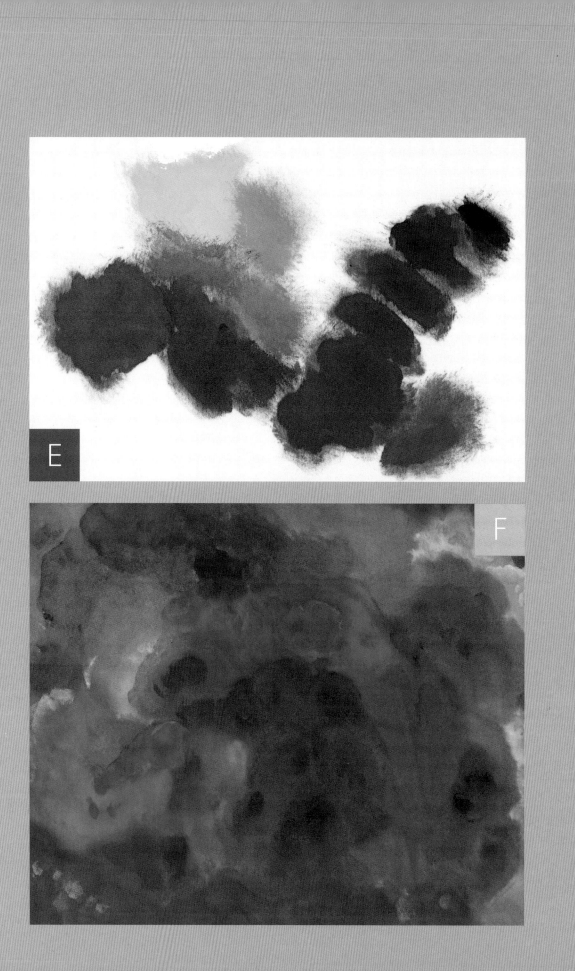

E

F

A BIT OF INFORMATION ABOUT COLOR   The term *color scheme* refers to satisfying relationships of color. The most common color schemes are monochromatic, analogous, and complementary. To a beginning student, knowing something about these color schemes gives important insight into why certain color expressions work.

Monochromatic cannot be discussed without understanding color value. Value refers to the lightness or darkness of a hue. A hue is a specific color. Monochromatic then is a single hue in various values.

Analogous refers to a limited range of neighboring hues on the color wheel.

Complementary refers to colors opposite each other on the color wheel. When mixed together, complements form a neutral color.

A good basic color resource from Liquitex is *How to Mix and Use Color*. Although this has much more information than you may want on acrylic and oil paints, it does have a handy color chart and value scale. See the Resource Guide under Liquitex on page 141.

Gray is referred to as achromatic. To gray any color, mix it with its complement. However, seldom will you get a true gray, but rather a neutral with overtones of one of the component colors. This is due in part to the difficulty of accurately blending two colors and the different saturation of pigments in the specific products. If a mixture of equal proportions failed to produce a neutral gray, the two colors mixed may not have been true complements.

VALUES

Color value is the lightness or darkness of a color. The strongest expression of light and dark is white and black. The scale of color intensity between the lightest and darkest hues forms the range of values.

To further educate yourself on color study, my recommendation is to find a copy of Johannes Itten's *The Art of Color*, published by Van Nostrand Reinhold. Not only is it easy for a beginner to read, but the color exercises suggested can also help someone develop a personal awareness of the workings of color.

The subject of working warm and cool colors together can be found in Itten's book and will not be discussed here.

COMPLEMENTS

E. A SINGLE HUE WITH WHITE AND BLACK ADDED CREATES DIFFERENT VALUES.

F. ANALOGOUS

WHEN AND WHY TO USE BLACK   Mixing yellow with black results in a bilious green color. The "call attention to itself" quality of the yellow is gone. Setacolor vermilion with black has the potential for creating a brick red, and blue with black moves toward the darkest indigo. This is why I like to mix black with my pigments; the mood of the color is subdued, the brightness is gone. See the colors of the tea pots below. For this quilt, the concept was a nineteenth-century tea party, and the colors I mixed reflected that somber quality. Too much black deadens a color, so be sure to use it sparingly. The "shade" of a color has black added to the basic hue.

VIOLET MAUD, RAPTURE, AND TEA, 59" x 37 1/2"

WHEN AND WHY TO USE WHITE   Conversely, white lightens a color and makes it appear cooler. Adding opaque white to a transparent pigment dulls the color because this white is not a glossy medium. In painting an artist can add gloss, semi-gloss, or matte white to a color for different effects. When I use transparent textile paints, I always dilute my colors with water, but with this method I also am diminishing the amount of pigment on the surface. Colorless extender for fabric paints can be added to the color for a different effect; it lightens the color but doesn't dilute the color. "Tinting" a color by adding white to the basic hue produces a wide range of light color values. See diagonal stripe resist on page 35.

"Know that there are several kinds of black colors. There is a black which is a soft, black stone; it is a fat color. . . . Then there is a black which is made from vine twigs; these twigs are to be burned; and when they are burnt, throw water on them, and quench them; and then work them up like the other black. And this is a color both black and lean; and it is one of the perfect colors which we employ; and it is the whole . . . [the conclusion of this sentence is lost] There is another black which is made from burnt almond shells or peach stones, and this is a perfect black, and fine. There is another black which is made in this manner: take a lamp full of linseed oil, and fill the lamp with this oil, and light the lamp. Then put it, so lighted, underneath a good clean baking dish, and have the little flame of the lamp come about to the bottom of the dish, two or three fingers away, and the smoke which comes out of the flame will strike on the bottom of the dish, and condense in a mass. Wait a while; take the baking dish, and with some implement sweep this color, that is, this soot, off on to a paper, or into some dish; and it does not have to be worked up or ground, for it is a very fine color."[11]

"A natural color, but still artificially prepared, is white, and it is made as follows: take good white air-slacked lime; put it, in the form of powder, into a pail for the space of eight days, adding clear water every day, and stirring up the lime and water thoroughly, so as to get all the fatness out of it. Then make it up into little cakes; put them up on the roofs in the sun; and the older these cakes are, the better the white will be."[12]

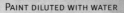

Paint diluted with water

COLOR STUDIES   Color is an intuitive thing. We all see color with different eyes, different perceptions, and emotions. Trying to teach another your personal sense of color is not an easy task. In this book I will offer you some samples which might help make mixing color easier for you.

Students of fine art spend many years testing and blending colors so it becomes second nature. For the past thirty-five years I have taught myself about color, and I am always learning more about the subject. My preference is to mix color intuitively, which results in very creative and unique colors. I begin with a color concept in my mind, then mix enough paint to color a variety of fabrics for use in a project.

A color study is a valuable tool you should create for yourself in order to have a record of how colors can be mixed. Make a color study for each new product since pigments vary with different manufacturers. See the samples below which use Setacolor Transparent.

Begin by selecting a good-quality white bleached or unbleached cotton muslin. Prewash and iron the muslin unless you are using a dyer's cloth which is free of sizing.

In an aluminum pie pan put about a $^1/_2$"-size spot of the following colors: Setacolor Transparent cardinal red, cobalt blue, buttercup, black lake, parma violet, emerald, bengal rose, and pearl white. I have chosen two reds for this color exercise, cardinal red and bengal rose. Another study could begin with vermilion for the red. I like to mix my own orange color, but you could add bright orange to your pan.

With a black fine line permanent pen, write the color names on the fabric. Using a size 8 pointed round brush, make a color sample of each one of the colors in your pan. You need a clean and nearly dry brush to make good samples, so wash the brush often and squeeze out the excess water.

LEFT: COLOR STUDIES

RIGHT: JACQUARD AND SETACOLOR

Begin at the top left side of the fabric and apply paint. Continue across to the right adding very small amounts of four variations of each color.

Row 1: Paint buttercup and add emerald; mix as described above. (Cobalt blue could be used instead of emerald.) Then add black to the fourth green mixed color. I made a seventh color sample by adding more emerald to the sixth color. With a clean brush, make a sample of emerald.

Row 2: Combine bengal rose with buttercup; mix paint as described above.

Row 3: Combine bengal rose with parma violet; mix paint as described above.

Row 4: Combine emerald with buttercup (or substitute cobalt in place of emerald); mix paint as described above.

Row 5: Combine cardinal red with buttercup; mix paint as described above.

Row 6: Combine emerald with bengal rose; mix as described above.

You can continue the color sample by adding your own color exercises.

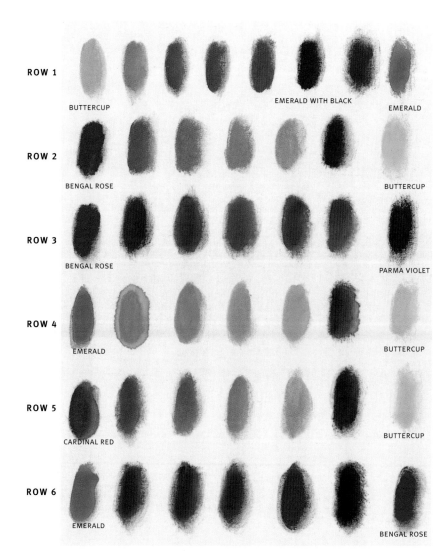

MIXING COLORS

ROW 1

BUTTERCUP   EMERALD WITH BLACK   EMERALD

ROW 2

BENGAL ROSE   BUTTERCUP

ROW 3

BENGAL ROSE   PARMA VIOLET

ROW 4

EMERALD   BUTTERCUP

ROW 5

CARDINAL RED   BUTTERCUP

ROW 6

EMERALD   BENGAL ROSE

Another practice sample includes the basic colors plus black and white. Paint a sample of each of your colors on the left side of the fabric. Use a clean brush and make four values of each pure color mixed with pearl white. You can substitute opaque white for the pearl. Start each row on the left with pure color and add black to the color. Then mix pure color with white to make four value changes.

COLOR WHEEL   The color wheel has twelve colors, beginning at the top center with red, moving clockwise to red-orange, orange, yellow-orange, yellow, yellow-green, green, blue-green, blue, blue-violet, violet, red-violet. Another good exercise is to make your own color wheel with your paint product. Each product brand produces a different color wheel.

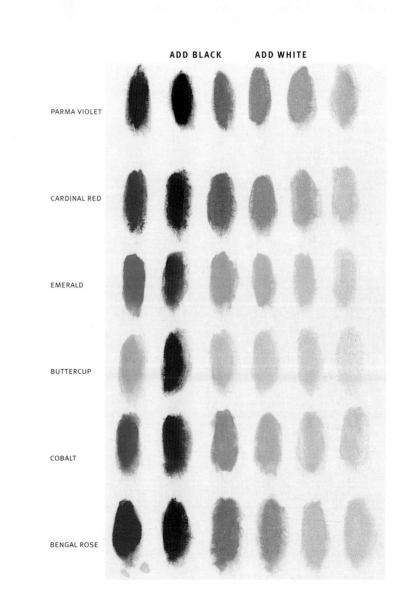

ADD BLACK   ADD WHITE

PARMA VIOLET

CARDINAL RED

EMERALD

BUTTERCUP

COBALT

BENGAL ROSE

COLOR WHEEL

surface
design

This chapter includes a variety of surface design techniques which use different methods to put paint onto fabric. To make the samples, begin with a variety of white cotton fabrics. Prewash and iron only if necessary for the project, or if the cotton has a permanent press finish such as "drip dry cotton." Dyer's cloth which has no sizing or finish can be used without prewashing. Cut fabrics approximately 18" x 22" or larger, if necessary. All painted fabric samples must be heat set with an iron when dry. Although some paint products are permanent on the fabric if allowed to dry for four days, be sure to check each product's recommendations for setting the color.

Cover the work table with a plastic drop cloth. Have water in a 64-oz. bottle nearby to clean your brushes. **HINT:** *Keep a piece of white fabric muslin or dyer's cloth near your work area. Clean your brush on this fabric. Some of these small areas of color may be usable in future projects.*

LEFT: INCOMPLETE
RESIST LINES ALLOW
COLOR TO BLEED.

RIGHT: PERFECTLY
APPLIED GUTTA
RESIST LINES

RESISTS   A resist is a barrier put on fabric to confine textile dye or paint to a specific area. It is used to separate colors and also to prevent the color from penetrating the fabric. Commonly used resists are wax, starch paste, or gutta. Wax resists are used in traditional batik fabrics; fine lines appear in these fabrics because the wax cracks, which allows the dye to penetrate into the fabric. Starch paste resists have been used in many forms, and can be found in traditional Japanese printed textiles and India wood block prints. Gutta resist is a rubber cement product, and is applied on fabric generally using fine lines to draw specific images. Notice above left where the red dye has penetrated through the weak resist lines into the blue. Controlling the thickness of gutta resist is a consideration.

Cennino states: "and there is a glue which is known as leaf glue; this is made out of clippings of goats' muzzles, feet, sinews and many clippings of skins. This glue is made in March or January, during those strong frosts or winds; and it is boiled with clear water until it is reduced to less than a half. Then put it into certain flat dishes, like jelly molds or basins, straining it thoroughly. Let it stand overnight. Then, in the morning, cut it with a knife into slices like bread; put it on a mat to dry in the wind, out of the sunlight; and an ideal glue will result".[13]

I have a strong feeling (although I have no personal experience with the fifteenth century), that this glue making created a very powerful odor. Other glues of that period were cheese and lime glue, fish glue, and goat glue. A dilute solution of glue or resin is called sizing and is used to coat the painted surface to reduce absorbency or porosity and to prepare the surface for paint.

". . . and there is a size which is made from the scrapings of goat or sheep parchment. Boil them with clear water until it is reduced to a third. Know that it is a very clear size, which looks like crystal. It is good for tempering dark blues. And apply a coat of this size in any place where you have happened to lay in colors which are not tempered sufficiently, and it will retemper the colors, and reinforce them, so that you may varnish them at will . . . . First take a size made of clippings of sheep parchments, boiled until one part remains out of three. Test it with the palms of your hands; and when you find that one palm sticks to the other, it will be right. Strain it two or three times. Then take a casserole half full of this size, and the third part water, and get it boiling hot. Then apply this size to your ancona [wooden panel] . . ."[14]

RESIST WITH GLUE   One of my favorite methods for resist, and a very quick one, is to use a water-soluble glue stick. This method works very well on lightweight fabrics such as silk, cotton muslin, or batiste. It will work on heavier fabrics, but the resist lines may not be as crisp.

Draw simple shapes or lines with a glue stick on the fabric and allow this to dry. When applying paint, do not brush vigorously across the fabric surface, but rather dip your brush into water-diluted Setacolor Transparent paint and touch the bristles to the fabric. The paint will wick into the fabric. Some paint may discolor the resist, but some areas of white will remain. Let the fabric dry and heat set with an iron; use a press cloth over the painted fabric to protect the iron from the resist. Wash the fabric in soap and water, gently rubbing off the resist areas with your hand to remove the glue. Then, rinse, air dry, and iron the fabric again.

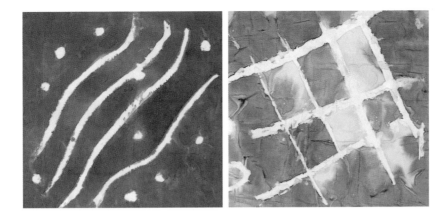

RESIST WITH MASKING TAPE   Resisting fabric with masking tape takes some time, depending on the size of the fabric. On a large piece, allow an hour to apply the tape. After painting, the tape should be removed as soon as possible to avoid transferring the gum adhesive to the fabric. The method for painting the sample below allows for experimentation with mixing new colors. Once you have started mixing colors it can be difficult to restart the process another day. By adding opaque white to any mixed color, an area painted with an undesirable color can be repainted. The opacity will mask out the undesirable color. **CAUTION:** *It also adds more paint to the fabric surface.*

For the sample use Jacquard Textile Paint opaque white, with Jacquard Transparent paints goldenrod, violet, true red, sky blue, emerald, and maroon, a 1" paint brush for wide stripes, and a size 8 round brush for narrow stripes. Refer to the section on brushes (page 8) for sizes. Select one yard of 48"-wide drapery lining fabric; sateen weave works better than broadcloth. This fabric is usually sold on a roll so it will not have a center crease.

MASKING TAPE RESIST

Space resist lines
randomly for an
interesting design.

Begin by spraying the fabric with water, and iron to remove any wrinkles. Be sure to have enough masking tape; two large rolls of $^1/_4$" wide and two rolls of $^3/_4$" wide. Buy the cheapest brand of tape so it will come off the fabric easily. Try an automotive parts store for $^1/_4$"-wide masking tape. This tape is made by 3M and sold as automotive refinishing tape. Some hardware stores also carry this width tape.

Don't worry about being accurate with the lines, just begin by placing tape across the fabric on the diagonal. Cover the fabric with tape, but leave enough fabric exposed where the paint will be applied. See the small sample with tape applied. A good rule is to leave $^1/_4$", $^1/_2$", 1", and $1^1/_2$" spaces, but these should be positioned randomly across the surface. Be sure the tape has adhered to the fabric so paint will not wick under the tape.

In an aluminum pie pan or dish, place about 1 tablespoon of yellow paint. Begin selectively painting the fabric, staying between the tape lines. Paint about four lines, and add a small amount of opaque white with a palette knife to the yellow and paint about four more stripes. Continue painting by adding colors to the pie pan, painting lines with each color: maroon; then add yellow to maroon to make orange; add blue; then yellow to blue to make green. Use a 1"-wide brush for wide stripes and a size 8 round brush for narrow stripes.

After all the fabric has been painted in various color stripes, allow this to dry. Remove the masking tape as soon as possible and discard the tape; heat set these colors onto fabric by ironing.

Put the fabric on the plastic again and begin retaping over the colored areas, exposing the white fabric. Apply colors to these areas. Allow to dry, remove the tape, and heat set again with an iron.

RESIST WITH OPAQUE WHITE PAINT

Opaque paint is exactly that: opaque. In contrast to transparent paint, it can be used to paint dark fabrics. Opaque white has great hiding ability and can be used as a resist. See sample (left) where the white opaque was painted first, then black paint was applied. Notice that even the black paint can be blocked from coloring the portions where the opaque white was painted.

Consider these to be test samples, so don't worry if the colors are not perfect for a project. Notice the colors in Sample One on page 37 (left).

1. Lay two 18" x 22" pieces of white fabric side by side. Use a palette knife or tongue blade to dispense small amounts of paint into a pie pan. A paper towel or piece of fabric can be used to clean the palette knife; it is important to wipe off excess paint before it dries on the knife.

2. Begin with about 1 teaspoon of Jacquard Opaque white in the pan and a size 8 round brush.

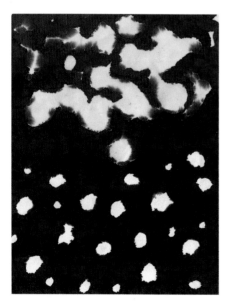

White opaque used as
a resist

3. For Sample One: Dab opaque paint onto the fabric in arch shapes. Opaque white is sometimes very thick. Be careful the paint is not too thick on the fabric; remove excess with your brush. Allow opaque to dry.

4. For Sample Two: Mix more opaque white with a tiny amount—the tip of the palette knife—of Jacquard goldenrod, using the brush to mix the yellow and white together just enough to allow some yellow and some white to remain. With the tip of the brush, dot yellow in flower-like shapes or circles in a random pattern. Allow to dry. Put 1 tablespoon of sky blue in the pie pan and load up your brush with blue paint. Now dip the brush quickly into the wash water, being careful to avoid transferring paint to the water. Dab the blue around the flower shapes, allowing the paint to wick up to the edge of the yellow. Some blue will wick under the yellow resist and appear green at the color interface. Continue with this method until the fabric is covered with blue. You can add small amounts of water to the pie pan to use up all the blue, but leave a little of this dilute blue water in the pan.

5. Return to Sample One. I tried to think about organic shapes when I began applying the paint. I mixed a color close to turmeric spice by mixing 2 teaspoons of goldenrod with 1 teaspoon of true red, then mixed in the small amount of dilute sky blue. Again I used the dab method to put this color at the top of the

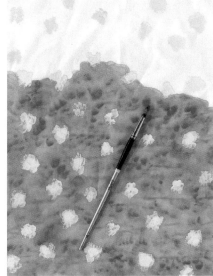

LEFT: SAMPLE ONE

RIGHT: SAMPLE TWO

white shapes, allowing the color to wick under the white. This technique requires adding water to the paint as described for Sample Two.

To the remaining turmeric mixture in the pie pan, add a small amount of true red to get a brick color. I needed a touch more of sky blue to make this color.

By now I have used up all the paint in my pan. I wanted a gray color, so I mixed up orange—two parts goldenrod to one part true red —then I added sky blue and got green! To correct this I added more red, which resulted in a dark aubergine color. I used some of this under the white shapes and then added more sky blue to the mixture, and finally added more blue. Eventually I added some emerald. This was definitely an experiment! I think it is very helpful to experience each textile paint and how the colors develop. Each hue is the manufacturer's combination, so it may give a different color than you might expect.

G

H

THE PATTERN OF SALT   Salt makes a wonderful pattern on fabric when it reacts with the liquid paint or dye. Some precautions should be taken to avoid getting salt all over your work space. Rock, kosher, or table salt can be sprinkled on wet painted silk or cotton fabric. The following example illustrates how color is moved by each grain of salt. The silk fabric is elevated from the table surface. Either textile paint or liquid dye will respond to the salt on silk or cotton.

The only secret to this technique is to use the salt sparingly. Do not pile up the salt. Each grain must have space to react. After the fabric has dried, gently brush off the salt into a garbage bag. Then heat set the fabric. After heat setting, wash the fabric to remove the excess salt.

LEFT: SALT PATTERN
WITH DYE ON COTTON

ABOVE: SALT PATTERN
WITH DYE ON SILK

DIFFERENT BRUSH STROKES   As a fabric painter you will discover the size and type of brush used can give you different results. To paint large amounts of fabric, consider using a 2" or 4"-wide brush. My favorite brush is the size 8 round; I can use just the tip, lay the bristles sideways, stroke the brush across the fabric, or just dab the brush on the fabric. Each technique will give a different pattern. *Dry brushing* is drawing the brush across the fabric to express all the liquid from the bristles. Use a dilute solution of fabric paint or undiluted liquid dye and practice making a variety of brush strokes.

For Sample G, I used Jacquard Dye-na-Flow true red, sky blue, golden-rod, emerald green, maroon, black, a size 8 round brush, and a gold metallic pen with a broad nib on white dyer's cloth.

I painted full-strength black in angular stripes which then were high-lighted with the gold pen. Next, the other colors were added. I mixed the colors in my pie pan and put them on in sequence, first the blue circles, then the purple, lime green, red, pink, orange, and finally yellow.

In Sample H the flowers were shaped with different brush sizes and strokes. A plastic syringe was used to achieve the fine lines. Paint was loaded into the syringe barrel and applied to the fabric. Also see syringe used on page 98.

G. ANGULAR BLACK LINES DEFINE
SPACES; THEN COLORS ARE FILLED IN.

H. DIFFERENT BRUSH STROKES MAKE
FLOWER FORMS AND THIN PAINT LINES
ARE EXTRUDED FROM A SYRINGE.

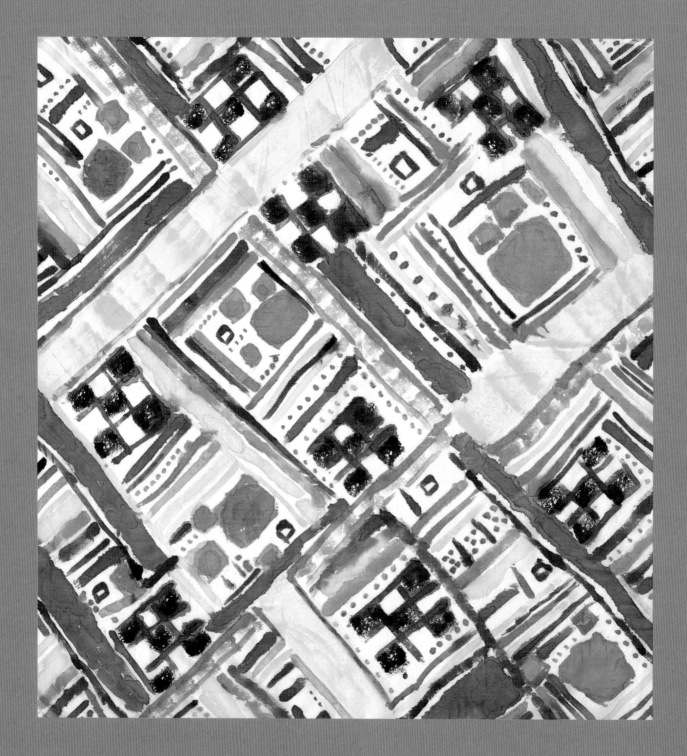

SPONGE STAMPING   A new kitchen sponge is an inexpensive tool used to create a design. The sponge can be stamped again and again to repeat the same shape. Choose a sponge with medium-size pores, but not a sea sponge, because they are expensive and not as easy to cut into shapes. When the sponge is dry, cut interesting shapes or a simple circle or square. Just about any fabric can be stamped.

Cover the table with plastic and lay the fabric on top. Into a pie pan pour 1 teaspoon of full-strength Setacolor Transparent paint in each of your choice of colors; space the paint around the edge of the tin. Moisten the sponge with water and squeeze the excess water out. You can decide whether to press the sponge lightly into some paint in the pie pan, or after mixing colors with a brush, brush the paint directly onto the sponge. Press the sponge onto the fabric with the palm of your hand. Dip the sponge lightly in water or spray water to moisten the sponge; stamp on the fabric again. This will lighten both the color and the clarity of the image on the fabric.

Re-stamp the fabric with other colors. You can go over the design with more paint to highlight colors. Allow the fabric to dry and iron to heat set. The *Sponge Stamped Vest* features one piece of stamped silk fabric combined with cotton fabrics. See page 109.

In the sample on page 40 different brush sizes and sponge stamps were combined to design a cotton gauze scarf. See the temporary lamp shade in photo on page 69.

STAMPING WITH PAINT
USING A SHAPE CUT
FROM A KITCHEN SPONGE

RUBBER STAMPS   Commercially-made rubber stamps can be used to make personal fabric designs. I have a collection of stamps, including four sets of alphabet stamps in different fonts and sizes which I purchased some years ago. One set of alphabet stamps is from my childhood, and even though the rubber is very old, I can still get a decent image. Rubber stamping has become an exciting addition to personal art projects and an adjunct design source. Now you can "just stamp it."

A COLLECTION OF
ALPHABET STAMPS

IN THIS SAMPLE DIFFERENT BRUSH
SIZES AND SPONGE STAMPS WERE
COMBINED TO DESIGN A COTTON
GAUZE SCARF.

Make your own stamp pad colors.

Liquid fabric dye can be used to transfer the stamp image onto fabric. I buy clean stamp pads—not saturated with ink—and make my own colors by filling the pad with dye. See stamping with black Dye-na-Flow on Deco Glaze fabric. Fabrico™ makes water-based fabric ink stamp pads in twelve colors. See Resource Guide on page 141.

You can also use Liquitex acrylic artist paints to cover the stamp. Squeeze enough paint into a pie pan and spread the paint out with a palette knife or brush. Gently push the stamp into the paint, look at the face of the stamp, use a brush to smooth out the paint on the stamp, and press the stamp onto the fabric. See the celebration banners on pages 135 and 138. Immediately clean the stamp with water, removing all the paint before it dries. You may have to use a small, stiff bristle brush to remove leftover paint which remains in the small design areas of the rubber stamp.

If you are interested in finding resources for unique stamping supplies, consider getting a copy of *Rubberstampmadness* magazine. Some retail stamping stores have the latest issue or will mail order a copy. See Resource Guide on page 141. You will be amazed at what is available in this medium.

TUBE OR POLE WRAP   This is my very simple variation of a traditional but complex Japanese tie dye technique. Fabric is first wrapped around a tube, manipulated, and securely tied. Dye is then added to the fabric after the tieing. In Japan masters of textile art are able to produce specific ancient tied patterns.

My technique is not pattern specific but offers a quick method where colors will migrate into the fabric to produce a dark to light value pattern.

Adding paint to the outside layer of the wrapping causes a diminishing amount of the color to wick into the inner layers.

A 12"-long small bore tube 1" in diameter works best with lightweight silk. When using cotton, select a larger 3" diameter tube. The tube can be a plastic plumbing pipe or a clear acrylic tube. If you are using silk, loosely roll an 18" x 18" piece of silk on the 1" tube, allowing excess fabric to hang over. If the silk is wrapped too tightly, static electricity will cause the fabric to cling to the tube, making it difficult to manipulate. Tie a 2-yard length of string or a piece of silk ribbon to the top end of the tube, securing the fabric. Twist the silk on the tube and force the silk up to the tied end until the silk now measures about 5 inches. Wrap the remainder of the string around the 5-inch section of silk, securing it at

Wrap fabric around a tube or pole; secure at the top with two yards of ribbon or string. Then push up fabric and secure with the remaining string.

the top and tieing it to the original knot. The exposed 7 inches of bare tube can then be used to hold the tube while applying the paint to the silk.

Use a dilute mixture of Setacolor Transparent paint and apply with a brush to the wrapped fabric. Try pushing the paint from the brush into the creases of the wrapping. Roll the tube on a piece of plastic drop cloth to force the color into the fabric. Now reapply full strength paint on the fabric and

THREE PIECES OF TUBE-
OR POLE-WRAPPED SILK
FABRIC ARE USED TO
MAKE THE BASIC VEST.

allow this to dry. Cut the string and remove the silk from the tube. Heat set
with an iron, and if necessary, spray the fabric with water and iron again to
remove the wrinkles. The fabric can also be left in the wrinkled state for a textured effect.

This technique using a small diameter tube restricts the painting to
small pieces of fabric. It may be necessary to repeat this process several times
to have enough fabric to make a vest. For the Basic Vest pattern I needed three
18" x 18" pieces. For the *Purple and Orange Vest* on page 116 only one piece
of that same size for the strip piecing was needed.

SPRAY PAINT   Just about any clean spray bottle can be used for spray painting fabric. The paint and water can be mixed right in the bottle. Pour $1/4$ cup
Setacolor Transparent paint into the bottle, fill with water, replace the top,
and shake to mix. Adjust the nozzle to stream or spray.

Any fabric can be used, although cottons and silks are shown in the
samples. The fabric can be laid flat on a plastic drop cloth and one or many
colors can be sprayed on. Use caution, and protect surrounding surfaces when
using this technique. Be aware that the paint will permanently stain any
porous surface such as walls, rugs, furniture, clothing, and concrete. After the
fabric is dry, heat set the color by ironing. The blue color is sprayed on the
white fabric. A secondary technique shown at right and on page 98 features
black gesso lines added to the sprayed fabric.

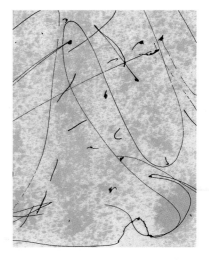

A DILUTE MIXTURE OF
BLUE IS SPRAYED ON
COTTON.

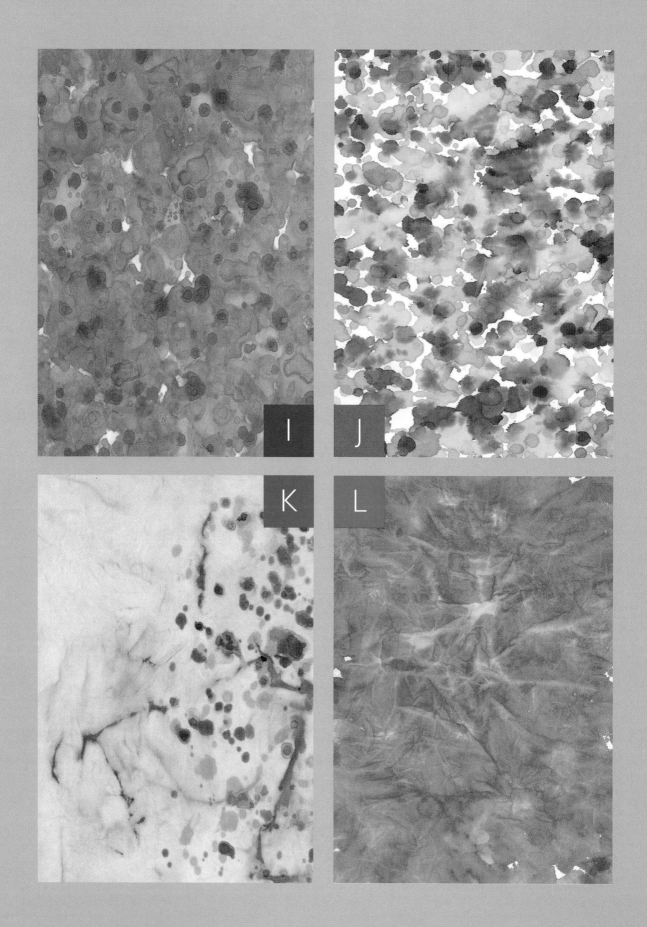

I J

K L

RAINDROPS   This is probably my favorite technique for achieving a unique fabric design. Sometimes the color mixtures are a wonderful surprise. Again, any fabric can be used. For this method I often spread a plastic drop cloth on the floor so I can drop the paint from a greater height to more closely simulate falling rain drops. See Sample I.

Use a dilute mixture of Setacolor Transparent paint and water, a ratio of about 2 tablespoons paint to $1/2$ cup of water. I usually use small jars to mix my colors. If this mixture is too dark, add water to dilute and further lighten the value. Use the 1" paint brush or the size 8 round brush and begin by dropping the paint off the brush onto the fabric one color at a time. Again, be careful of the surrounding surfaces and don't be too vigorous shaking the brush or the paint may stain the carpet or floor. Continue dropping different colors onto the fabric. Transparent paint colors will layer on the fabric if allowed to dry between each color as shown in Sample J. If paint is not allowed to dry between applications, the colors will mix together on the fabric to create a different effect.

See *The Flowers That Bloom in the Spring* on page 77 and Sample K. The gold fabric on the sleeves was painted first and heat set, then the purple and blue colors were dropped on.

Further dilute the paint and completely cover the fabric with drops. The fabric will be very wet. Immediately go back with another color for a second application of paint. The pattern will now be very subtle. See Sample L.

I. Raindrops. Use a size 8 brush.

J. Use a 1"-wide brush to drop the paint. Allow paint to dry slightly before adding more paint.

K. First gold colored paint is brushed onto fabric and allowed to dry. Then other colors are dropped on top.

L. Notice how the colors orange, yellow, and red blend together.

TIDE LINES Another one of my favorite surface designs requires more control of the paint on the cloth. The pattern looks like the water at the edge of the ocean: bands of color and foam as the water recedes. Any color is suitable for this technique. In Sample M dark colors were painted on dyer's cloth with yellow. I prefer using the size 8 round brush to apply the paint even if I am painting a four-yard piece.

Use either a dilute mixture of Setacolor Transparent paint or a more concentrated solution. Too much paint on a lightweight cotton or silk fabric may cause a buildup of acrylic residue on the back side of the fabric. I usually dilute the paint with water.

Begin on one edge of the fabric and press the paint from the brush into the fabric. Continue applying paint in this method until a nice shape develops; change colors and apply more paint. Each time you load the brush with paint and express the liquid onto the fabric, you will encourage a unique pattern. See the turquoise color in Sample N.

The *Landscape Vest with String Piecing* project on page 106 was painted using this method. The fabric for the outside surface was spun silk painted in turquoise and sienna colors, and embellished with metallic pens and metallic paints after the vest was completed.

tide

M. Press paint from the bristles of size 8 brush onto the fabric to create the Tide Line effect.

N. Each paint-loaded brush, when pressed onto the fabric, will leave a mark.

O

P

PAINT OVER A DRAWN GRID Taking the time to first draw a grid on the fabric provides a unique system for painting colors in assigned spaces. Choose a cotton fabric with a smooth surface, such as an unwashed glazed fabric.

Using a sharp #2 lead pencil, draw a 2" x 2" grid pattern on the fabric. Select the colors you would like to use and the size 8 round brush. Into a pie pan, pour 2 teaspoons full-strength Setacolor or Jacquard Transparent paint. Saturate the brush with paint and make a circle shape inside one of the grid squares. Add water to the brush and repaint the circle. Continue filling the squares with different colors in this manner. You can also try adding opaque white to your colors. See Sample O, which has opaque white added, and Sample P, which was painted using pure color diluted with water. The sample above was painted using a mixture of dilute and concentrated paints with opaque white. See *Yo Yolanda* on page 90 and notice this grid fabric used at the top and bottom of the quilt. **NOTE:** *Be aware that the pencil lines will remain on the fabric.*

OPAQUE MIXTURES AND WATER DILUTED COLORS ARE PAINTED TO OVERLAP THE DRAWN GRID LINES.

MONOPRINT A monoprint is a single print. It is made by spreading paint onto a smooth hard surface, making marks in the paint, placing fabric on top of the painted surface, and applying pressure to transfer the paint to the fabric.

I use a 16" x 20" x $^1/_8$"-thick sheet of plastic or acrylic purchased at the plastic store. (Look in the Yellow Pages for a local source.) A piece of glass can be used, but first fold a piece of 1"-wide masking tape ($^1/_2$" on top and $^1/_2$" folded over the edge to the back side) over all four edges to prevent cutting yourself on the sharp edge of the glass. The size of the plastic or glass sheet determines the size of the print. See the purple silk piece (right) which has green paint printed over the already-painted silk. A small 8" x 11" plastic sheet was used as the printing surface.

Begin this technique by covering a large area with a plastic drop cloth in order to have a place to lay out the wet fabric after it has been printed.

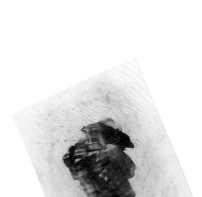

ABOVE: MONOPRINT IS A SINGLE PRINT MADE BY SMEARING PAINT ON A SURFACE. FABRIC OR PAPER IS LAID ON TOP AND PRESSURE IS APPLIED TO TRANSFER THE IMAGE.

LEFT: GREEN PAINT IS PRINTED ONTO PRE-PAINTED PURPLE SILK FABRIC.

O. OPAQUE PAINT ADDED TO TRANSPARENT PAINT

P. PURE COLORS DILUTED WITH WATER

To make a double print, begin with a tongue blade or a palette knife and an 18" x 44" piece of cotton dyer's cloth folded in half to be 18" x 22". (This technique can also be done by cutting the fabric into two pieces and printing one piece at a time.) Dispense emerald and then parma violet Setacolor Transparent paint onto the plastic. Use a large plastic putty knife or squeegee to spread the paint lightly and evenly; use a light hand to prevent scraping up the paint. After the paint is spread, use a large-tooth comb to make a pattern in the paint. Work quickly before the paint dries.

Then lay the doubled fabric over the paint and draw a clean squeegee across the surface of the fabric. Carefully pick up the fabric and lay wet side up on the plastic drop cloth. Spray the plastic print surface with water from a spray bottle to keep it moist. Be careful not to smear the previously printed fabric half as you now open up the folded fabric. Use the unprinted half of the fabric to make a print using the method described above. (A small amount of color may have wicked onto this side when the paint was squeegeed the first time.) In Sample Q you can see the effect this technique offers: a lighter image of the print on the same piece of fabric.

In the dyer's cloth sample (above left) I sprayed water over the paint, which was spread on the plastic first, before placing the fabric on the plastic. Adding water to the paint first made the print image slightly "out of focus."

I do not like to waste any paint, so in the sample (above right) I cleaned the squeegee tool, the comb, and the tongue blade on the piece of fabric laid flat on a plastic drop cloth. I sprayed each tool with water and tapped or scraped it onto the fabric to force the paint off the tool onto the fabric.

Another example of a monoprint is shown in Sample R. This is a large piece of fabric printed on a large sheet of glass. (Since we changed the window panes in my studio to double panes I had the old window glass to use as a print surface.) After the print was made, a secondary design was made using fabric marking pens and metallic pens. See information on pens on page 55.

Q. MONOPRINT IMAGE IS VERY INTENSE; SECOND DILUTED PRINT IS LIGHTER.

R. A LARGE PRINT MADE ON A GLASS WINDOW. THE PRINT IS DECORATED WITH METALLIC AND FABRIC PENS.

transferring images

There are many methods for transferring images to fabric. Most fabrics are suitable, but the samples shown are on cottons and silks. Transferred images on fabrics are usually the size of an original picture or a print. The picture or print can be enlarged using an opaque projector and reduced or enlarged using a copy machine.

PHOTOCOPY ON
PAPER OF ORIGINAL
PHOTOGRAPH

CHAPTER FOUR

WHICH IMAGES TO CHOOSE

It is important you select images that are not protected by copyright. Most studio portraits and magazine photographs have been copyrighted by the photographer. It is better if you take your own photos, use old photos, or select images which are in the public domain.

CARBON TRANSFER

Make a photocopy of the item you want to copy. Commercial copy machines use carbon to make the photocopy transfer on paper.

When the carbon transfer is fresh and has not had time to completely bond with the paper, the image can be transferred to fabric with a solvent. The following method is not suited for everyone, and you should exercise caution since the solvent used is volatile and flammable. (Do not use near an open flame.) I have successfully transferred images onto silk organza, cotton batiste, and cotton broadcloth.

Prepare an ironing surface in an area with good ventilation. Layer newspapers on a board and cover the top with a few sheets of white tissue paper. Put a fresh photocopy of the selected image face up on the tissue paper. Using a soft bristle 1/2"-wide brush, gently and quickly brush the surface of the image with turpentine. Do not restroke over the image. Immediately lay white fabric over this image, then layer about six pieces of white tissue paper

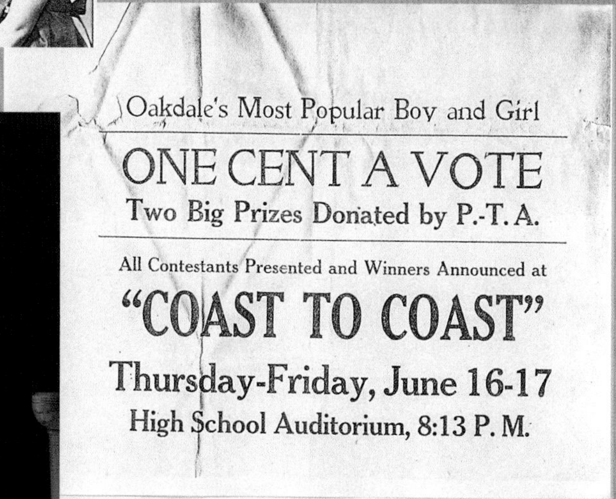

Oakdale's Most Popular Boy and Girl

ONE CENT A VOTE

Two Big Prizes Donated by P.-T. A.

All Contestants Presented and Winners Announced at

"COAST TO COAST"

Thursday-Friday, June 16-17

High School Auditorium, 8:13 P. M.

VOTE FOR

NE BECHIS

on top of the fabric and apply a dry iron for approximately 30 seconds. The heat will lift the carbon off the paper and into the fabric. Remove the tissue paper and place the fabric on another surface to air. The turpentine will evaporate, leaving no residual odor. See where the image on page 52 in the top left and lower right is the reverse of the original copy, which is on the top right. This method which reverses the image is not suitable for images with lettering. See the sample below and notice a copy of the original is on the left, and fabric transfer on the right is reversed.

NOTICE HOW IMAGE ON
THE RIGHT IS REVERSED.

ACRYLIC MEDIUM   Bonding the whole picture to a piece of fabric can be done by using either matte or glossy acrylic medium. This process involves painting a heavy film of acrylic on the front side of a picture. When the acrylic is dry the paper is soaked off, leaving an image on the acrylic film which can then be glued to fabric. Some of the paper may remain, so I recommend this be used only for wallhangings. In my sample you can see where the image has been reversed, illustrating that the acrylic was painted on the back side of the copy paper.

Coat the image to be transferred with five coats of acrylic gloss medium. Dry the medium between each coat and further dry it overnight. Soak the image in warm water for fifteen to thirty minutes. Gently rub off the paper and the image will remain on the film of acrylic medium. Glue this image onto your fabric with another coat of acrylic medium, or sew the film onto fabric.

LIGHT BOX   You can make your own light box by suspending a piece of opaque plastic sheeting over a light bulb. I find a commercial light box to be a valuable studio tool. I purchased one many years ago from an art supply mail order catalog for a reasonable price and it has served me well.

PERMANENT PENS AND FABRIC MARKING PENS Tracing over a picture using permanent pens is another method for transferring images and one which has secondary benefits. I used the same photograph in the carbon transfer and acrylic medium methods. The original photo was a cropped photograph of me taken many years ago (top left). I made a photocopy of the photograph (top right), taped it securely to the light box, and then taped white cotton dyer's cloth over the copy. With fine-line permanent marking pens I traced the image onto the fabric (middle left). Notice how the middle right image is the reverse in the acrylic medium transfer of the photocopy. Tracing over a familiar image helped awaken the creative side of my brain to feel the contours of each shape. I think this is a valuable technique to help people learn how to draw, since tracing reduces the picture to lines and shapes. Concentrate on the form under the fabric instead of consciously trying to draw, and suddenly the image appears before you. Also, you can enhance the image if desired. Note how I added to the hair line, filling it in at the top edge.

Another version of the same photo is drawn with permanent pens (bottom left). This time the image is abstracted and reduced to just contour lines in an attempt to distort the original photograph.

THE SAME IMAGE USING
DIFFERENT TRANSFER
TECHNIQUES

This reproduction of an old Japanese print is a good example of a copyright-free image. Japanese prints were very popular in the seventeenth century, and they have been reproduced ever since. The image featured was printed on a thin cotton hankie (left). I made an $8^1/_2$" x 11" photocopy of the hankie (middle) and placed the copy on my light box. Various nib widths of permanent marking pens were used to imitate the directional lines in the original (right).

ORIGINAL HANKIE, PHOTOCOPY, AND PERMANENT PEN TRACING

Different textures can be explored using the light box method and various pen nibs (top of page 57). The heart shape was traced from an original painting which was secured to the light box (lower left). Thick and thin black lines give a feeling of volume to the flowers. In the next example repetitive lines portray a rendering of a tile roof (upper right). Contour drawing—lines and dot patterns—gives a realistic image similar to an old lithograph print in this image of a woman (upper left). Gesture drawing using lines for shading renders a mood to a lonely tree (lower right). The drawing was done from memory and is not a traced image. Again, different pen nibs were used to achieve the effect.

Permanent ink pen drawings further enhanced by adding color with permanent fabric pens can personalize a special quilt. The quilt *In Loving Memory* on page 58 features hand-colored tracings of family photographs. The original photographs were photocopied, and some were enlarged and traced onto the fabric using an opaque projector. For this method, the photo must first be copied to simplify the image to just black and white values. The copied image must also be small enough to fit on the glass screen of the projector. Begin by taping the fabric on a wall, and center the copied photo on the opaque projector. Adjust the size of the enlargement by focusing the lens on the projector. It may be necessary to move the projector toward or

away from the wall to get the focus and size you want. Trace the image onto the fabric using black permanent marking pens. **CAUTION:** *Protect the wall; pens can bleed through the fabric.*

For the tracing method the images for the quilt were transferred to fabric and colored with fabric marking pens. If you personally do not feel you can manage the task of coloring your drawings, think about asking an artist friend to do it for you. My good friend Steve Kalar did these images for me, and his talent as an artist is evident in the coloring of each of these special images. Nine images were selected, colored, and then added to a variety of cotton fabrics to make the quilt. Each fabric print was chosen because it conveyed the history and mood of the story surrounding the photos.

When designing the quilt I realized my photo, which I traced and colored to use in the upper right corner, was too strong for the rest

of the quilt. A second transfer image of the same photo using the turpentine method was transferred onto silk organza, and this was layered over the colored drawing to give a shadow effect to the image.

The muslin backing fabric for the quilt was also painted by Steve Kalar. A small photograph of two sisters riding bicycles was enlarged on the opaque projector. The image was centered on a large piece of muslin backing fabric, and the image was traced. The two sisters are riding bicycles down the emerald green pathway of life. Family history and stories, which might be forgotten, are written in permanent pen on the backing, recording memories for future generations.

In Loving Memory, 82" x 89"

BACK VIEW OF
In Loving Memory

This chapter will cover various general surface embellishments such as beading, textured surfaces, and overpainting for quilts and garments. See *Totally Embellished Vest* project on page 102. The following techniques were used to embellish the vest sample using fabrics compatible with the vest color scheme.

DETAIL OF *TOTALLY*
EMBELLISHED VEST

CHAPTER FIVE

FABRIC REQUIREMENTS

Muslin: two 12" x 12", one 12" x 24" (folded in half to 12" x 12"), and one 8$^1/_2$" x 9"

Blue cotton: one 7" x 8$^1/_2$" and one 9" x 9"

Black woven damask: one 7" x 10"

Red cotton: one 10" x 10" (canvas weight) and one 9$^1/_4$" x 9$^3/_4$"

Yellow cotton: one 10$^1/_2$" x 16$^1/_2$", one 9" x 9", and one 9$^1/_4$" x 10"

Red, yellow, blue, red-violet, orange, green cotton: one 2" x 9" strip of each color

Orange cotton: one 9" x 9"

Green cotton: one 9" x 9"

Red netting: one 10" x 10"

Painted silk organza: one 6" x 6"

Woven cheesecloth: one package (Purchase at gourmet food or paint store.)

Wonder Under or other 2-sided fusible transfer web: two yards

Lace curtain: 22" x 18"

ments

OTHER SUPPLIES

Seed beads (colors compatible with fabrics)

New kitchen sponge

Stencil brush: $1/2$"-wide tip

Stencil: $1/4$" to 1" checkerboard grid

Liquitex Iridescent: gold

Color Mist: highlight gold, blue

Template material

Heart patterns

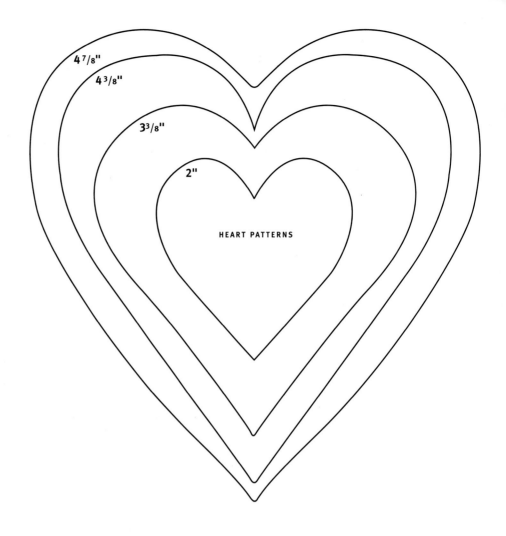

4 7/8"

4 3/8"

3 3/8"

2"

HEART PATTERNS

BEADING   Choose seed beads compatible with your fabric. See detail of *Totally Embellished Vest* on page 60. The detail shows beading sewn around a small iron-on appliqué heart. After machine satin-stitching the heart to outline the edges, begin the beading. Use regular hand-sewing thread in a very small needle which has a small eye. Secure the first stitch by back stitching, and then load four seed beads on your needle. Stab stitch along the edge of the appliqué the length of the beads on your thread. Come back up to the top with your needle as close to the last stitch as possible and continue adding beads, stab stitching until the whole appliqué is surrounded with beads. Then mount another thread on the needle and go over the beaded edge again, catching every two beads.

THREAD FOUR SEED BEADS
ON SEWING THREAD AND
STITCH; THEN SECOND-
STITCH PATTERN ANCHOR-
ING EVERY TWO BEADS.

FABRIC MARKING PENS   Enhance a piece of solid-colored fabric by adding designs with fabric marking pens. Make a template from the 2" heart pattern (page 62), draw six small hearts on the 7" x 8$^1/_2$" blue fabric, and add lines, dots, or stripes with colored fabric pens. Heat set 6$^1/_2$" x 8$^1/_4$" fusible web to the back of the blue fabric. Cut out three of the hearts.

Fold the 12" x 24" muslin in half and baste the edges. Spray blue Color Mist onto the muslin, using a piece of lace as a stencil, and allow the paint to dry. See the photograph on page 61. Heat set the heart shapes on the muslin. You can add a larger heart shape (cut out of the organza overlaid on yellow fabric) after trying this Fabric Marking Pen technique. See Painted Silk Organza Over Fabric Pens on page 64. As described in Beading on page 62, add seed beads to one of the small heart shapes.

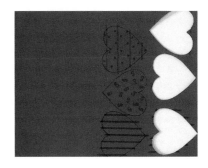

FABRIC MARKING PENS
ON BLUE FABRIC

CONFETTI STITCHING   Layer a 9$^1/_4$" x 9$^3/_4$" piece of red fabric over a 12" x 12" piece of muslin. Cut snips of red, orange, blue, yellow, and green fabrics from the 2" x 9" strips onto the red fabric. Arrange the snips of fabric into a pleasing composition. Then layer a 10" x 10" square of red netting on top and pin through the surface, including the muslin base fabric. Pick the square up carefully, keeping it flat.

Take the sample to the sewing machine. First stitch a diagonal pattern across the surface, using a 2.75 stitch length and red thread. Stitch beyond the edges of the red fabric, turn, and pivot back in another direction. Try to stitch all the small snips, catching them in the stitching. For the secondary stitching, stitch again from the middle in a smaller diagonal pattern to catch all the edges of the small snips.

LEFT: SNIPS OF FABRIC
STITCHED WITH RED
NETTING OVERLAY

RIGHT: THREAD COLOR
FOR DEMONSTRATION
PURPOSES ONLY

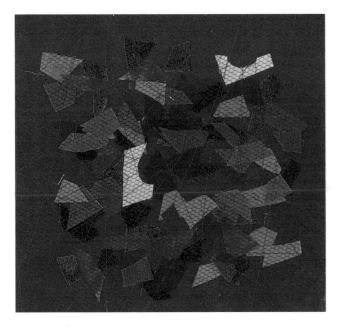

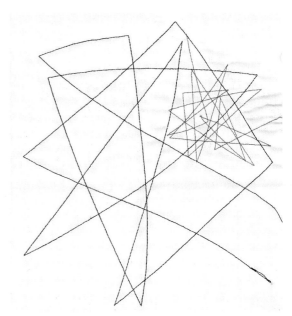

THREAD PAINTING   Heat set a piece of fusible web to the 9" x 9" pieces of blue, green, yellow, and orange fabric. Follow product directions for heat setting. Cut two 2" squares of blue and two 2" squares of green, an orange triangle whose sides measure 3^1/$_2$", 3", and 2^1/$_2$", and two yellow shapes approximately 5" x 1" tapering to ^{1}/$_2$ inch, and 3^3/$_4$" x 1^1/$_2$" tapering to 1 inch. Heat set these shapes to a 10" x 10" red canvas square with a damp press cloth according to the product instructions.

Change the bobbin thread in your machine to blue; change the top thread to orange. Set the machine on straight stitch with a 2.75 stitch length. Activate continuous reverse if you have a Bernina® machine.

Place sewing machine needle at the edge of the green fabric square and with your left hand steering the fabric square stitch forward. With the right hand resting on the reverse button, activate the reverse and stitch backwards. Deactivate the reverse and stitch forward. Continue stitching forward and backward all around the shapes. Stitch all the raw edges. Change the color of the top thread for contrast over the different colored shapes and continue to stitch all the edges. For this technique also see the Athlete on page 96.

LEFT: FORWARD AND BACKWARD STITCHING OVER FUSED SHAPES

RIGHT: PAINTED ORGANZA FUSED OVER PEN-MARKED YELLOW FABRIC

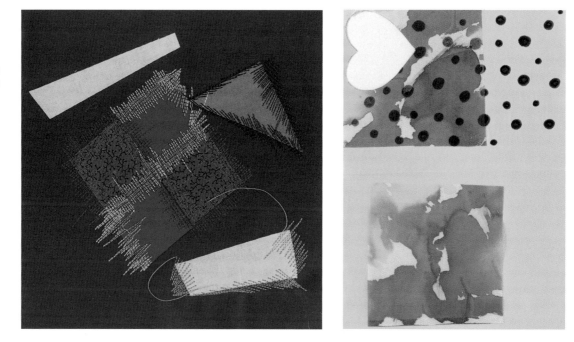

PAINTED SILK ORGANZA OVER FABRIC PENS   On one end of the 10^1/$_2$" x 16^1/$_2$" piece of yellow fabric, draw different size polka dots with a black fabric marking pen.

Cut a 6" x 6" and a 7" x 9^1/$_2$" piece of fusible web. Heat set the 6" x 6" fusible web to a 6" x 6" piece of painted silk organza. **CAUTION:** *Please note the difference; organza is a loosely woven fabric—the fusible web may stick to the iron surface. Use a press cloth over the organza for the first fusing process. Gently lift off the press cloth.* Fuse the silk organza to the yellow-with-black-dot fabric. When the fabric is cool, heat set a 7" x 9^1/$_2$" piece of fusible web to the back side of the yellow fabric. Cut a heart shape which can be fused onto the vest or the blue Color Mist muslin shown on page 61.

COLOR MIST ON FABRIC   Use a piece of lace as a stencil and layer this over the 7" x 10" black fabric. Spray Color Mist highlight gold over the lace. Also see Stenciling with Metallic Paint, page 67. This will make a lovely pattern on the black fabric. See the same pattern using blue Color Mist on muslin (page 61) and gold on black (Scrap Heart Sample below).

SCRAP HEART SAMPLE   Layer the gold-sprayed black fabric over an 8$\frac{1}{2}$" x 9" piece of muslin. Cut snips of yellow, red, orange, green, and blue fabrics from the 2" x 9" strip. Choose different shades of these colors to make the design more interesting. Arrange the snips in the center of the black fabric approximating the size of the 3$\frac{3}{8}$" heart pattern on page 62. Without pinning, keep this arrangement of snips level, and carefully take it to the sewing machine. I use my Bernina 1630 and set it to A-1 with a stitch length of 1. This is a long, open zigzag stitch. Begin anywhere on the surface of the scraps and random stitch over all the scraps, rotating the work under the presser foot until all the small scraps are sewn enough to be secure. Be sure not to fold over the scraps; lift the presser foot to straighten scraps if necessary. Repeat this same technique on the 9$\frac{1}{4}$" x 10" piece of yellow cotton which has been layered over the 12" x 12" muslin.

Cut fusible web to 6" x 8" and heat set this to the muslin side, centering the fusible web under the scraps.

Make a 3$\frac{3}{8}$" heart template from the pattern on page 62, position the template over the scraps, and trace the heart on the scrap side with a permanent marking pen. Cut out the heart shape and reserve this to use in your project. This heart shape can be heat set to your project. Satin stitch around the edges of the heart to finish the edges after fusing to the project. See the examples of scrap hearts on page 103.

LAYER LACE OVER BLACK FABRIC AND SPRAY ON GOLD COLOR MIST.

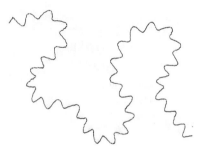

BERNINA STITCHING PATTERN

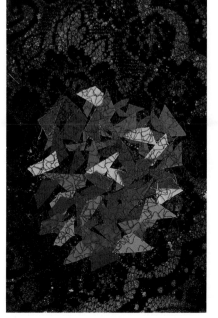

SCRAPS STITCHED TO A BACKGROUND FABRIC. MAKE INTERESTING COLOR PATTERNS LARGE ENOUGH FOR THE HEART PATTERN SIZE.

STENCILING WITH METALLIC PAINT   In the *Totally Embellished Vest* on page 103, metallic paint is used to decorate the vest. This is done after the vest is finished and the binding sewn. Gold metallic paint is added to the black fabric and to the print binding fabric as follows: apply Liquitex Iridescent gold paint to the binding with a cut piece of kitchen sponge. Squeeze the gold paint into a disposable dish or pie pan. Moisten the sponge with water and stamp the paint on the fabric following the directions on page 41. Use a piece of kitchen sponge, a paint brush, or a $^1/_2$"-wide tip stencil brush to apply the paint to the grid stencil.

USE A GRID STENCIL, THEN APPLY GOLD PAINT ONTO THE BLACK FABRIC.

OVERPAINTING BLACK FABRIC   This technique is similar to the Stenciling with Metallic Paint technique described above. For the quilt *Violet Maud, Rapture, and Tea* (page 26) I diluted Liquitex gold, silver, and copper paint in water. To achieve a similar effect squeeze an inch of paint into a small glass jar and add about $^1/_4$ cup of water. Stir this very well with a size 8 round brush until all the paint has dissolved. Drop paint from the brush onto the black fabric (Sample S).

CHEESECLOTH   This wonderful fabric can be used as an embellishment. First paint a selection of one-yard pieces of cheesecloth in your desired colors. Apply paint to cheesecloth with a 1" brush, forcing color into the cloth. Allow this to dry in a lump on a piece of plastic drop cloth. It may take overnight to dry. Open out the cheesecloth and cut it into small strips. These can be stitched onto projects (Sample T), or cheesecloth can be the total focus of the design for a garment; see the *Bella Luna Half Circle Jacket* on page 112. Another alternative to traditional cheesecloth is the drapery material called "scrim." This is a woven cotton gauze fabric slightly heavier than cheesecloth.

S. DILUTE METALLIC PAINTS WITH WATER AND DROP OR SPLATTER ONTO BLACK FABRICS AROUND THE APPLIQUÉ SHAPES.

T. PAINTED CHEESECLOTH MACHINE STITCHED OVER PAINTED SILK

decorat
the home

PRIMARY COLORS Painted projects detailed in this book liven up a neutral-colored contemporary bedroom. *Hearts For Robbie*, pattern on page 84, is hung over the sleigh bed. *The Opaque Hearts* wallhanging, pattern on page 92, doubles here as a pillow cover. The Athlete panel, pattern on page 96, from the quilt *Success* seen on page 97, when quilted and bound, makes a seat cover for an antique folding chair. The temporary lamp shade is a painted cotton gauze scarf, found on page 40. A piece of masking tape resist fabric, technique described on page 35, covers a pillow.

Additional painted objects add to the decor. Although no patterns are given in this book, each was painted using products and techniques covered in the book. The paper mâché heart-shaped box on the bed was textured with gesso and allowed to dry before burgundy Color Mist was painted on with a brush. Paint was brushed on by removing the spray assembly from the container.

DETAIL OF *OPAQUE HEARTS*

CHAPTER SIX

The side table, rescued from a 1940s bedroom set, was first coated with gesso, then sanded. Acrylic artist paints were used to design the painted surface using simple motifs of checkerboard, circles, stars, and stripes. Masking tape was used as an aid to mark off the areas of color.

On the bed is a small, painted wooden chair which serves as a sewing thread caddie and pincushion. Blue, gold, pink, green, and purple acrylic artist paints were used to decorate the chair.

ing

VICTORIAN MEMORIES   On the wall the quilt *Violet Maud, Rapture, and Tea* captures the spirit of a Victorian lady. The quilt is embellished with burned silk appliqué (described on page 26 of *Colors Changing Hue* by Yvonne Porcella) and seed beads accent the hand-appliqué stitches. Tea pots shaped like triangles and roses decorate the center surface of the quilt and overpainting with silver, gold, and copper metallic paint has been applied to the black background fabric. The paint drops convey the feeling of the night sky and to enhance the concept of looking out a window, drapes were added to each side of the quilt. The drape fabrics used are painted silk chiffon and silk organza which were also sprayed with Color Mist highlight gold.

THE ABSTRACT KIMONO   A commissioned 91" x 72" triptych silk hanging echoes the colors of nature and carries the restful palette of the evergreen wooded exterior into the interior of this home. Red tones, complementary to the green, reflect the redwood, copper, and carnelian accent pieces of the room's decor.

Contemporary versions of primitive shapes—spiral, triangle, and square—are scattered across the surface of the kimono pieces. An abstraction of the traditional obi or kimono tie is placed diagonally across the middle panel.

Hand quilting, hand appliqué, and copper metallic paints all serve to make this a unique artistic expression. A single motif pertinent to the homeowner has been hand quilted on the surface.

Using emerald mixed with black, silk twill was painted for the background and backing of each panel. Complementary colors were painted using a variety of surface design techniques on silk twill and pongee to have several choices for the appliqué as the design progressed. Metallic copper paint was added to areas near the bottom borders after the piece was finished to avoid having to stitch through the heavily painted surface.

THE ABSTRACT KIMONO

A LARGE PAINTED SILK WALL PIECE COMPLEMENTS A REDWOOD WALL.

JONES' QUILT, 91" x 72"; QUILT COURTESY OF DR. AND MRS. JERRY JONES

VICTORIAN MEMORIES

QUILT, TABLE, AND DECORATIVE ACCENTS CONVEY A SENTIMENTAL MOOD.

A PLEASANT INTERLUDE   Burned silk appliqué decorates the wall quilt *On Dwight Way*, as well as the *Shades of Romance* coat (pattern on page 128). Across the ottoman is a piece of purple/ lavender painted silk chiffon which can be used as a colorful room ornament or worn as a summer wrap.

On Dwight Way was designed using burned silk appliqué and overpainting techniques described in *Colors Changing Hue*. This quilt was made after visiting the Monet exhibition at the Fine Arts Museum of San Francisco. A later painting by the artist was hung at the end of the chronologically arranged exhibition. Many viewers thought this final piece was a poor rendering of the artist's oeuvre, when in fact he was almost sightless at the time of the painting's execution. Gesturing with broad colored brush strokes, Monet again painted his beloved *Wisteria*. My attempt in this quilt was to capture that feeling of spring on Dwight Way, at the Julia Morgan house in Berkeley, where the pergola is burgeoned with cascading blossoms.

A Pleasant Interlude

Complementary colors capture nature's bounty with a profusion of heavily-laden purple clusters played against a yellow sun-drenched sky.

OAK LEAVES WITH INDIGO AND MADDER   Some years ago I was commissioned to make a 6' x 6' wall quilt for a specific home interior wall. The homeowners had used another of my painted fabric wall pieces in their previous ultramodern home, and wanted this new piece to harmonize with the antique furniture and oriental carpets of their new environment. Since the quilt was a perfect square I mentioned that it could also be used as a bed covering if desired.

Shades of old gold with madder and indigo as accent colors were used to bring the dominant hues of the carpets into the quilt surface.

Since a very large oak tree anchored the home exterior, an abstraction of the oak's leaf was used as a quilting pattern on one of the quilt borders. Tracings of family hands, as well as alphabet characters representing the names

Detail of On Dwight Way

Echoing the Songs of Splendor, 72" x 72"; Quilt courtesy of Mr. and Mrs. A. E. Buzz Carrade

of the family, were added to the quilting pattern. Other elements of design were translated from complex shapes found in the living room carpet. A pattern for each motif was drawn and then traced onto the quilt surface and hand quilted in gold threads.

The quilt was made in sections, each hand quilted before being joined to the next. The cotton backing fabric was painted indigo and gold, and each section was joined using the alternate color as a binding over the seam. When viewed from the back, a very interesting pattern developed from the juxtaposition of these two colors.

The bed skirt is painted silk organza fabric, used as an overlay on a heavy woven Indian silk fabric, making a temporary change to the bed coverings. Rust-colored, painted, sand-washed silk covers the side table.

The wrapped poles on either side of the bed add a touch of whimsy to this classical room. Closet poles were gilded with several metallic paint colors. Eight-foot lengths of painted silk fabrics were torn into narrow strips which were then wrapped around the poles. The tassels that cascade off the tops of the poles were made by tearing strips of fabric, painting the torn edges with metallic paints, adding antique beads, and tieing this collection to the pole.

OAK LEAVES WITH INDIGO AND MADDER

A SILK QUILT ADDS A BIT OF ELEGANCE WHEN PAIRED WITH COTTON DAMASK PILLOW CASES.

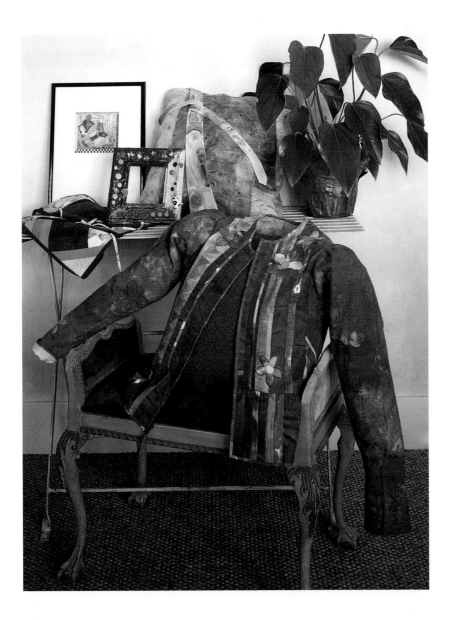

THE JACKET SETUP

Beyond Roses JACKET MIXES WITH VARIOUS PAINTED FABRICS AND ACCESSORIES.

THE JACKET SETUP   Would you believe that a wonderful Peplum Jacket could be used as room decor? I should first explain the rather eccentric vanity bench that supports the jacket. This treasure from an antique store had to be rescued! The 1930s bench had been painted a cheddar cheese color with dark green trim. The tired velvet upholstery was an early 1960s shade of lime green. I painted just the velvet on the inside surfaces with a mixture of bengal rose and black. It was a stroke of luck that the decorator pillow matched my raspberry paint mixture and that the pillow fit so well as a support for the *Beyond Roses* jacket.

Items on the antique table behind the bench include another pillow which has silk scarves as coverings and a jaunty hand-painted necktie as trim.

The *Sponge Stamped Vest* becomes a casual ornament on the table top, and the hand-painted picture frame captures some of the vest colors. The frame was first textured with gesso, then acrylic paints were applied in a very thick application. Before the paint dried, buttons and embellishments were pressed into the wet paint.

One of my small drawings is featured in the black frame. I used the small black and white drawing in an opaque projector to enlarge the image which served as a cartoon for a large quilt. Here the original drawing was hand colored using fabric and paper marking pens.

CERAMIC AND SLATE   Tuscany water jars set on the second floor landing contrast the gray slate floors and spiral stairway of this Mediterranean-inspired room. The custom-made iron railing seemed the perfect place to tie a child-sized painted kimono.

The Flowers That Bloom in the Spring is a cotton and silk painted kimono measuring 40" x 40". This small kimono is traditionally fastened with a large silk tie at the front. However, for this version, silk ribbons were made using a lightweight silk fabric and serging the edges.

The flowers of spring—hyacinth, daffodil, crocus, and iris—were the inspiration for the kimono. The Raindrops technique, shown on page 45, served as the painting technique for the gold sleeves. Painting Over a Drawn Grid, the technique shown on page 49, was used on polished cotton fabric, but the grid was omitted. This fabric was used for the edges of the sleeves and the body of the kimono. Other fabrics used were silks painted in a variety of techniques and painted cotton muslin used for the lining fabric.

Another small piece of painted fabric, painted in marble fudge color, is used as a discreet table runner under the giant ceramic lemons.

THE FLOWERS THAT BLOOM IN THE SPRING, 40" x 40"

CERAMIC AND SLATE

THE FLOWERS THAT BLOOM IN THE SPRING HANGS IN THE STAIRWELL.

THE COLORS OF NATURE   Terra-cotta and sage; rust and forest; orange and malachite; brick and viridian all speak of reds and greens. All the colors of nature can easily be painted on fabric. Every time I mix either a red or green color, I get a different variation. This is because I never precisely measure the paint portions when mixing them.

There are many ways to showcase hand-painted fabrics in a home interior. A beautiful cinnabar-colored tansu (Japanese chest) seemed the perfect place to wrap a painted green obi. Twisted silk chiffon makes a perfect rope to tie the obi. Simple pillows are covered with painted cotton fabric, and again a silk chiffon rope is used as a tie for the chair pillow. The floor pillow is in fact a pillow case tied with two silk scarves.

As a casual element, one arm of the antique chair is wrapped in painted fabric before the turquoise and sienna-colored *Landscape Vest* is draped over the arm of the chair. The vest pattern is on page 106.

THE COLORS OF NATURE

PAINTED FABRICS ENLIVEN
A RENAISSANCE ROOM.

BLUES BY THE PIANO A beautiful old piano seemed like a perfect backdrop to celebrate the color blue. The oriental antique carpet flagrantly portrays the complementary colors of blue and orange, but in such a profuse pattern that it becomes the perfect neutral floorcovering. The painted fabric decorations on the piano are all shades of blue with different accent colors. The *Celestial Jacket*, shown at left and on page 117, was painted using cobalt blue with navy and gold.

A simple, painted cotton string bag becomes a unique ornament. This bag also functioned as a travel bag, holding a large scarf when the weather turned too warm to wear it. The large silk stole, a piece 40" wide and 86" long, was painted yet another shade of blue in the center portion and a yellow gold color at each end. The scarf can be worn over the shoulder cascading over the body, or worn in the traditional manner. For the brave of heart, it can be tied as a wrap skirt. Even the pillow cover is blue with a touch of green, and a silk scarf painted in gold and blue snugly ties around the pillow, providing a casual yet elegant feeling.

On the floor is a heart painted blue and decorated with red, white, and blue beads and sequins. Red, white, and blue are comfortable colors playing off books in the library, and can be elegant when done in silk fabrics.

BLUES BY THE PIANO

AN INTERESTING MIXTURE OF
PAINTED FABRICS ARE SCAT-
TERED IN THE LIBRARY.

CONSIDER THE FLOOR   Consider using a framed painted fabric heart not as a traditional wall picture but, instead, as a floor picture. There is a casual elegance about placing a gold shadow frame box on the floor. The frame contains a painted silk heart shape. The pattern is the same as for the heart in *Hearts for Robbie* on page 88. The technique to make the heart is the same as the *Harvest Heart* on page 85 in *Colors Changing Hue*.

This heart was made using green painted silk pongee which was embellished with thirty-seven pink silk fabric roses. The heart shape was strengthened by machine quilting diagonal lines on the finished heart in a $3/4$" grid using a walking foot.

Cut and paint three yards of silk twill. Paint each yard in a slightly different shade of rose or red. Shades of green and rose were painted on $5^1/2$ yards of 1"-wide wire edge ribbon and on $18^1/2$ yards of 4 mm. silk ribbon. These ribbons were cut into manageable lengths and then painted either green or rose. Refer to *Colors Changing Hue* for directions on painting ribbons.

To make each rosebud, tear a $1^1/2$"-wide strip of silk twill and then cut 12"-long pieces. Fold the strip in half to $3/4$" wide and sew gathering stitches along the torn edge, catching both layers. Pull up the gathers to make the strip approximately five inches long. Make a triangle at the end of the strip and begin rolling the gathered edge, stitching through all layers as you roll to form the rosebud. Secure the fabric end to the stitching at the bottom.

To make each leaf, cut a 5" piece of painted wire edge ribbon, find the center, then make a 45 degree angle fold toward the center on each side. This will make a triangle with two long ends. Run a gathering stitch along the cut edges of the ribbon, gather to $1/2$", and stitch to the bottom of the rose.

Cut an 18"-long piece of 4 mm. ribbon. To make a 2" bow, wrap the ribbon in a figure 8 around two fingers and secure the middle by stitching with thread. Stitch this between the rosebud and leaf.

Use a hot glue gun to secure thirty-seven silk roses to the green pongee heart. Use two-sided mounting tape to attach the heart to a piece of foam core (an artist's material: two pieces of heavy white cardboard with a thin layer of foam between) which has been cut into a slightly smaller heart. Take this to a professional framer and select the backing and frame molding.

CONSIDER THE FLOOR

A HEART OF ROSES IN A
$17^1/2$" X $17^1/2$" FRAME
ANCHORS THIS ROOM.

quilts

Hearts for Robbie This quilt features three pieces of hand-painted fabric along with a selection of commercial fabrics from my supply of quilter's cottons. My style is never to calculate the fabric necessary for a quilt; I just cut and sew. If I need more fabric or another color, I generally purchase at least one yard, knowing that I can use any extra fabric in another project. Therefore, I do not have the exact fabric measurements needed to make this quilt, except for the painted fabrics.

CHAPTER SEVEN

DETAIL OF *HEARTS FOR ROBBIE*

PAINT, SUPPLIES, AND EQUIPMENT

Setacolor Transparent: bengal rose, bright orange, cobalt blue, ultramarine blue, emerald, buttercup, cardinal red, parma violet

Brush: acrylic size 8 round

Plastic drop cloth

Six containers to mix paints and a 64-oz. jar for washing brushes

Chalk wheel

Sewing and **quilting thread**

Template material

Pencil or **marking pen**

Sewing machine

Rotary cutter and **mat**

Rotary cutting ruler: 6" x 24"

Rose, star, and **heart patterns**

FABRIC REQUIREMENTS

Dyer's cloth: 22" x 48" cut into two pieces 22" x 24"

Deco Glaze: 22" x 27"

Purchased cotton fabrics in various amounts and colors

Backing fabric: 55" x 58" (can be hand-painted or purchased fabric)

Batting: 55" x 58"

Binding: 1 yard red print

The quilt is constructed in a modified Court House Steps/Log Cabin style. Finished sizes for widths of strips are given. Lengths are cut to fit as the quilt progresses.

Center Panel: 18" x 18$^1/_2$"

1: 1" red
2: 1$^1/_2$" red
3: 1" orange
4: 1$^1/_2$" pink;
5: 1" royal
6: 1$^1/_2$" blue
7: 1" red print
8: 2$^3/_8$" painted
9: 2$^3/_8$" painted
10: 1" x 1" red/red print checkerboard
11: 1" x 1" red/blue checkerboard
12: 1" lime
13: 2$^3/_8$" green
14: 1$^1/_2$" red/orange print
15: 1$^1/_2$" red/orange print
16: 1$^1/_2$" red
17: 1$^1/_2$" x 1$^1/_2$" red/blue checkerboard
18: 2$^3/_8$" painted
19: 2$^3/_8$" painted
20: $^1/_2$" red
21: 7" checkerboard
21a: 1$^1/_2$" yellow
21b: 1$^1/_2$" red
21c: 1$^1/_2$" red/orange print
22a,b,c: repeat **21a,b,c;**
23: 1$^1/_2$" yellow
24: 3$^3/_4$" blue;
25: 1" x 1" red/pink checkerboard
26: 1" x 1" red/pink checkerboard
27: 1$^1/_2$" red
28: 1$^1/_2$" red
29: 1" x 1" red/green checkerboard
30: 1" lime
31: 2$^3/_8$" painted

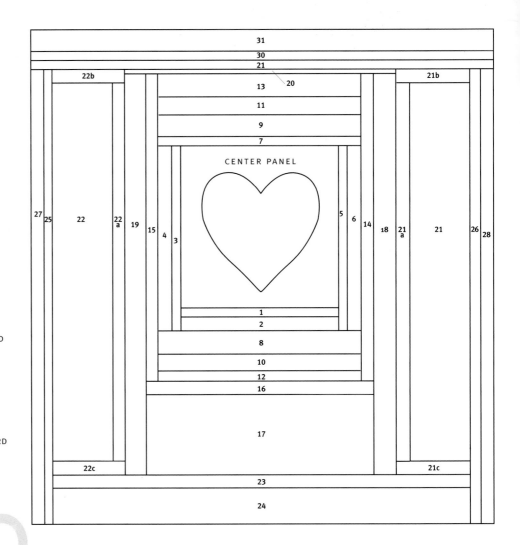

CENTER PANEL   The center square features two pieces of dyer's cloth, 22" x 24" each: one painted using diluted red and orange and one painted in diluted blues: each color is diluted 1 tablespoon color to $^1/_2$ cup water. Pieces of this same fabric were used for the appliqué hearts and a blue rose. One piece of 20" x 27" Deco Glaze was painted in an abstract pattern using full-strength mixtures of six colors, each diluted with a small amount of water.

To begin the quilt I hand-stitched the center appliqué panel and then added strips of colored fabrics and pieced checkerboard strips until the quilt reached 53" x 50". I had to be very creative with my Deco Glaze painted fabric, since I had only painted one small piece which I cut into 3" x 27" strips to be used in five places. Red print fabrics used to bind the edges finished the quilt.

BEGINNING THE QUILT   Paint two pieces of dyer's cloth with red and orange for one piece and blue for the other piece. When dry, iron to heat set the color.

The center panel is done in reverse appliqué; the finished size is 18" x 18$^1/_2$". Enlarge and trace the 12" heart pattern onto template material. Center the heart template onto the blue painted fabric. Given the size of the finished center piece, try to position the heart to conserve as much blue fabric as you can. Trace around the heart template with chalk. Remove the heart template and draw another chalk line $1/4$" inside the heart shape. Cut on the inside chalk line.

Position the red and orange fabric under the blue fabric directly under the heart opening. Baste $3/4$" outside the first chalk line on the heart. Clip the blue fabric $1/4$" along the inside edge of the heart. Turn this seam allowance under and hand appliqué or machine stitch the blue fabric to the red and orange fabric. After stitching the edges of the heart, turn the piece over and trim away the surplus red and orange fabric. Reserve this for the smaller heart appliqué.

Trim the blue appliquéd panel to $18^1/2$" x 19". Begin sewing strips around the center panel in a Court House Steps version of Log Cabin until the quilt is the desired size. See quilt diagram on page 86.

SMALL HEART, ROSE, AND STAR APPLIQUÉ   Trace the $3^1/8$" heart, star, rose, and leaf patterns onto template material. Cut out the templates and trace two heart shapes each on the red and orange and the blue painted fabrics. Add seam allowance before cutting out the shapes. Cut out the hearts. Then trace the rose petals onto the blue painted fabric and cut the petals out. Repeat using green fabric for the leaf templates and then cut out the leaf shapes. Trace and cut out the star pattern on fabrics of your choice. Appliqué designs on the quilt top, scattering them on four sides around the center panel. I stitched the rose below the center panel and the small hearts on the right and left sides. The stars were scattered, allowing the color and design to dictate placement of each of the five stars.

FINISHING THE QUILT   Layer the quilt top, batting, and backing; then baste the quilt. Begin quilting by stitching around the large heart shape and the appliqué shapes. Continue quilting in a pattern of your choice. Finish the quilt with a $2^3/4$" binding. Press the binding in half and sew the raw edge of the binding with a $3/8$" seam to the edges of the quilt. Press the binding toward the seam. Hand stitch the folded edge of the binding to the backing.

In order to hang the quilt, add a quilt sleeve to the top edge of the backing. The quilt sleeve is a folded fabric casing added to the top edge of the back; it should be at least 4" wide. The sleeve is made in two pieces separated in the center, and extends the length of the top of the quilt.

THE CENTER PANEL HEART FEATURES TWO PIECES OF HAND-PAINTED FABRIC.

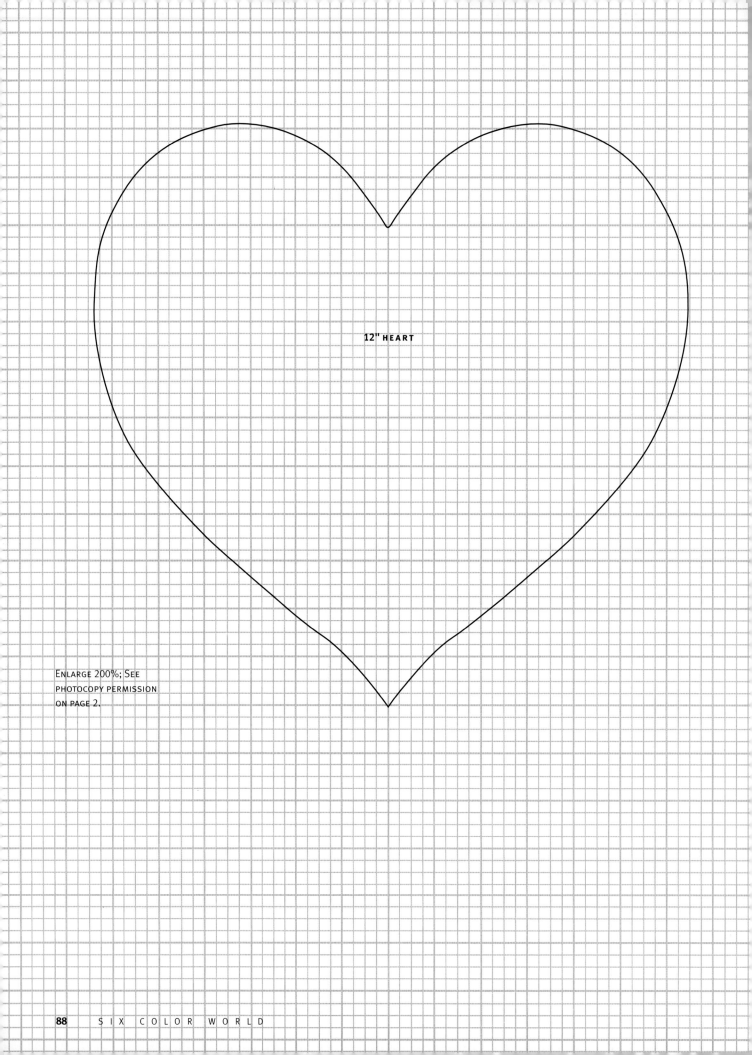

12" HEART

ENLARGE 200%; SEE
PHOTOCOPY PERMISSION
ON PAGE 2.

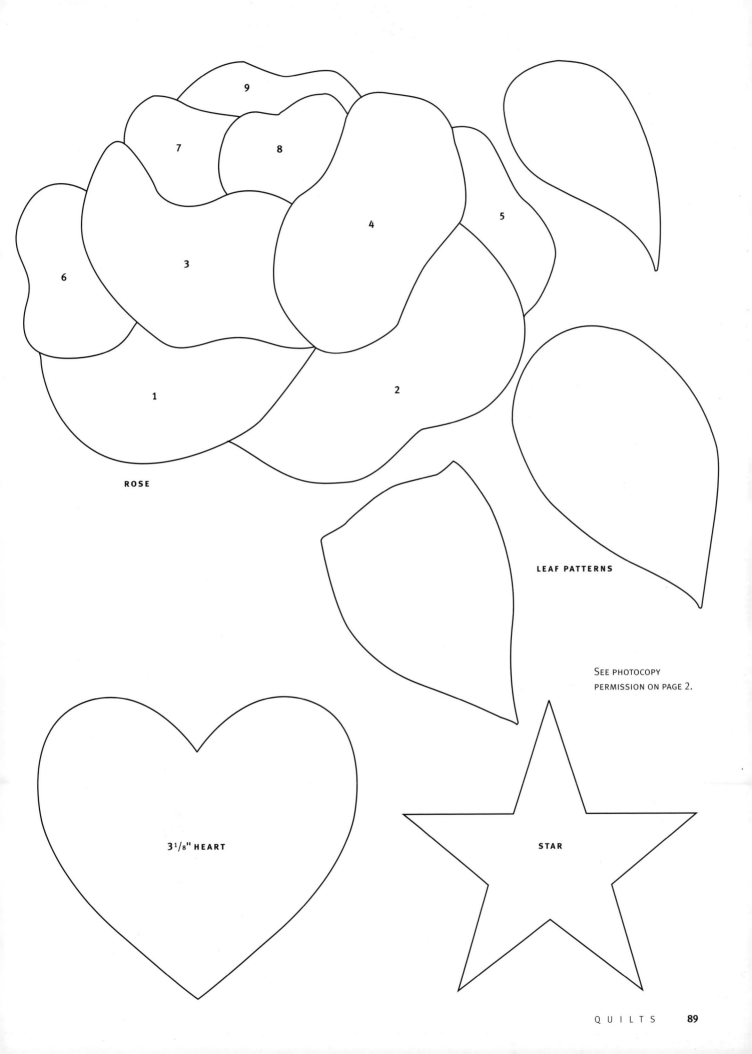

ROSE

LEAF PATTERNS

SEE PHOTOCOPY
PERMISSION ON PAGE 2.

3 1/8" HEART

STAR

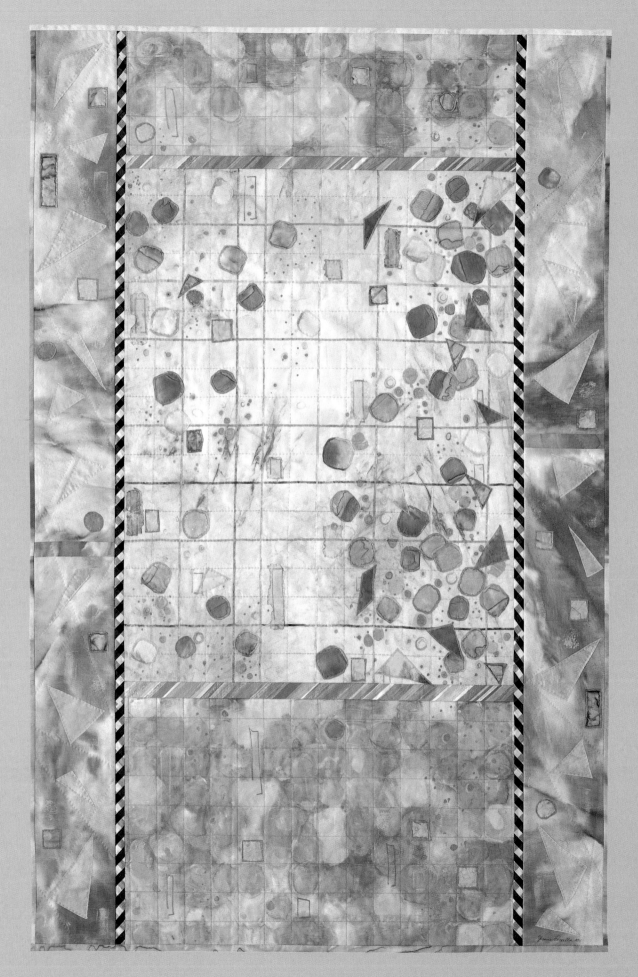

Yo Yolanda   *Yo Yolanda* was selected for the 1995 Quilt National exhibition. The surface of this quilt is hand-painted, quilted, and appliquéd using a variety of circle, triangle, and square shapes. Many of the techniques offered in this book were used to design the cotton and silk fabrics.

The title refers to the ubiquitous yo-yo quilt pattern of the 1930s. In this quilt the circle shapes on the center portion of the quilt are actually small circles cut out of silk, whose edges are sealed using different colors of Pearlescent Liquid Acrylic. Each circle was hand-stitched to the quilt surface. The center panel grid was outlined with painted silk ribbons sewn on by hand, and the circle shapes were added.

The narrow band of diagonal colored stripes were cut from fabric painted using the Resist with Masking Tape technique found on page 35. Fabrics on the top and bottom of the quilt were designed using the Paint over a Drawn Grid technique found on page 49.

I like to add a small area of black and white fabric to my quilts as a place for the eye to escape from the bright colorful fabrics. Many of these quilts and wearables were the subject of my 1986 book *A Colorful Book*. In *Yo Yolanda*, which is made using hand-painted fabrics, the black and white appears again. Here it is in the form of a purchased Indian silk gingham which acts as a break between the center panel and the border.

Since this is an art quilt there are no specific dimensions, directions, or patterns. The center panel is silk pongee painted gold, layered over batting and backing. The painted 4 mm. silk ribbons were hand sewn in a grid pattern. Square, circle, and triangle shapes were painted with Pearlescent Liquid Acrylic onto painted silk twill fabrics. After the paint dried, the shapes were cut. The paint sealed the raw edges.

The center panel was lengthened by stitching narrow bands of diagonal painted fabric to the silk pongee. Then fabrics painted over a drawn grid were added to the top and bottom. These three panels were further embellished with metallic and fabric pens.

The left and right borders were made as separate pieces and added to the center panel using binding to cover the vertical seams. To make the borders, painted muslin was layered over batting and backing, and triangles, squares, and circles were hand sewn. The borders were stitched to the center panel with the silk gingham. After the quilt was bound further painting was applied to the surface to enhance the design.

Yo Yolanda, 64^1/$_2$" x 42"

OPAQUE HEARTS,
APPROX. 25" x 25"

Opaque Hearts This irregularly-shaped, small wallhanging has a completely painted surface using Setacolor Opaque paints on white fabric. The design features a painted curved frame, which borders a center medallion of painted diagonal stripes and heart shapes. To accomplish the detailed spacing of the colors, use masking tape as a resist. See Resist with Masking Tape on page 35.

PAINT, SUPPLIES, AND EQUIPMENT

Setacolor Opaque paint: red, black lake, lemon yellow, light green, parma violet, bengal rose, vermilion, cobalt blue, buttercup

Fabric marking pen: black

Permanent marking pens: black with fine, medium, and large nibs

Brushes: acrylic size 4 round or acrylic size 2 bright flat

Plastic drop cloth

Bob Ross black gesso

Masking tape: $^3/_4$" and 1" wide

Tracing paper: 28" x 28" to make the pattern for the painted frame

Ruler: Omnigrid with 1" x 1" markings

X-acto knife with #11 blade

Pencil

Template material

Three heart patterns: 2", $3^1/_8$", 5"

FABRIC REQUIREMENTS

Deco Glaze fabric: 26" x 26"

Backing fabric: 26" x 26"

Quilt batting: 26" x 26"

Bias binding: $^1/_2$ yard of black cotton fabric

Ribbon: 12" of 1"-wide ribbon, cut into three pieces

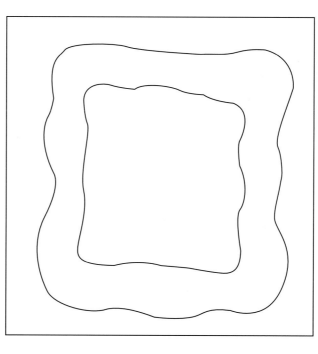

FRAME

MAKING THE FRAME

To make the undulating $2^1/_2$" to $6^1/_2$"-wide curved frame border pattern, begin with the 28" x 28" paper and draw a square 24" x 24". With a pencil draw curving lines, in and out to make an interesting shaped outer edge, and repeat for the inner edge. Keep the corners rounded. The inside measurement of the frame is approximately 14" x 16". Cut the pattern out of the paper. Be sure to save the paper pattern.

Trace the paper pattern frame shape onto a 26" x 26" piece of Deco Glaze fabric with a large nib permanent pen. I used this fabric because it has a nice glazed surface on which the paint sits well. However, if the painted wallhanging is washed, some of the glaze will come off, damaging the clarity of the painted design.

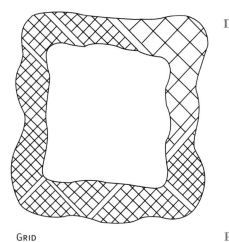

GRID

DRAWING THE GRID   Choose an arbitrary spot on the frame and with a fine nib marking pen begin to draw 1" grids and $^3/_4$" to 1" stripes. Use a ruler which has a 1" grid to plan out the spacing. The $^3/_4$" or 1" stripes break up the color patterns. When you draw the permanent pen lines, keep the lines inside the frame and do not go into the center area. These lines may show through the center panel design. Accuracy of the grid is not critical because this is a hand-painted piece.

With the X-acto knife cut masking tape strips into pieces the size necessary to cover the grid on either side of the drawn stripes.

PAINTING THE FRAME   Paint red opaque stripes between the grid drawings. When the red paint is dry, use the small size 4 round brush and make tiny marks on the red paint with black opaque paint. After the black paint is dry, discard the masking tape and press the painted areas to heat set. Use a press cloth over the painting, or the small raised areas of paint may adhere to the iron surface, where they will transfer to other areas of the fabric and appear as smudges.

Cut 1" squares of masking tape and place them over every other drawn square of the grid. Paint one color to make a checkerboard pattern on the

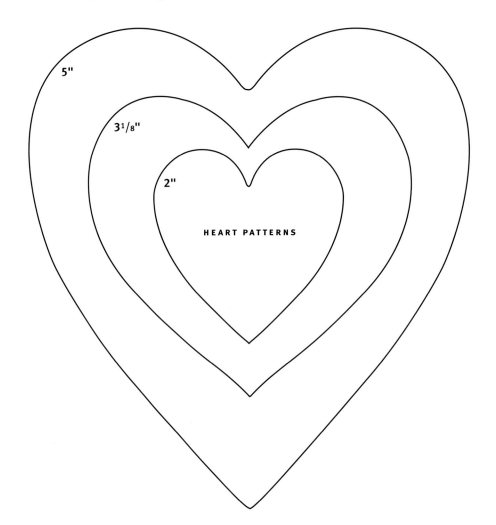

5"

3$^1/_8$"

2"

HEART PATTERNS

untaped squares of the grid, and remove the tape from the taped squares as soon as the paint is dry. Taping gets very tedious and it should not be done on a painted surface. I usually do it only once for the first checkerboard color. Then I carefully paint in the second color with the size 4 round brush or use the bright flat brush. **HINT:** *Using a small brush, begin by painting around the edge of the square first and then fill in the center. Continue painting the checkerboards in colors of your choice.*

DESIGNING THE CENTER PANEL

Trace the three heart patterns onto the template material and cut them out. With a pencil lightly trace the heart templates onto the center panel, spacing as desired.

Divide the center panel background into diagonal sections and draw pencil lines, making sure to stop the line at the edge of each of the heart shapes.

PAINTING THE CENTER PANEL

Using the small brush, color in the heart shapes. When the paint is dry, add dots or stripes to the hearts.

Paint in the background using different colors in each area. When the paint is dry, use a press cloth and heat set the paint.

Use the black gesso to paint around the inside edge of the curved checkerboard frame. The black gesso will hide any imperfections in your painting where this edge meets the center panel. If the edges of your lines are not crisp you can use a black fabric marking pen to smooth over the edges.

HEART PLACEMENT

FINISHING THE WALLHANGING

Since the opaque paint sealing the fabric makes for a very stiff surface and any pinholes in this surface will show, I deliberately pinned through the black line which divides the frame and the center panel. When I removed the pins, I painted over the holes in the black lines with black gesso, thereby hiding the pinholes.

To finish the wallhanging, layer the painted panel, the backing, and the batting. Baste all the layers together along the black line. Then machine stitch with black thread following the curves of this line.

Trim the outside edge $1/2$" beyond the painted edge and pin through the unpainted fabric. Bind the edge with 3"-wide black bias binding folded to $1 1/2$". Stitch the binding using a $1/2$" seam, adjusting for the curves as you stitch. Carefully press the binding toward the seam allowance. Do not touch the opaque paint with the iron. Hand stitch the folded edge of the binding to the backing.

PREPARING FOR HANGING

In order to mount this wallhanging, sew three pieces of 1"-wide ribbon by hand to three spots on the back top edge. Adjust the length of these ribbon pieces to accommodate the width of your rod.

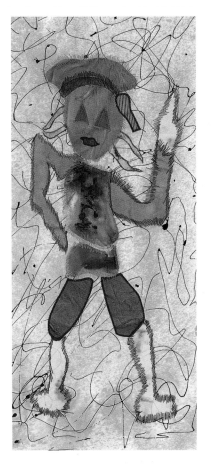

ATHLETE. THE FIGURE PATTERN PIECES ARE CUT FROM HAND-PAINTED COTTONS. AFTER FUSING, THE EDGES ARE FINISHED WITH DIFFERENT MACHINE STITCHES.

Success   After viewing the gymnastics trials for the 1992 Olympics on television I was inspired to draw a small illustration about that event. Later I enlarged the drawing into a 45" x 68" cartoon to use for the quilt *Success*. The quilt has four central panels, and I painted a different color on each of the background fabrics. Commercial cottons were selected for the appliqué and the remainder of the quilt. The designs on the appliquéd center panels and borders were cut freehand, and the quilt was hand sewn except for the machine-sewn vertical strips joining the four panels and the binding.

In panel one, the figure represents the universal athlete. Panel two depicts the exercise equipment used for workout training. Panel three symbolizes the fans who sit and watch sporting events. Panel four is about numbers and time trials.

Only the pattern and instructions to make the figure using hand-painted fabric are included here. The sewing technique, Thread Painting, is described on pages 63-64. **OPTIONAL:** *Sew the figure by hand or machine appliqué.*

FABRIC REQUIREMENTS

Wonder Under or **two-sided fusible web:** one yard

Muslin: 22" x 44" and 20" x 36", prewashed and ironed

Pellon Sof-Shape fusible nonwoven interfacing or a **tear-away stabilizer:** one yard

White cotton sateen: 17" x 36" background fabric

Multicolored painted muslin wipe-up cloth: 18" x 22"

PAINT, SUPPLIES, AND EQUIPMENT

Bob Ross black gesso or **black opaque fabric paint**

Setacolor Transparent: cobalt blue, vermilion, buttercup, cardinal red, emerald, parma violet

Brush: acrylic size 8 round

2 spray bottles and water

6 small empty jars to mix paint

Plastic painting syringe

Plastic drop cloth

Tracing paper and **template material**

Pattern Pieces for the Athlete

Permanent marking pen: black

Fabric marking pen: red

Fabric softener (Downy® is preferred)

Iron for heat setting fabric

Sewing machine and **sewing threads** to match fabrics

PAINTING THE FABRIC   Use the 22" x 44" piece of prewashed muslin.

To begin, paint six hues: cardinal red, vermilion, yellow, emerald, blue, and parma violet. Spread the prewashed and ironed muslin out on a plastic drop cloth. Think of the piece of muslin as being divided into six sections so you can paint each of the six colors on each part of the fabric. Notice how much painted fabric you will need for each template piece: hat, hat band, hat flap, left and right upper arms, left and right hands, lower legs, face, left and right upper legs. The eyes and mouth can be cut out of leftover pieces. Have an 18" x 22" piece of muslin available to use as a wipe-up cloth when you clean your brush. This will be used for the hair, torso, and hip fabrics.

Use the size 8 round brush and begin painting one section cardinal red for the face. Use about 1 teaspoon of paint to $1/4$ cup of water in a small jar. Add more paint and more water for the desired color. In the other small jars dilute the remaining colors the same way with water. Use 2 teaspoons of buttercup with 1 teaspoon vermilion and add about $1/2$ cup of water to make a red orange for the left and right arms. Paint diluted emerald for the hat in one section; touch a bit of buttercup paint to the green fabric to make an interesting patterned fabric. Dilute buttercup paint for the lower legs and then add a bit of the emerald mixture to the painted fabric. The upper leg fabric is painted cobalt blue, then a bit of dilute emerald is added. Diluted parma violet is painted in a small portion of the remaining fabric to use for the hat band and mouth. The torso and hips are cut from the wipe-up cloth which you used to clean up your brushes. After the paint is dry, heat set the fabrics.

BEGINNING THE FIGURE   Trace the patterns for the appliqué shapes onto tracing paper or template material and cut out the shapes. Heat set a piece of fusible web, large enough to accommodate each of the shapes, onto the wrong side of each of the painted six sections of the fabric. On the paper side of the fusible web, trace the reverse image of the shape patterns. To make the flap for the hat, draw red lines with a fabric marking pen onto a piece of the orange fabric to make stripes for the flap on the hat.

Success, 45" x 68"

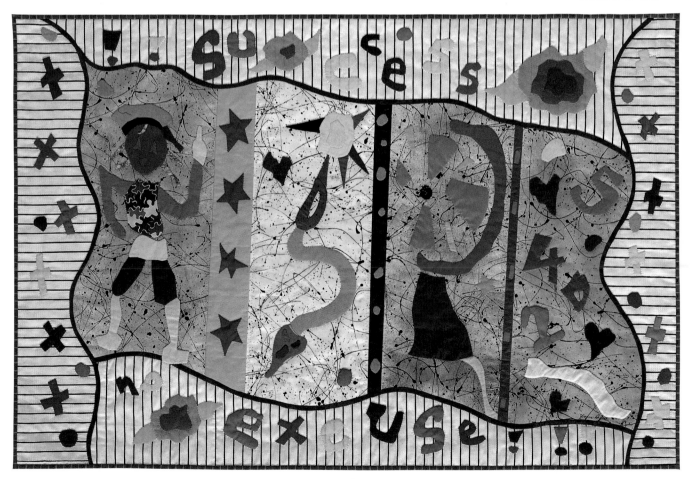

PAINTING THE BACKGROUND FABRIC   Begin by adding 1 tablespoon of fabric softener to the water in a large spray bottle. Spray the sateen fabric with this mixture and iron any wrinkles out of the fabric.

Lay the ironed fabric on a large plastic drop cloth. The background color will be sprayed on and you must protect surrounding surfaces from the spray. Mix a very dilute solution of cobalt blue and water, about 2 teaspoons color to 2 cups of water. Pour this into the second spray bottle. Spray color on the fabric. This background should be a fairly pale color to allow the colors of the figure to stand out. Let this dry.

ADDING THE BLACK LINES   Prepare the black gesso or opaque black paint to make the fine lines on the blue background fabric. If you use gesso, remove the plunger from the syringe and pour a small amount of black gesso into the barrel. You may not be able to pull up the gesso through the narrow tip. Carefully replace the plunger. (The black opaque paint may be thin enough to pull up into the barrel by pulling back on the plunger.) Be careful that the air space inside the barrel does not force the paint out of the tip before you are ready.

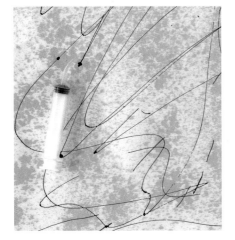

BLACK GESSO LINES ARE APPLIED WITH A SYRINGE ONTO BLUE SPRAY-PAINTED FABRIC.

Push on the plunger to spread very thin black lines over the blue sprayed fabric. Thick gesso lines will just sit on the surface of the fabric. They may be difficult to sew through, or the lines may just peel off, if they are not entirely bonded to the surface fabric. If you get thick splotches of gesso or the lines are too thick, use the following suggestion. Take a piece of muslin 20" x 36" and just spray it lightly with the fabric softener mixture to moisten the fabric. Carefully lay this moistened fabric over the painted sateen fabric and gently pat the muslin to remove the extra gesso. Be careful not to pat too vigorously or you may have black gesso all over your hands. You can wash this piece of muslin to remove the excess gesso, or lay it out to dry. If the latter, it then can be used as the backing fabric for another project. When the gesso has dried completely on the sateen, iron it with a damp press cloth. Do not touch the hot iron directly to the gesso surface.

HEAT SETTING THE FIGURE   Remove the paper backing from the fusible web of the figure shapes and arrange them on the background fabric. The design for this figure is suggestive of a body in motion. The arrangement of arms, legs, torso, trunk, head, and hat can be speculative. Try different configurations to make your own unique action figure. Notice there is a subtle difference in the figure on the quilt *Success* and the project sample. Heat set the shapes onto the prepared blue-with-black-gesso fabric according to the fusible product directions.

ADDING THE STABILIZER   Before stitching around the fused shapes, heat set the whole background fabric to Pellon Sof-Shape to stabilize the fabric; or use a tear-away stabilizer if desired.

STITCHING THE FIGURE Machine sew around the pattern pieces with the Thread Painting technique as described on pages 63-64. Use different color thread on each shape. I used satin stitching for the eyes, mouth, hat flap, upper legs, and hair.

Use this panel to make your own quilt. It can also be set into a garment or used as a chair seat cushion See Primary Colors on page 69.

PATTERN PIECES FOR THE FIGURE. SEE PHOTOCOPY PERMISSION ON PAGE 2.

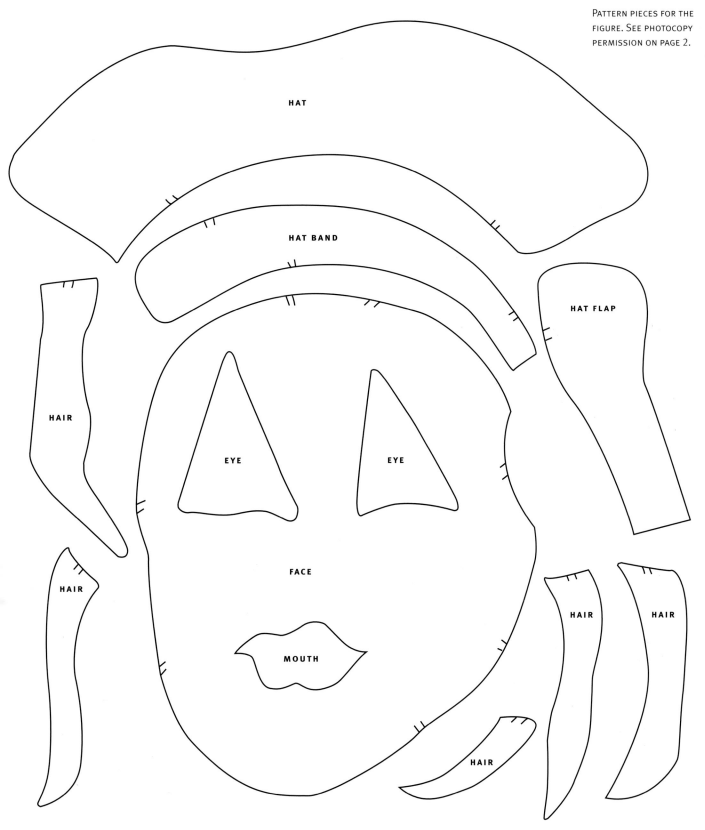

HAT

HAT BAND

HAT FLAP

HAIR

EYE

EYE

HAIR

FACE

HAIR

HAIR

MOUTH

HAIR

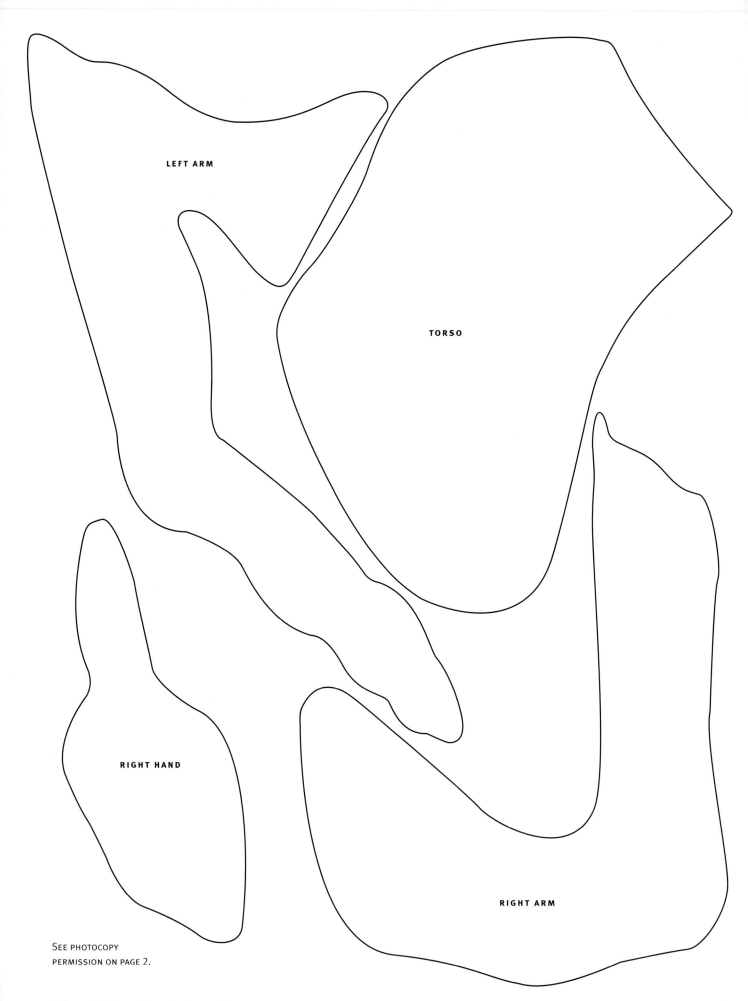

LEFT ARM

TORSO

RIGHT HAND

RIGHT ARM

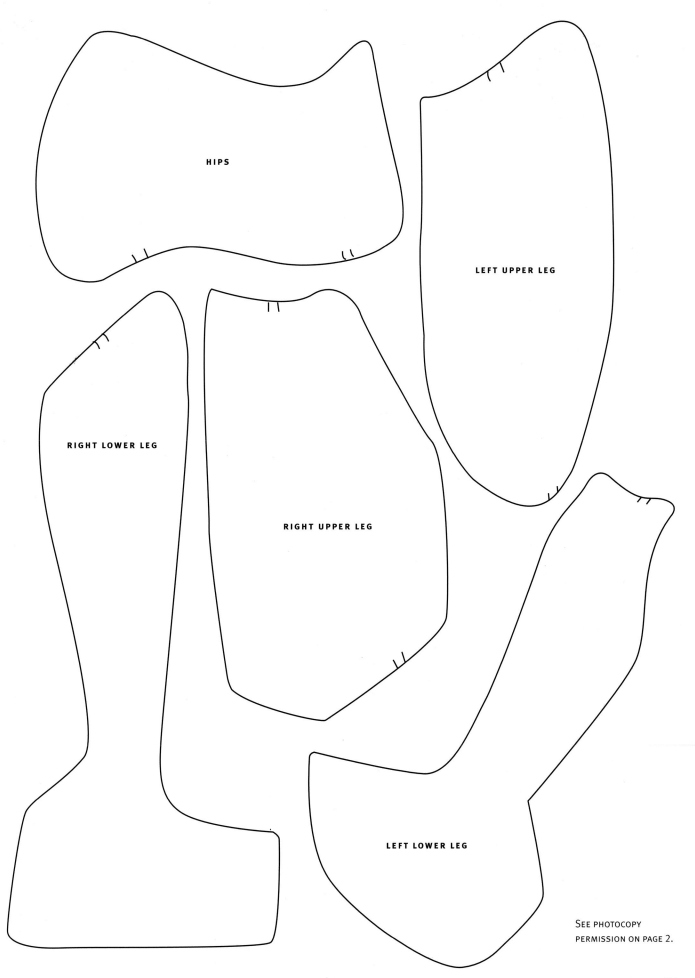

HIPS

LEFT UPPER LEG

RIGHT LOWER LEG

RIGHT UPPER LEG

LEFT LOWER LEG

wearables

Totally Embellished Vest The pattern for this vest is the same as the *Pleated Surface Vest with Appliqué* on page 54 of *Colors Changing Hue*. However, any pattern of your choice is suitable. Many of the suggested embellishments offered in Chapter 5 are used on the sample vest to varying degrees. The muslin lining is also painted and embellished with a variety of painting techniques. The heart patterns can be found on page 62. Other shapes on the vest are scrap squares, triangles, and strips.

A complete pattern suggesting where each embellishment is placed on the sample is unavailable since this was one of those projects which just developed—the "design-as-you-go" method.

FABRIC REQUIREMENTS

(Yardage given is for a medium-size women's vest.)

Black damask woven fabric: 1 yard

Muslin: $1^1/_2$ yards for lining and 1 yard for underlining

Woven fusible transfer web: $1^1/_2$ yards

Woven fusible interfacing: 1 yard used for pleated lining

Checkerboard print fabric: $^1/_4$ yard

Stripe fabric: $^1/_4$ yard

Additional fabrics for hearts, triangles, and squares

Commercially printed fabric for binding: $^1/_2$ yard

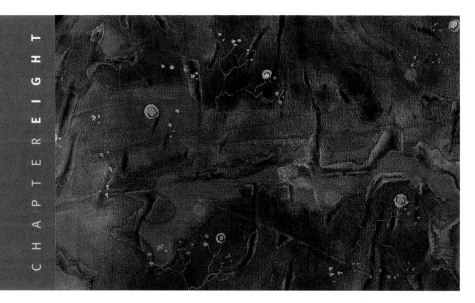

CHAPTER EIGHT

EMBELLISHMENT OF THE *LANDSCAPE VEST*

PAINT, SUPPLIES, AND EQUIPMENT

Setacolor Transparent: cardinal red, bright orange

Color Mist: highlight gold

Liquitex Iridescent: gold

Pearlescent Liquid Acrylic: volcano red

Brushes: 1" wide and size 4 round

Stencil brush: $1/2$"-wide tip

Stencil: $1/4$" checkerboard grid

A piece of lace to use as stencil

Fabric marking pens: red, black

A small piece of kitchen sponge

Plastic drop cloth

FRONT AND BACK VIEW OF *TOTALLY EMBELLISHED VEST*

HEARTS, TRIANGLES, SQUARES, STRIPS, AND BEADS

For a medium size vest add a piece of fusible transfer web to the back of each:

Two 4⁷/₈", one 4³/₈", and two 2" hearts in the Scrap Heart technique described on page 65

One 4⁷/₈", one 4³/₈", one 3³/₈", and two 2" organza overlay hearts (One heart on the back of the vest has organza pleated before the heart shape is fused.)

Two 3³/₈" and five 2" hearts cut from commercial fabric prints

Eight different size squares or rectangles and two triangles cut from checkerboard fabric

Three 20" x 1" strips cut from stripe fabric

Seed beads to match the heart shapes: small container or tube in each color

8 mm. sequins to match beads: 1 envelope of each color

Tube beads: ¹/₄" long

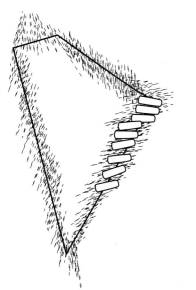

FUSED TRIANGLE WITH
THREAD PAINTING AND
¹/₄" TUBE BEADS

ACTUAL SIZE
8 MM. SEQUINS

ACTUAL SIZE
¹/₄" TUBE BEADS

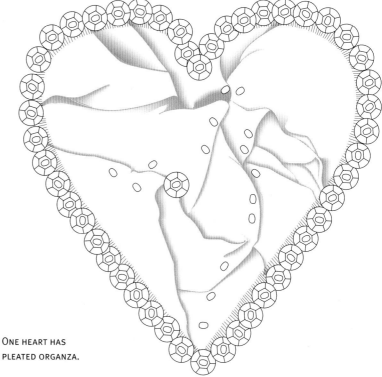

ONE HEART HAS
PLEATED ORGANZA.

SMALL HEART
SATIN STITCHED WITH
BEADS ADDED.

BEGINNING THE VEST   Cut the vest pattern back and two fronts out of the black damask fabric and the muslin underlining. Layer the black fabric over the muslin and pin the layers together.

ADDING THE EMBELLISHMENTS AND BEADS   After the vest pattern is cut from black fabric and interfaced with muslin, fuse three 1" stripe strips on the diagonal, one on the back and one on each front. All the heart shapes are made and then fused to the black damask fabric around the strips. Machine satin-stitching secures the hearts to the vest and edges of

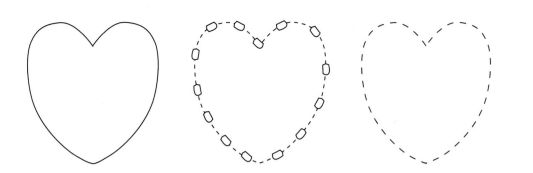

LEFT: HEART PATTERN

CENTER: SEED BEADS
AND QUILTING

RIGHT: QUILTED HEART

the strips. The different size squares and strips are placed around the heart shapes and stitched with the Thread Painting technique described on pages 63-64. Seed beads and large sequins are added to some of the heart shapes over the satin stitching. Some beads and sequins are stitched on the hearts and along the strips. See page 62 for Beading techniques. Seed beads also are used as a quilting stitch in the shape of hearts in the blank spaces.

STENCILING THE VEST   Iridescent gold paint is stenciled on the remaining blank spaces using a $1/4$" checkerboard grid stencil and $1/2$"-wide stencil brush.

PREPARING THE LINING FABRIC   Dilute 2 tablespoons cardinal red with $1/2$ cup of water and paint with the 1"-wide brush onto $1 1/2$ yards of moistened unbleached muslin. Then dilute 2 tablespoons bright orange with $1/2$ cup water and paint this over the still-damp red with a 1"-wide brush. Allow this to dry and heat set by ironing. Now re-dampen the fabric and twist it in order to deliberately wrinkle it. Then, using your iron, try to iron into the fabric as many wrinkles as you can.

Next, take the vest pattern pieces and lay them onto woven fusible interfacing and cut them out; see the cutting guide for fusible interfacing *Landscape Vest* on page 106. Now, take these woven fusible interfacing vest pieces and lay them on the wrong side of the painted wrinkled muslin. Heat set the interfacing according to product directions. Trim the muslin to the edges of the interfacing.

Two decorative Bernina sewing machine stitches were used to secure the pleats and wrinkles. Color Mist highlight gold was then sprayed over the lining through a piece of lace used as a stencil. Heart shapes drawn with black and red fabric marking pens, along with volcano red Pearlescent Liquid Acrylic, further embellish the lining.

ADDING THE BINDING   Sew a $1 1/2$"-wide bias binding with a $1/4$" seam, fold, and hem to the lining side covering all the raw edges. Iridescent gold paint was sponged with a piece of kitchen sponge onto the neck and hem binding.

SECURE PLEAT WITH
DECORATIVE STITCH. PAINT
HEART SHAPES ON LINING.

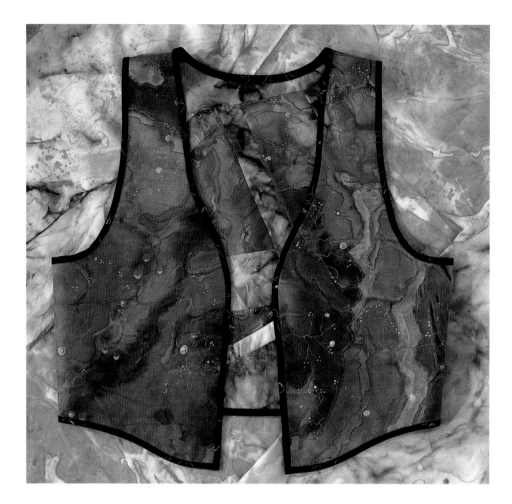

Landscape Vest with String Piecing

This is a reversible vest, with side one constructed from a single piece of spun silk painted using the Tide Lines technique described on page 47. Side two is pieced using scraps from the front side and a silk twill painted in a light gray/green.

The vest pattern for the sample is the same one used for the *Totally Embellished Vest* on page 102 and can be found on page 54 of *Colors Changing Hue*. Any vest pattern is suitable for the techniques shown here.

CUTTING DIAGRAM FOR
FUSIBLE INTERFACING

BACK:
CUT 1 ON FOLD

FOLD

FRONT: CUT 2

BLACK FUSIBLE INTERFACING

FABRIC REQUIREMENTS

Spun silk: 1^1/$_3$ yards

Silk twill: 1 yard

Muslin for the underlining: 1 yard

Black woven fusible interfacing: 36" x 24" folded to 18" x 24"

Black silk fabric for binding: ^{1}/$_2$ yard

PAINT, SUPPLIES, AND EQUIPMENT

Setacolor Transparent: emerald, black lake, bright orange

Liquitex Iridescent: copper, white

Pearlescent Liquid Acrylic: birdwing copper

Brushes: size 8 and size 4 round

Plastic drop cloth

Metallic pens: gold, silver

Small piece of kitchen sponge

Make two paint mixtures of emerald with black lake. The first mixture is predominantly emerald, with $1/2$ cup emerald to 2 tablespoons black lake plus $1/4$ cup water. The second mixture is predominantly black, with $1/2$ cup black lake to 2 tablespoons emerald plus $1/4$ cup water. A third mixture, used as a sienna accent color, is $1/2$ cup bright orange mixed with 2 teaspoons black lake and a small amount of Liquitex Iridescent copper squeezed from the tube and mixed with $1/4$ cup water. For side one of the vest, paint $1\ 1/3$ yards of spun silk using the Tide Lines technique described on page 47.

Cut the vest pattern pieces, one back and two fronts, from black fusible interfacing. Fuse by ironing these pattern pieces to the painted spun silk to stabilize this lightweight silk fabric. (See cutting diagram.) Reserve the remaining fabric cut from the neck opening and armholes and cut this fabric into strips or rectangles of varying widths.

For side two, paint 1 yard of moistened silk twill in a light value using the second predominantly black paint mixture above, diluted again with $1/2$ cup of water. Heat set this fabric when dry. Cut out the back and two front vest pattern pieces from muslin underlining. Tear four strips of the silk twill, 2" to 3" wide, and begin string piecing with this fabric along with the cut pieces from the spun silk scraps. Sew the strips to the muslin underlining. See the directions for Strip Piecing to the Underlining on pages 119-120. The leftover scraps from the cut spun silk should be irregular in size. Pin one scrap onto the muslin and string piece around the shape. Add strips of twill and scraps of spun silk until the muslin is completely pieced.

ASSEMBLING THE VEST   Trim the string-pieced back and fronts to the same size as the pattern pieces. Sew the shoulder and side seams of both side one and side two. Press seams open. Pin both sides, wrong sides together, around the neck and front edge, lower edge, and armhole openings. Cut enough $1 1/2$"-wide black silk bias binding to hem all the raw edges, beginning with the neck edge, then the lower edge, and the armhole openings. Sew the binding to side one of the vest with a $1/4$" seam, fold, and hem to side two covering the raw edges.

PAINTED EMBELLISHMENT   After the vest is finished gold and silver metallic pens and Pearlescent Liquid Acrylic applied with a size 4 round brush are used to embellish side one and the black binding. Iridescent white paint on a kitchen sponge was stamped on side two.

LANDSCAPE VEST, SIDE TWO, STRING PIECED

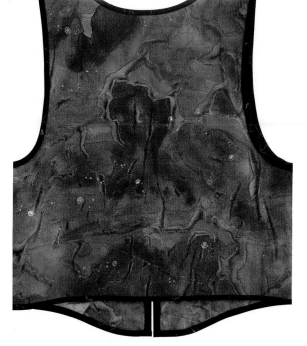

METALLIC PENS AND PAINT DECORATE THE *LANDSCAPE VEST*.

Sponge Stamped Vest   This vest pattern is the basic pattern featured on page 6 in *Pieced Clothing Variations*, my 1981 book on vests. The pattern features a center panel back and front and two side panels. The neck edge, front edges, top of the side panels, and lower edge are all covered with contrasting color binding.

This vest is made using what I call the "chop suey" method, in which blocks and fabrics from previous quilts or garments are recycled into a vest. Four cotton Nine Patch blocks and a variety of strip pieced units were combined with a leftover piece of sponge-stamped silk pongee. See Sponge Stamping on page 41. All the blocks and strips were sewn to a muslin underlining. (Directions are on pages 119-120.) The sponge painted silk was cut into triangle shapes, added as an accent to the cotton patchwork, and used for the vest lining. This vest differs slightly from the original pattern in that the front binding edge on this vest has a 2"-bias-cut binding which covers a $^3/_4$" welting cord; the ties were cut from 1"-bias binding and the side panel top edge was shaped. See the optional side panel diagram on page 110.

FABRIC REQUIREMENTS
Since this vest was made using leftover patchwork blocks and strips of fabric, it is impossible to determine exact measurements. See Determing the Fabric Needed below. The sponge-stamped fabric was a scrap approximately 9" x 24".

PAINT, SUPPLIES, AND EQUIPMENT

Setacolor Transparent: buttercup, parma violet, cardinal red, bright orange, black lake, bengal rose

New kitchen sponge: cut into circle, triangle, rectangle, and square shapes

Plastic drop cloth

THE PATTERN
This is a waist-length vest pattern with a back, two fronts, and two side panels. The pattern shape is suitable for patchwork, appliqué, or hand-painted fabrics. The strip piecing or embellishment is sewn directly to an underlining, and a lining is added before the vest is sewn together. Straight and bias bindings (1$^1/_2$" wide) sewn with a $^1/_4$" seam, folded, and hemmed to the lining side cover the raw edges.

DETERMINING THE FABRIC NEEDED
A medium size vest can be made using $^1/_2$ yard of fabric for the outside and $^1/_2$ yard of fabric for the lining. An additional $^1/_2$ yard of fabric is needed for the bias binding to cover raw edges. The vest is underlined and requires $^1/_2$ yard of muslin or cotton flannel or very thin batting. Various amounts of different fabrics are required if the surface is patchwork. See directions for Strip Piecing on page 119.

The measurements given are for a medium size. To change the pattern size for personal fit, use the following directions.

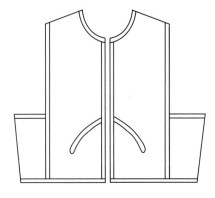

BASIC VEST

HOW TO CHANGE PATTERN SIZE   To make

a larger or smaller size for personal fit, measure around
your bust with a tape measure. To your bust measure-
ment add two or more inches for garment ease. This adjusted bust measurement will be divided among the pattern pieces.

Hold a tape measure across your upper chest. Look in the mirror to
determine the width of your center panel. The tape should be positioned from
inside left armhole to inside right armhole.

The center panel provides both the front and back of the pattern. Take
center panel front measurement plus the same width for the back panel and
subtract from your adjusted bust measurement. The answer is the amount
needed for the side panels. Divide the answer in half to determine the width
of each side panel.

SPONGE STAMPED VEST
FEATURES ONE SCRAP OF
PAINTED SILK PONGEE
COMBINED WITH COTTON
PATCHWORK.

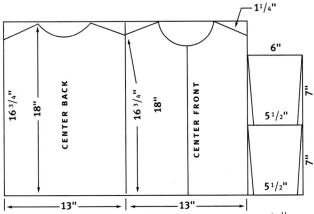

DIMENSIONS OF PATTERN
PIECES FOR A MEDIUM
SIZE VEST

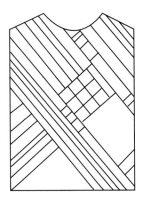

STRIP PIECE CENTER
BACK.

SIDE PANEL

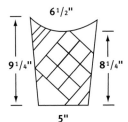

OPTIONAL SIDE PANEL

For waist length, measure from shoulder to waist to determine length of center panel. Depth of armhole is measured from shoulder to underarm. Allow an extra one to two inches for ease underarm. Subtract armhole depth from length of center panel to determine length of side panel. Add $^1/_4$" seam allowance to all pieces before cutting except the lower edge, the front edge, the neck edge, and top of the side panel, which are covered with binding.

To measure for shaped shoulder seam, hold a ruler horizontally against your neck where shoulder meets neck. Measure the distance between ruler and tip of shoulder. Medium size is $1^1/_4$" drop from ruler to tip of shoulder. Angle shoulder seam on pattern from neck opening to tip of shoulder. Add $^1/_4$" seam allowance to pattern before cutting. See drawing to measure for shaped shoulder seam on template neck opening on page 132.

DIMENSIONS OF PATTERN PIECES   Center panel has front and back panels 13" wide by 18" long sewn together at the shoulder. Shape shoulder seam with a $1^1/_4$" drop. Add $^1/_4$" seam allowance to pattern piece for shoulder seam. Neck opening is from template found on page 132. It is finished with a bias binding. No seam allowance is necessary on neck edge. Armhole is approximately 9" from shoulder seam to top of side panel. Side panel length is approximately 9" shorter than center panel. Width of side panel is 6" wide by 7" long. Side panel can be shaped to allow for narrower look at waistline. Medium is 6" wide at top and $5^1/_2$" wide at bottom and 7" long. For small and large sizes refer to page 133.

BEGINNING THE VEST   Cut out center panel for a strip-pieced vest by drawing a rectangle on the underlining fabric. Trace template for back neck opening in center of top edge. Shape shoulder by drawing from neck opening to armhole edge, adding $^1/_4$" seam allowance. Make a paper pattern using the dimensions as described, or mark the pattern directly on the underlining. Cover center back panel underlining with strip piecing. Directions for Strip Piecing are on page 119.

Repeat for center front. Slash center front for front opening after drawing neck opening. Vest edges just meet in front; there is no overlap. Cover center fronts with strip piecing.

Cut two side panels in underlining fabric and strip piece the same as for center front and back panels.

LINING THE VEST   Line back, fronts, and sides by laying these pieces wrong sides together on the lining fabric. Pin the pattern pieces to the lining fabric and trim the pattern pieces to the correct size; at the same time cut out the lining fabric. If you made a paper pattern, use this as a guide to cut the lining, or trim the pattern pieces to the correct size using your measurements.

BINDING THE FRONTS AND SIDES   Bind the center front raw edges with $1^1/2$"-wide straight grain binding. Pin and sew binding with a $1/4$" seam, fold, and hem to the lining side, covering all the raw edges. If ties are desired as front closure, add ties in the binding seam. Ties are 6" long and cut from a $1^1/2$"-wide strip of fabric finished to $1/2$" wide. Fold strip in half length-wise; press. Open fold, and then fold in long raw edges to center. Fold in one short end $1/4$". Top stitch on long side and across folded end.

Bind the tops of the side panels with $1^1/2$"-wide straight grain binding. **OPTIONAL:** *A $1^1/2$"-wide bias binding was needed to cover the shaped top edge.*

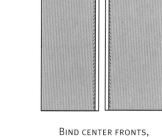

BIND CENTER FRONTS,
SEW SHOULDER SEAMS,
AND BIND NECK EDGE.

SEWING THE SHOULDER SEAMS   Pin the back and fronts, right sides together, at the shoulder; pin through the three layers of the back (pieced layer, underlining, and lining) and two layers of the front (pieced layer, underlining). Hold the front lining out of the way, and stitch the shoulder seam with a $1/4$" seam. Press the seam toward the front. Hand hem the front lining over the machine stitched seam.

BINDING THE NECK EDGE   The bias binding needs to be one inch longer than the neck edge. Pin $1^1/2$"-wide bias binding around the neck edge allowing $1/2$" extension at each end. Stitch using a $1/4$" seam, then press seam toward binding; fold in ends at neck edge. Turn in raw edge, and hem binding to lining over machine stitched seam.

ASSEMBLING THE VEST   Pin the side panels to the center panels, lining sides together. Lay the $1^1/2$"-wide bias binding on the center panel, and using a $1/4$" seam, stitch through the binding, center panel, and side panel. Repeat on the other side. The hand stitching for the binding will be on the lining side of the center panels. This joins the panels together and finishes the armhole opening.

Finish the lower edge of the vest with $1^1/2$"-wide straight grain binding, and fold the side panel binding seam toward the side panel. The lower edge binding will lay flat over this junction.

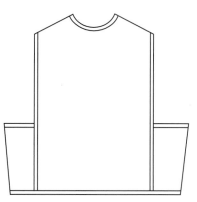

ASSEMBLE VEST.

OPTIONAL FRONT BIAS BINDING   This vest has a front binding which was put on after the vest was assembled. The binding is a 2"-wide pieced bias strip long enough to cover the front edge openings on right and left, with extra for hem allowance at neck edge and bottom edge. Stitch the bias onto the front opening using a $1/4$" seam. Fold the bias over a $3/4$"-wide welting cord. Then fold under the raw edge of the bias and hem to the lining covering the stitching line. The ties on this sample vest were made from a 1"-wide by 6"-long piece of bias which was sewn into a tube.

Bella Luna Half Circle Jacket

The Basic Vest pattern from *Pieced Clothing Variations* can be expanded into a variety of shapes by lengthening the body of the garment into a long vest or adding sleeves. The Half Circle Jacket uses the Basic Vest pattern with sleeves cut from a full circle of fabric, with half making each sleeve. The diameter of the circle is joined to the jacket at the armhole edge. All the raw edges except the shoulder seams are finished with 1^1/$_2$"-wide binding.

The *Bella Luna Half Circle Jacket* has painted cotton cheesecloth arranged over painted cotton flannel accented with silk and silver ribbon. A final unpainted layer of cheesecloth laid over the surface is channel stitched to join the layers. The sleeves and lining are painted silk.

THE *BELLA LUNA HALF CIRCLE JACKET* FEATURES PAINTED SILK FABRICS AND CHEESECLOTH.

FABRIC REQUIREMENTS

Cotton cheesecloth: 3 yards painted in a variety of colors, blue, peach, turquoise, violet

Cotton cheesecloth unpainted: 1 yard (Cheesecloth can be narrower than 45" in width.)

Cotton flannel: 1 yard painted blue, peach, and turquoise used as underlining

Silk twill: 3 yards painted blue, peach, and turquoise for the sleeves and lining

Silk faille: ^{1}/$_2$ yard painted blue and turquoise for the binding

Ribbon: approximately 4 yards each of 4 mm.-wide silver and silk

PAINT, SUPPLIES, AND EQUIPMENT

Setacolor Transparent: turquoise, cobalt blue, parma violet, buttercup, bright orange

Brush: 1" wide or size 8 round

Plastic drop cloth

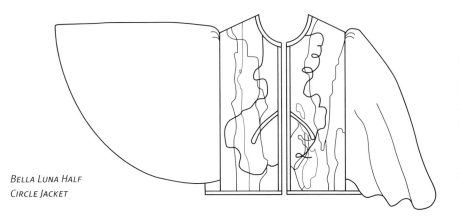

BELLA LUNA HALF CIRCLE JACKET

PAINT MIXTURES

Make a diluted mixture of each color: 2 tablespoons paint to $^1/_2$ cup water of each of the following paints: turquoise, cobalt blue, and parma violet. To make the peach color, mix 2 teaspoons buttercup to 1 tablespoon bright orange, then add $^1/_2$ teaspoon cobalt blue and $^1/_2$ cup water. Test the color and add more cobalt blue or buttercup to get peach.

Use the paint mixtures to paint cheesecloth, cotton flannel, silk twill, and silk faille. See the example of painted flannel right. This napped fabric can be painted using any method. Place the flannel on a plastic drop cloth. When painting, the moisture will sink to the bottom of the napped fabric. As the fabric dries the color will wick back to the top. After the fabric dries, heat set with an iron.

PAINTED COTTON FLANNEL

DETERMINING THE FABRIC NEEDED

The Half Circle Jacket is waist length and can be made from $^1/_2$ yard of fabric for the outside, $^1/_2$ yard for underlining, and $^1/_2$ yard for lining. An additional $^1/_2$ yard is needed for bias binding to cover the raw edges. Allow 1 yard of fabric for sleeves and 1 yard for optional sleeve lining. About 3 yards of painted cheesecloth and 1 yard of unpainted cheesecloth is needed to decorate the body of the vest, but not all is used.

DETERMINING THE JACKET SIZE

The measurements given are for medium size. To change the size for personal fit, follow instructions on pages 109-110.

DIMENSIONS OF PATTERN PIECES

Center panel has front and back panels 13" wide by 18" long sewn together at the shoulder. Shape shoulder $1^1/_4$". Then add $^1/_4$" seam allowance to pattern piece for shoulder seam. Neck opening is from a template found on page 132. Neck opening is finished with bias binding. No seam allowance is necessary on the neck edge. Armhole is approximately 9" from shoulder seam to top of side panel. Side panel length is approximately 9" shorter than center panel. Width of side panel is 6" wide by 7" long. Side panel can be shaped to allow for narrower look at waistline.

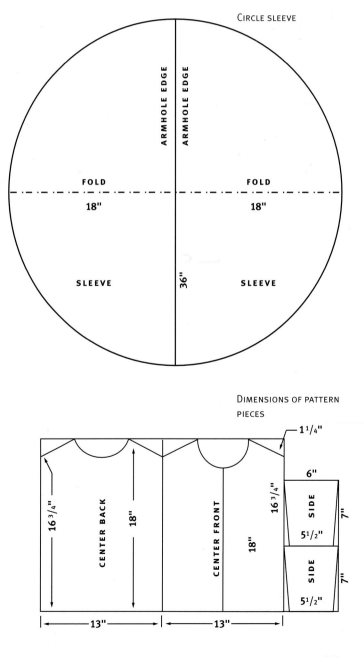

CIRCLE SLEEVE

DIMENSIONS OF PATTERN PIECES

DESIGN CENTER BACK.

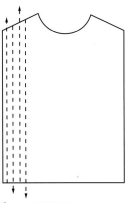

CHANNEL STITCH
CHEESECLOTH.

SIDE PANEL

DETAIL OF BACK SHOWS
PAINTED CHEESECLOTH
DESIGN, WITH THE TOP
LAYER PLAIN CHEESECLOTH
WITH CHANNEL STITCHING.

Medium is 6" at top and 5¹/₂" at bottom and 7" long. Sleeve is a half circle 36" on the diameter. The sleeve is slightly gathered at shoulder fold to fit into shaped armhole.

CUTTING OUT THE JACKET   To cut out the jacket, begin with center panel back. Draw a rectangle on the underlining fabric. Trace template for back neck opening in center of top edge. Shape shoulder by drawing from neck opening to armhole edge, adding ¹/₄" seam allowance. Repeat for center front. Slash center front for front opening after drawing neck opening. Jacket edges just meet in front, there is no overlap.

DESIGNING THE CENTER BACK   Cut small pieces of painted cheese-cloth and layer them over the painted cotton flannel in a pleasing color pattern. Directions for painting cheesecloth are on page 67. When the flannel is covered with cheesecloth, add pieces of silver and silk ribbon on top. Carefully layer an unpainted piece of white cheesecloth over the decorated flannel. Pin in place. Stitch with pale color thread through all the layers in a ¹/₂"-wide vertical channel pattern. Stitch from top to bottom and then reverse and stitch from bottom to top until the back is completely stitched.

DESIGNING THE FRONTS AND SIDE PANELS   Repeat the same design of cheesecloth over flannel on the fronts and side panels. When the machine stitching is complete, layer the wrong side of all the panels over the wrong side of lining fabric. Pin the layers together and trim the pattern pieces at the same time you cut out the lining.

FINISHING THE FRONT EDGES   Make the two ties from a 1" x 15" bias strip; fold right sides together, stitch using a $1/4$" seam, turn into a tube, and turn right side out. Divide this in half, hand hem two ends, and pin raw ends onto the center fronts. Bind center fronts with $1^1/2$"-wide straight grain binding, catching the ties in the seams.

SEWING THE SHOULDER SEAMS, NECK EDGE, AND SIDE PANELS   Sew the shoulder seams as described on page 111 for the Sponge Stamped Vest and then bind the neck edge with $1^1/2$"-wide bias binding. Finish the top edge of the side panels with $1^1/2$"-wide straight grain binding.

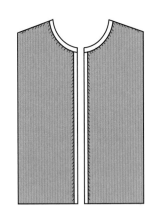

SEW SHOULDER SEAMS, BIND CENTER FRONTS, AND BIND NECK EDGE.

CUTTING OUT THE SLEEVES   The sleeves are cut from a circle 36" on the diameter. Draw a circle on a 36" x 36" piece of fabric. Cut the circle in half. The diameter of the circle, when cut, will be the armhole edge of the sleeve, and be sewn into the armhole edge of the jacket. The sleeve may be lined with a very lightweight fabric. If so desired, cut sleeve lining the same size and sew sleeve and lining together along the circular edge. Turn wrong sides together and press the circular edge. Handle sleeve and lining as one fabric. Otherwise the circular edge of the sleeve can be finished with a narrow hem and omit the lining.

Find the center fold of sleeve along diameter. Mark and sew two rows of gathering stitches for 12" along sleeve armhole edge; that is, 6" on either side of center fold of sleeve.

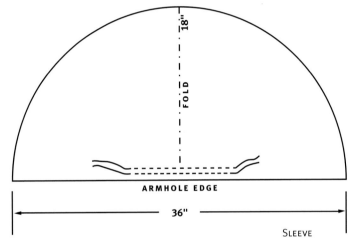

SLEEVE

ASSEMBLING THE JACKET   Join the side panels to the center back and fronts and put the half-circle sleeve into the seam. The sleeve on the fold measures 18". Pin the center mark on the sleeve to shoulder seam on the jacket. Adjust gathers at shoulder and pin sleeve around armhole edge, right sides together. Then pin side panel to center panel, starting at lower edge. Sew armhole seam with $1^1/2$"-wide bias binding over the seam. Press and fold in raw edge of binding and stitch flat to the lining side, covering the seams.

FINISHING THE LOWER EDGE
The lower edge is finished with a $1^1/2$"-wide straight grain binding. Follow directions found on page 111.

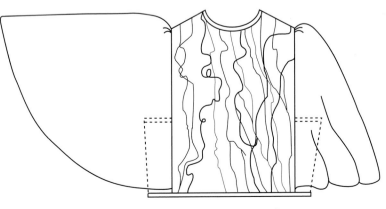

ASSEMBLE JACKET.

Purple and Orange Vest   This vest pattern, Vest with Armhole Band, is featured on page 46 of *Colors Changing Hue*. This sample features a variety of painted silk fabrics which are strip pieced to an underlining. Several of the strips of fabric were painted in the Tube or Pole Wrap technique described on page 42, Raindrops technique described on page 45, and Spray Painting technique described on page 43. Burned silk appliqué (further described in *Colors Changing Hue*), prairie points, and silk ribbon also decorate the vest. The pattern is a variation of the Basic Vest pattern, with a shaped lower edge and band added to the armhole edges in place of the half-circle sleeves.

PURPLE AND ORANGE VEST IS MADE USING A VARIETY OF SILK FABRICS.

After the fabrics were painted, the vest pattern was cut out of underlining. The fabrics were cut into strips and then pieced onto the underlining according to directions for Strip Piecing on page 119.

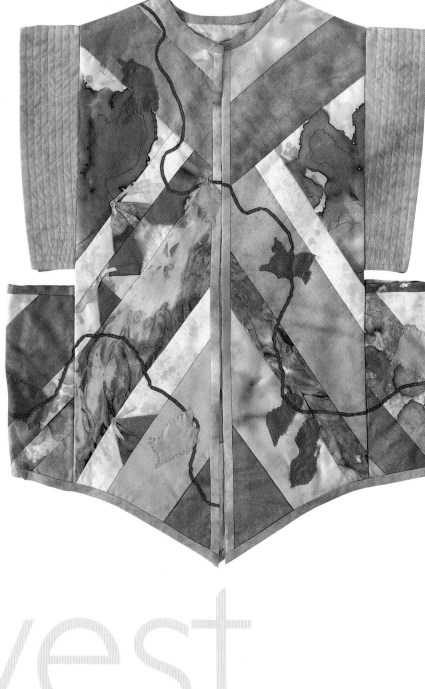

DETAIL OF THE BACK SHOWS TUBE OR POLE WRAPPED FABRIC, RAINDROPS, AND SPRAY PAINTING.

Peplum Jacket   In 1982 I designed a full-sized jacket pattern where three different style jackets were presented in one envelope, Peplum, Fitted, and Hip Length. The printing of this project was complicated due to the sizes of the pattern pieces and instruction page, necessitating the use of a map printing press. The pattern has been out of print for a number of years, but those who have the original pattern still like to make it using a variety of surface designs. The Peplum Jacket instructions will be presented here with instructions on how you can enlarge the pattern from a grid.

The body of the Peplum Jacket is the same as the Basic Vest pattern, with slight shaping at the lower edge of the center panel back. A peplum in the form of a straight piece of lined fabric is gathered to the lower bodice edge. The sleeve pattern has a high cap and tapers at the wrist. It is sewn to the top of the side panel and set into the jacket with binding covering the seams. Two versions of this jacket can be found below and on page 118.

Celestial Jacket   This jacket is made using hand-painted cobalt, navy blue, and gold silk fabrics with metallic pen embellishment, buttons, metallic paints, and hand quilting. The pattern is the Fitted Jacket with the peplum pattern piece added to the lower edge of the jacket. In the Fitted Jacket the front and back panels are slightly curved at the lower edge, and the side panels have been modified to an hourglass shape.

BACK VIEW OF *CELESTIAL JACKET*

CELESTIAL JACKET IS MADE USING PAINTED SILK, SATIN, AND CHARMEUSE. THIS JACKET VARIATION COMBINES THE PEPLUM JACKET WITH THE FITTED JACKET.

BEYOND ROSES PEPLUM
JACKET FEATURES STRIP
PIECING WITH HAND-PAINTED
COTTONS AND SILKS.

Beyond Roses

In *Beyond Roses*, made by Cathie I. Hoover, the fabrics used were hand-painted cottons and silks. Strip piecing, machine reverse appliqué, machine quilting, and pearl metallic paint decorate the jacket. Both of the sample jackets have a separating zipper as a front closure. In *Celestial Jacket* the zipper teeth show in the front; in *Beyond Roses* the zipper is hidden.

FABRIC REQUIREMENTS

Yardage is given for 45"-wide fabric. Purchase the same amount for the underlining and lining. Suggested fabrics for the underlining are cotton flannel, cotton muslin, thin cotton, or fleece-type batt. Different amounts of fabric will be necessary for the jacket surface if it is done in strip piecing or patchwork. Usually three yards total will be sufficient for piecing the surface.

PAINT, SUPPLIES, AND EQUIPMENT

Jacquard Dye-na-Flow: true red, yellow, green, orange, violet, black

Setacolor Transparent: ultramarine, bengal rose

Setacolor: pearl white

Brushes: size 8 round and 1" hardware store brush

FABRIC PAINTED FOR BEYOND ROSES

Cotton and silk painted fabrics included but all were not used:

8" x 11" each of red, orange, yellow, cobalt blue, emerald, violet cotton

36" x 27" red cotton

41" x 45" orange cotton

38" x 45" violet silk

34" x 45" lime silk

35" x 45" pink silk

12" x 44" lime cotton

15" x 45" turquoise cotton

18" x 45" multicolored print cotton

BACK OF *BEYOND ROSES* PEPLUM JACKET

The following pattern is for the Peplum Jacket. The exact measurements for the surface design by Cathie I. Hoover are not included. The center back, fronts, and side panels were strip pieced with a vertical set of painted fabric strips and half-square triangles sewn into a sawtooth strip. Then the reverse appliqué was cut into the piecing. The sleeves were cut from one piece of painted fabric and machine quilted in a grid pattern. The peplum was strip pieced. The lining features the orange, pink, and lime painted fabrics. Pearl metallic paint was sponged over the finished jacket sleeves.

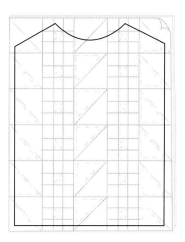

GENERAL DIRECTIONS   In keeping with the patchwork or pieced clothing tradition, the jacket is designed to be sewn in the three-layer method. Each pattern piece is pieced to an underlining or batting and then lined. All seams in the jacket are then covered with a binding similar to the edging on a quilt. The jacket is completely finished on the inside.

The Basic Vest pattern can be worn under the Peplum Jacket pattern for a jacket/vest combination.

MAKING UNITS FOR STRIP PIECING   Begin by selecting various colors of prints and solid fabrics. Cut enough strips of each color to have a selection during the piecing process.

Fold 45"-wide fabric in half (22^1/$_2$") matching selvage edges. Fold fabric in half again (11^1/$_4$") so fold line is even with selvage to make four layers of fabric.

Cut various width strips of fabric using a plastic ruler with a rotary cutter: 1", 1^1/$_2$", 2", and 2^1/$_2$". The horizontal lines of the ruler should match up with the folded edges of the fabric. Cut different width strips of fabric in different colors to have a selection during the piecing process. Extra cut strips can always be used in another project.

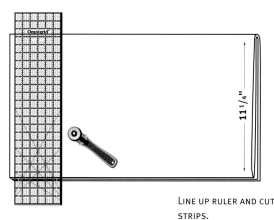

11^1/$_4$"

LINE UP RULER AND CUT STRIPS.

STRIP PIECING   A unit of strips refers to four, five, or more colors sewn together. Sew two strips together and press the seams in one direction. Join two strips to two more to make four strips (add more if desired). Always press seams after sewing. Reverse the direction of the stitching when joining two or more strips; sew two strips top to bottom, but reverse the stitching line from bottom to top when joining with two more. This now makes a "unit" of four different fabrics sewn together lengthwise.

Units can be cut vertically across the horizontally sewn colors. Widths can vary, and these can be pieced with units or sewn end to end to make a single strip of pieces.

UNIT

CUT STRIPS FROM A STITCHED UNIT.

STRIP PIECING TO THE UNDERLINING   The underlining serves as a foundation in machine piecing. Begin by pinning one strip unit to underlining.

Place strip 1 wrong side down on the left edge of the underlining. Pin the left edge of strip 1 to the edge of the underlining. Place strip 2 right sides together on top of strip 1. Line up right edge of both strips. Pin in place. Stitch

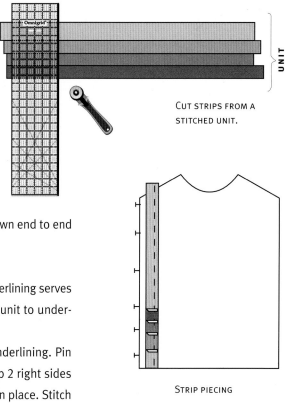

STRIP PIECING

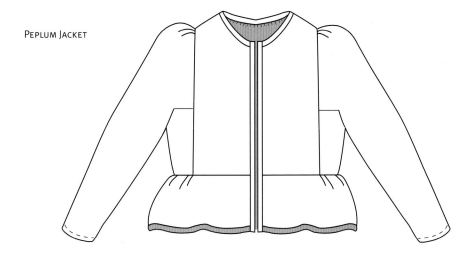

PEPLUM JACKET

through all three layers: underlining, strip 1, and strip 2. Turn strip 2 to right and press. Continue with strip 3, and so forth, until the underlining is covered.

CAUTION: *Each strip should cover all of the underlining pattern piece before stitching. If necessary, piece strip to make it long enough to cover the underlining. Then trim excess fabric after pressing top fabric to the right.*

If the pattern piece does not have straight edges such as in the Peplum Jacket center back pattern, draw a straight vertical line on the underlining as a guide to begin strip piecing. Fill in angles, etc., with another piece. Draw additional lines on underlining, if desired, for accuracy in keeping piecing straight.

CUTTING AND SEWING DIRECTIONS   Use pattern pieces 1A, 2A, 3A, 4A, and 5A on pages 124-127. To begin, cut all jacket pattern pieces from underlining.

Cut lining. **NOTE:** *All lining pieces are cut from same pattern pieces except peplum (5A). Cut the peplum lining 1" wider.*

Prepare fabrics for painting, piecing, or patchwork as desired for the surface design.

BACK   Cover back 1A underlining with strip piecing. If the strip piecing method is used, sew pieces directly onto underlining. Pin lining to back, wrong sides together, around all edges.

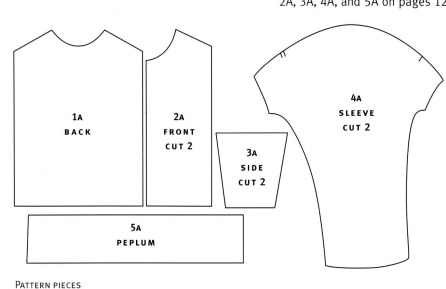

PATTERN PIECES

FRONTS   Cover fronts 2A underlining with strip piecing. Pin lining to fronts with wrong sides together.

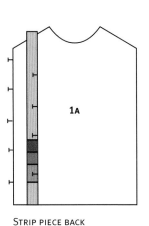

STRIP PIECE BACK

PIN LINING WRONG SIDES TOGETHER

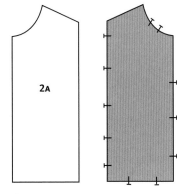

FRONTS

SEWING THE SHOULDER SEAMS Pin back to fronts at shoulder seams; pin through all three layers of back (pieced layer, underlining, lining) and two layers of front (pieced layer, underlining). Hold the front lining out of the way, stitch the shoulder seam using a $1/4$" seam. Press seam toward the front. Hand hem the front lining over the machine stitched seam.

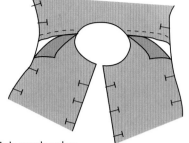

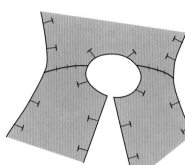

LEFT: SEW SHOULDER SEAMS.

RIGHT: HAND HEM LINING.

BINDING THE NECK EDGE Finish neck edge with $1^1/2$"-wide bias binding. Refer to Binding the Neck Edge on page 111.

SIDE PANELS Cover side panels (3A) with strip piecing. Pin lining to side panels with wrong sides together.

SLEEVES Cover sleeve (4A) underlining with a single piece of fabric or strip piecing. Try to keep piecing at a minimum on cap of sleeve. The sleeve cap will be gathered to fit into the armhole, and excessive piecing makes gathering difficult.

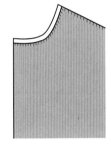

BIND NECK EDGE.

SIDE PANELS

Pin sleeve and lining right sides together at wrist edge. (Pay close attention to front and back notches on sleeve cap. Select correct sleeve lining to match notches.) Stitch sleeve and lining along wrist edge using a $1/4$" seam.

Open out flat the sleeve and lining, and press wrist seam toward the sleeve fabric.

With right sides together, fold sleeve and lining in half along straight grain line.

Pin underarm seam on sleeve and lining. Stitch seam using a $1/4$" seam and leave both ends of seam open at curve.

Press seams open on sleeve and lining. Turn sleeve right side out. Pin sleeve and lining along wrist edge and pin together along cap.

LEFT: STRIP PIECE SLEEVE

RIGHT: PIN AND STITCH SLEEVE AND LINING AT WRIST.

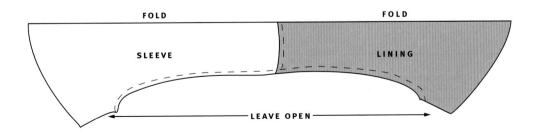

SEW SLEEVE AND LINING SEAM.

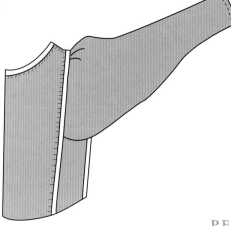

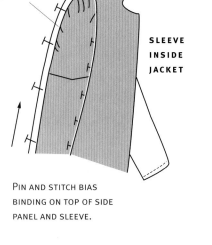

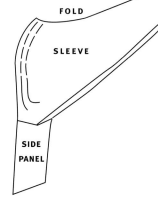

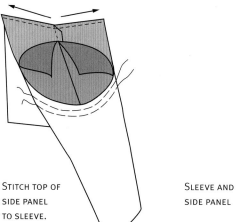

Top stitch wrist edge $^1/_4$" away from edge to secure lining.

To gather cap of sleeve, stitch two rows of gathering stitches between notches through both sleeve and lining.

SEW GATHER STITCHING ALONG CAP.

STITCH TOP OF SIDE PANEL TO SLEEVE.

SLEEVE AND SIDE PANEL

FOLD

SLEEVE

SIDE PANEL

BIAS BINDING

SLEEVE INSIDE JACKET

PIN AND STITCH BIAS BINDING ON TOP OF SIDE PANEL AND SLEEVE.

SLEEVES AND SIDE PANELS   Pin back and front edge of underarm sleeve to top of side panel. Stitch using a $^1/_4$" seam through all layers of the side panels, and sleeve and underlining fabric only, omitting sleeve lining. Press seam toward sleeve. Hand hem edge of sleeve lining over machine stitched seam. This seam assembles sleeve and side panel unit.

ASSEMBLING THE JACKET   Pin sleeve and side panel unit to back and fronts. Match shoulder seam with sleeve center; match front and back notches of sleeve with notches on front and back; match bottom edge of side panel with bottom edge of front and back. Pin side panel along front and back; pull up bobbin threads to ease in gathers on cap to fit into armhole.

IMPORTANT: *This joining seam is sewn with a very narrow $^1/_4$" seam. Be sure all three layers of each pattern piece have been trimmed evenly. This will ensure all edges will be caught in seam.*

Stitch this seam with a $1^1/_2$"-wide bias binding on top of the sleeve and side panel unit to finish this raw edge. Use purchased single-fold bias or cut your own. Clip curve through all layers at shoulder. Press binding toward center panel. Turn in raw edge and hand hem bias binding down to center front and back panel lining over machine stitched seam.

HEM BIAS BINDING TO CENTER PANEL LINING.

PEPLUM   Cover peplum (5A) underlining with strip piecing. **NOTE:** *Peplum lining should have been cut one inch wider than peplum.*

Pin peplum and lining right sides together along one long edge. Stitch using a $^1/_4$" seam. Turn right side out and press. Peplum lining should show $^1/_4$" along lower edge of peplum.

Pin raw edges together at top edge of peplum. Raw edges of center front of peplum will be finished with binding on center front opening. **OPTIONAL:** *Pin peplum and lining wrong sides together and hem*

5A

PEPLUM

lower edge of peplum with binding, as in Beyond Roses *jacket.*

Sew two rows of gathering stitches along top edge of peplum. Sew through peplum and lining.

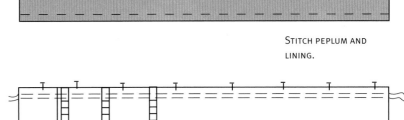

STITCH PEPLUM AND LINING.

Pin peplum to bodice. Match center back of peplum with center back of bodice. Pull up bobbin stitches to ease in gathers so peplum fits along lower edge of bodice. Pin on peplum side to guide the gathers.

SEW TWO ROWS OF GATHERING STITCHES.

Put a 1^1/$_2$"-wide binding over peplum and stitch using a ^{1}/$_4$" seam. Binding can be straight grain. Press seam toward bodice. Turn in raw edge and hand hem binding to bodice. This holds the gathers flat at waistline.

FINISHING THE JACKET Pin binding, right sides together, over front edges of center front, including neck binding and peplum raw edge. Binding is 1^1/$_2$" wide and can be straight grain or bias. Allow a ^{1}/$_2$" extension at each end. Stitch using a ^{1}/$_4$" seam. Press binding toward seam. Fold in ends at neck edge and peplum. Turn in raw edge and hand hem binding over machine stitched seam.

PIN AND STITCH PEPLUM TO BODICE.

OPTIONAL: *Add shoulder pads to lift cap of sleeve.*

Celestial Jacket and *Beyond Roses* have a jacket separating zipper as front closure. The zipper is set in by hand after the jacket is finished. Hand stitch a binding on the lining to cover the edge of the zipper tape.

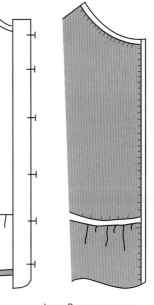

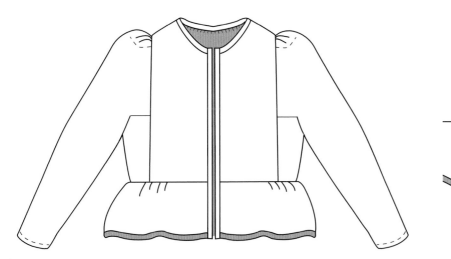

ADD OPTIONAL SHOULDER PADS.

LEFT: BIND FRONT EDGE.

RIGHT: INSIDE FRONT OF JACKET WITH BOUND EDGES

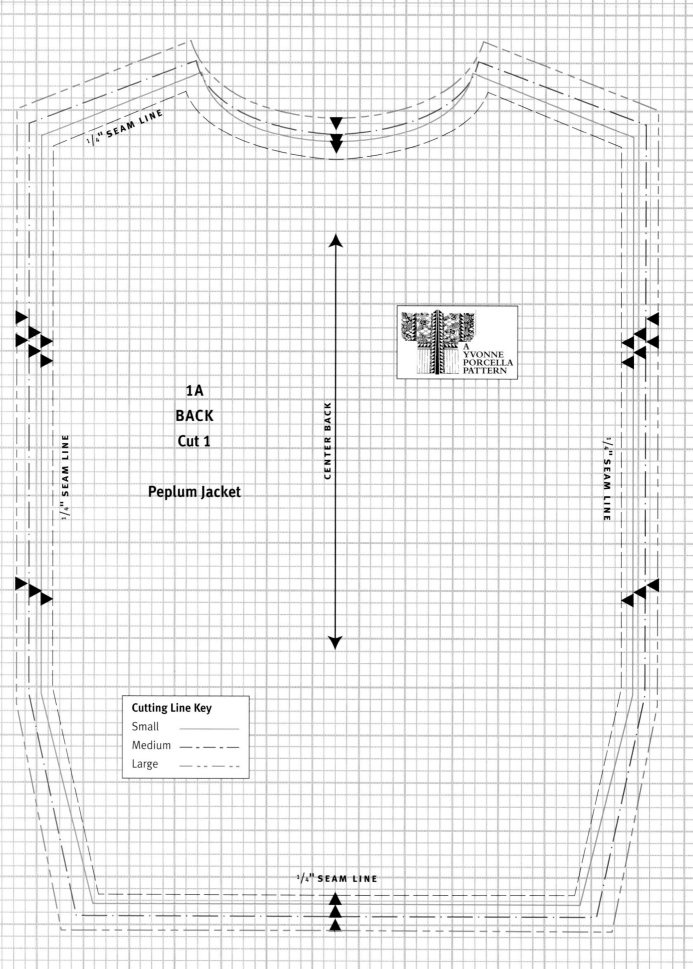

1/4" SEAM LINE

1A

BACK

Cut 1

Peplum Jacket

CENTER BACK

1/4" SEAM LINE

1/4" SEAM LINE

A YVONNE PORCELLA PATTERN

Cutting Line Key

Small ——————

Medium —·—·—·—

Large —— — — —

1/4" SEAM LINE

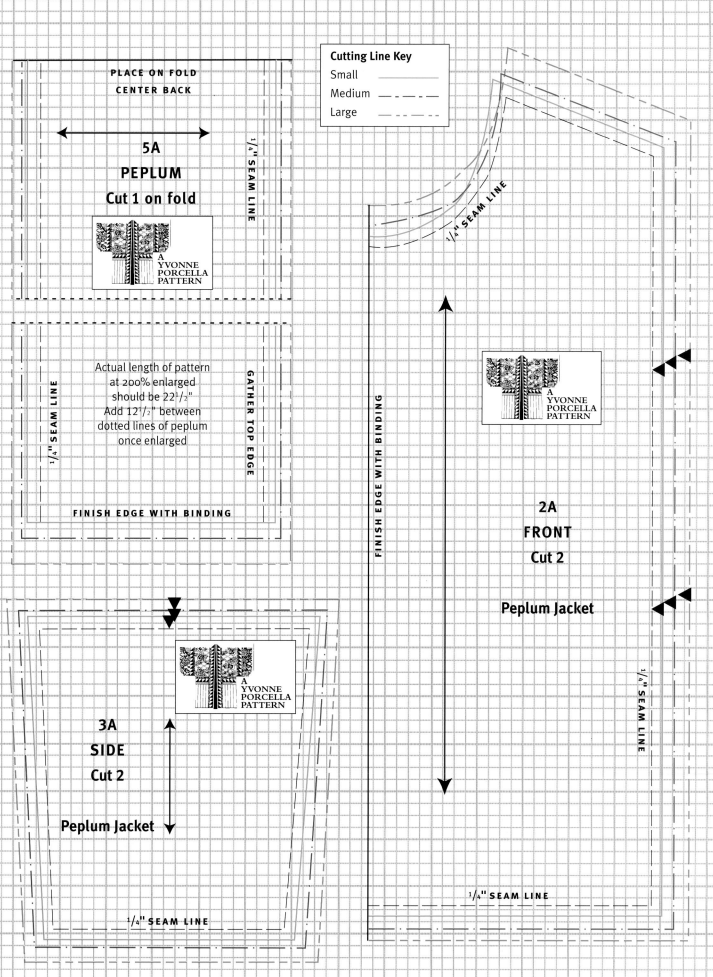

PLACE ON FOLD
CENTER BACK

5A
PEPLUM
Cut 1 on fold

A YVONNE PORCELLA PATTERN

¹/₄" SEAM LINE

¹/₄" SEAM LINE

GATHER TOP EDGE

Actual length of pattern
at 200% enlarged
should be 22¹/₂"
Add 12¹/₂" between
dotted lines of peplum
once enlarged

FINISH EDGE WITH BINDING

¹/₄" SEAM LINE

FINISH EDGE WITH BINDING

A YVONNE PORCELLA PATTERN

2A
FRONT
Cut 2

Peplum Jacket

¹/₄" SEAM LINE

A YVONNE PORCELLA PATTERN

3A
SIDE
Cut 2

Peplum Jacket

¹/₄" SEAM LINE

¹/₄" SEAM LINE

ENLARGE 200%. SEE PHOTOCOPY PERMISSION ON PAGE 2.

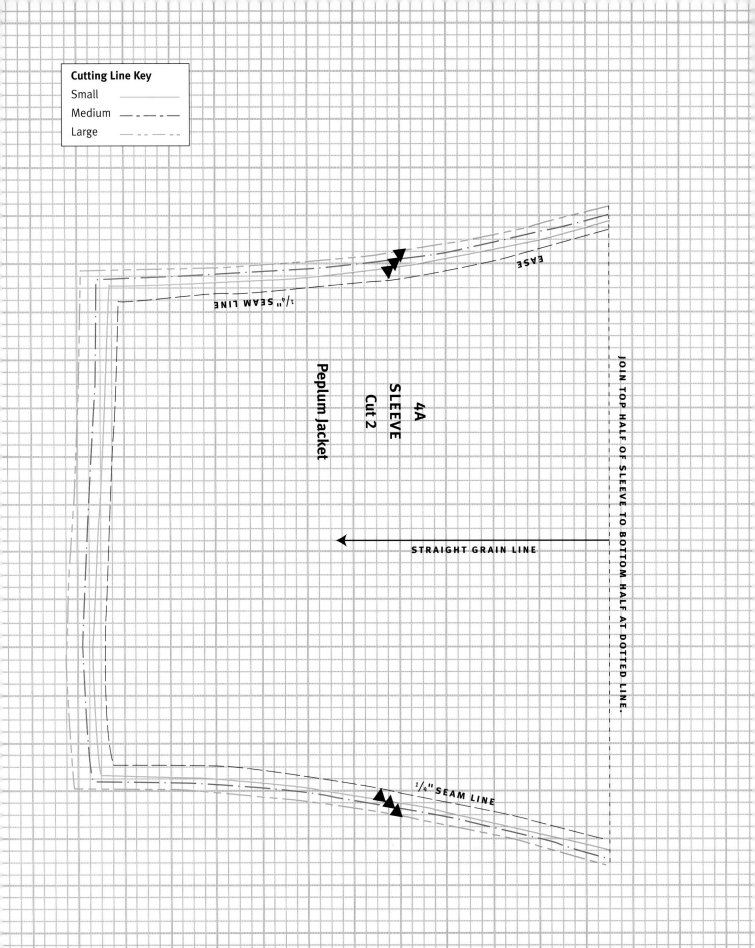

Cutting Line Key

Small

Medium

Large

Peplum Jacket

4A
SLEEVE
Cut 2

EASE

1/4" SEAM LINE

1/4" SEAM LINE

← STRAIGHT GRAIN LINE →

JOIN TOP HALF OF SLEEVE TO BOTTOM HALF AT DOTTED LINE.

ENLARGE 200%. SEE PHOTOCOPY PERMISSION ON PAGE 2.

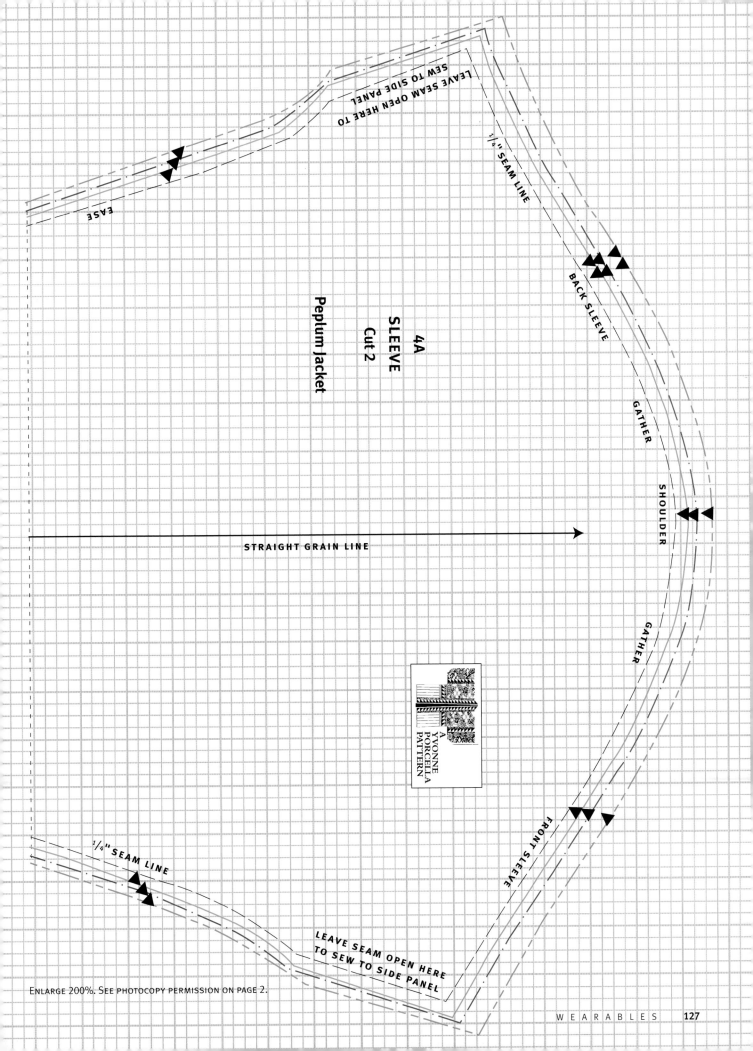

4A
SLEEVE
Cut 2

Peplum Jacket

STRAIGHT GRAIN LINE

EASE

LEAVE SEAM OPEN HERE TO
SEW TO SIDE PANEL

1/4" SEAM LINE

BACK SLEEVE

GATHER

SHOULDER

GATHER

FRONT SLEEVE

1/4" SEAM LINE

LEAVE SEAM OPEN HERE
TO SEW TO SIDE PANEL

A
YVONNE
PORCELLA
PATTERN

ENLARGE 200%. SEE PHOTOCOPY PERMISSION ON PAGE 2.

BACK VIEW SHOWING
BLOUSE OPENING. BOW
IS ATTACHED TO BLOUSE
WITH SNAPS.

SKIRT BACK WITH SASH

Shades of Romance This complete outfit is hand-painted and includes a coat, blouse, skirt, waistband, shoes, and hand piece. The coat and blouse were made using patterns adapted from *Pieced Clothing Variations*. The blouse is the Basic Vest modified to open down the center back; the front has a shaped lower edge and the side panels have a shaped top edge. The coat is a long version of the Basic Vest with a shaped back lower edge; the sleeves are from the Peplum Jacket pattern. The skirt is made with an elastic band at the waist and a top layer of silk organza over a silk pongee lining. The blouse and sleeve fabrics were pleated in the method described on page 55 of *Colors Changing Hue*. The shoes were purchased white and painted to match the outfit.

The coat surface design is made using the Burned Silk Appliqué technique found on page 26 of *Colors Changing Hue*. Silk ribbons, seed beads, machine, hand quilting, and various types of paint decorate the finished surface. The half belt on the back features silk roses made from painted silk twill fabric and painted wire-edged ribbons. Ribbons that decorate the coat front and back of the bodice are made using the rolled hem feature of a Bernina serger on cut strips of painted silk fabric. These ribbons are decorated with metallic pens and Pearlescent Liquid Acrylic.

One of the advantages of the patterns from *Pieced Clothing Variations* are that they are based on rectangular shapes. These flat shapes can then be adapted into many different styles. *Shades of Romance* is one example of the Basic Vest made longer, with sleeves from the Peplum Jacket, belt, and shaped lower back edge added. The following pattern is for the Basic Long Vest. Try adapting it for yourself and then let me know what variations you have made.

BLOUSE FRONT

BELT

**BACK VIEW OF COAT;
BLOUSE; SKIRT**

The Long Vest Variation   The Long Vest pattern comes below the knee. The pattern consists of center panel front and back and two side panels. In the *Shades of Romance* coat, the center back panel lower edge is slightly curved. The side panels should also be modified to reflect the curve. See center back extension on page 131.

DETERMINING THE FABRIC NEEDED   The Long Vest can be made from $2^{1}/_{4}$ yards of fabric for the outside and the same for lining and underlining. An additional $^{2}/_{3}$ yard is needed for bias binding to cover raw edges. If the sleeves are added, plan for another 1 yard of fabric. Additional fabrics are necessary for a strip pieced surface.

DETERMINING THE VEST SIZE   The measurements are for a medium size. To change the pattern size for personal fit, follow directions on pages 109-110. In the Long Vest the side panel lower edge width (13") is the same as the center panel width (13").

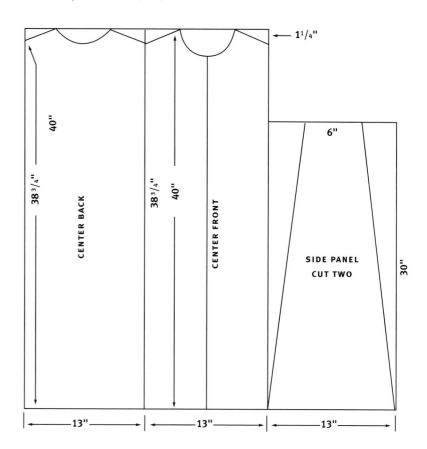

LEFT: LONG VEST

RIGHT: DIMENSIONS OF
PATTERN PIECES

DIMENSIONS OF PATTERN PIECES   Center panel has front and back panel 13" wide by 40" long sewn together at the shoulder. Shape shoulder seam $1^{1}/_{4}$". Add $^{1}/_{4}$" seam allowance to pattern piece for shoulder seam. Neck opening is from template found on page 132. It is finished with $1^{1}/_{2}$"-wide bias binding. No seam allowance is necessary on neck edge. Armhole is approximately nine inches shorter than the center panel. Width of side panel is six inches wide at top, thirteen inches wide at bottom, and thirty inches long.

BEGINNING THE LONG VEST   Draw the pattern shapes on the underlining fabric. Trace the template for the back neck opening found on page 132 in the center on the top edge of center back. If you would like to shape the lower back edge of the center back panel, draw the shape on the underlining before cutting out the center back. Shape shoulder by drawing from neck opening to armhole edge, adding $1/4$" seam allowance. Repeat for center front. Slash center front for front opening after drawing neck opening. Front edges just meet in front; there is no overlap.

Cover center back panel underlining with a single piece of fabric and begin embellishing or strip piecing the back. Continue on center fronts and side panels. Line all panels in the method described for the *Sponge Stamped Vest* on page 110.

CENTER BACK

FINISHING THE CENTER FRONT   Bind center front raw edges with $1^1/2$"-wide straight grain binding. Add ties or ribbons if desired, as seen in *Shades of Romance* on page 128.

SEWING THE SHOULDER SEAMS   Follow directions for shoulder seams found on page 121. Now finish neck opening with $1^1/2$"-wide bias binding.

If this is to be a vest, finish the tops of each side panel with $1^1/2$"-wide straight grain binding. For a coat with sleeves, follow directions for sleeves found on pages 121-122 of the Peplum Jacket pattern. Make sleeves and attach to tops of side panels.

ASSEMBLING THE VEST   Pin side panels to center panels, starting at lower edge. Using a $1/4$" seam, stitch the side panels to center back and fronts with $1^1/2$"-wide bias binding on top of the seam to finish the raw edges. Press binding toward seam. If necessary, grade the seam allowance to eliminate any bulkiness. Turn in raw edge and hem binding over the machine-stitched seam. For a coat with sleeves, follow assembly directions for Peplum Jacket on page 122.

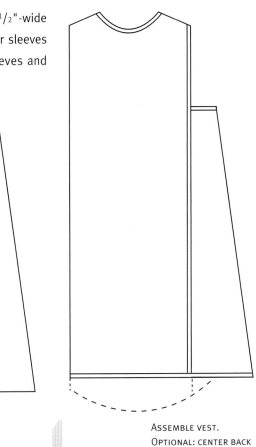

SIDE PANEL

ASSEMBLE VEST.
OPTIONAL: CENTER BACK
PANEL EXTENSION; NOTE:
MODIFY SIDE PANEL ALSO.

FINISHING THE LOWER EDGE   Finish the lower edge with $1^1/2$"-wide straight grain binding. If the lower edge has been shaped, finish with $1^1/2$"-wide bias binding. See *Shades of Romance*, page 129.

TEMPLATE FOR NECK OPENINGS

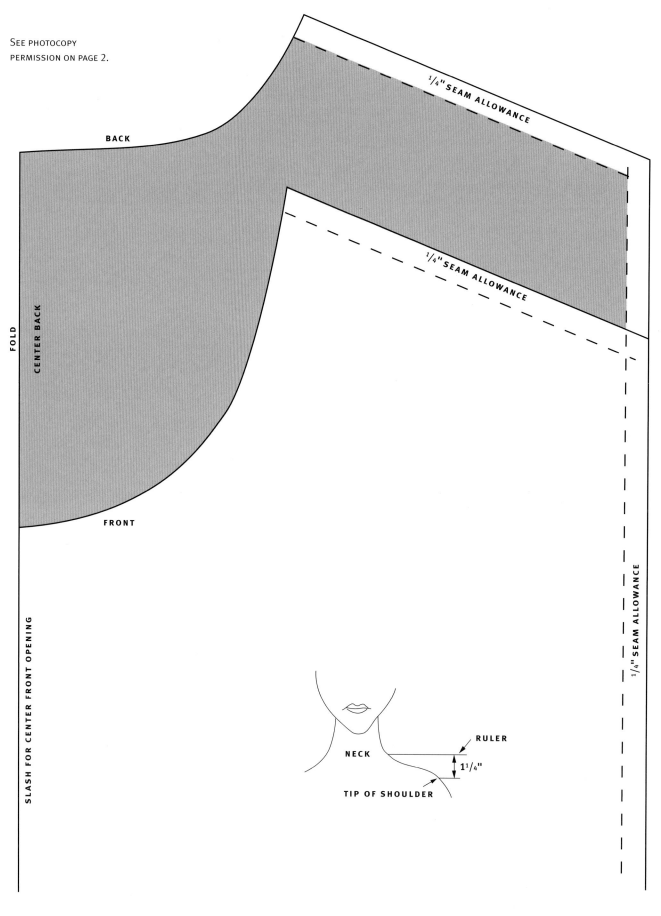

BACK

¹/₄" SEAM ALLOWANCE

¹/₄" SEAM ALLOWANCE

FOLD

CENTER BACK

¹/₄" SEAM ALLOWANCE

FRONT

SLASH FOR CENTER FRONT OPENING

RULER

NECK

1¹/₄"

TIP OF SHOULDER

ADDITIONAL PATTERN SIZES   To change pattern sizes, follow directions on pages 109-110. The following two diagrams show a larger size vest and a small vest which can be used as a guide for different sizes.

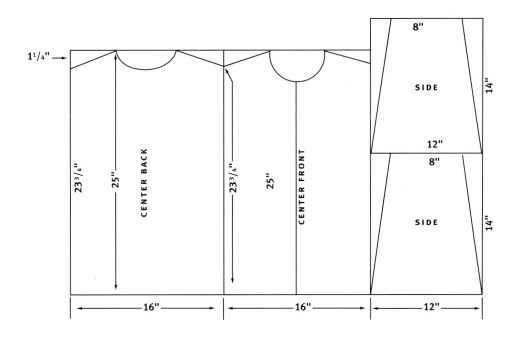

LARGE SIZE

The Basic Vest can be lengthened and the pattern pieces can be made wider to accommodate larger body measurements. To add length to the vest, the hip measurement must be calculated. Measure how long the vest will be and then measure around the hips. As seen in the diagram for the larger size, the side panel is wider at the bottom edge.

Dimensions for this pattern are for a small vest. Assembling the vest is the same as for the Basic Vest.

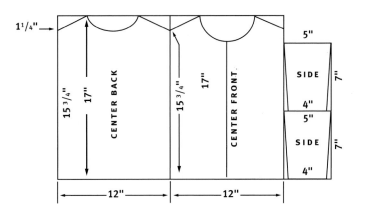

SMALL SIZE

celebration banners

These painted projects are not intended to be hand quilted. Oftentimes you may want a banner for a special occasion and do not want to spend the time making a quilted one. By using black gesso on fabric, in about twenty minutes you have a usable black fabric surface to decorate in any manner. The samples have photocopied images adhered to the surface. Other decorative painting and fabric techniques are added.

The two examples of celebration banners are made using white cotton duck purchased at the fabric store. This fabric is a type of canvas, but is not as stiff as commercial canvas. Both samples *Four Five Six* and *So Special* have a coating of black gesso; see photograph on page 15 showing application of gesso with a squeegee or large putty knife, to make the background solid black. The edges of *So Special* were left unfinished to demonstrate how the gesso covers the fabric. In *Four Five Six* the edges were hemmed and gold leaf was applied.

CHAPTER NINE

DETAIL OF
FOUR FIVE SIX

Four Five Six   This banner requires art supplies as well as additional fabrics. It is part painting and part collage. It was fun to make, and illustrates how opaque paints differ from transparent and can completely cover a surface. Finished size is 27" x 27".

PAINT, SUPPLIES, AND EQUIPMENT

Cotton duck, white: 28" x 28"

Serger (optional)

Plastic drop cloth

Bob Ross black gesso

Squeegee: 4" wide

Masking tape: 1" wide

Composition gold leaf sheets
($5^1/_2$" x $5^1/_2$")

Gold leaf liquid quick sizing

Brushes: acrylic bright flat about 1"
wide and size 8 round

A piece of cotton or **a soft bristle brush**
to wipe the finished gold leaf

Liquitex acrylic matte medium

Opaque paint: white

Liquitex Iridescent: white (or
Setacolor: pearl white)

64-oz. water bottle to wash brushes

Liquitex Iridescent: gold

Optional: Liquitex artists acrylic paint
in purple, blue, red

Paper towels

Aluminum pie pan or **disposable dish**
(to mix paints for panels)

Setacolor Transparent: buttercup

Carbon transfer of an image onto white
silk organza

Turpentine

Bits of colored foil candy wrapper

Gold paper seal

Bits of painted silk organza

Rubber stamps

Scissors

HEMMING THE EDGES OF THE COTTON DUCK Serge all four edges of the 28" x 28" piece of cotton duck, fold in all four edges $1/2$" so finished piece is 27" x 27". Stitch along all four sides to secure the hem. (The duck may shrink after the gesso is applied.)

Place the hemmed side of the duck down on a plastic drop cloth. On the front surface, pour black gesso along the top edge. With a 4" squeegee pull the gesso across the duck to spread it out evenly. Continue adding gesso until the surface is completely covered, it should have a smooth black color. Let this dry.

A BIT OF INFORMATION ABOUT GOLD LEAF Real gold leaf is 23K leaf. The most common leaf used by artists is a composition leaf which is sold in packages containing twenty-five sheets measuring $5^1/2$" x $5^1/2$". Composition leaf is available from mail order art supply catalogs or in some local craft stores. Composition leaf comes in a variety of colors: gold, silver, and copper.

Porous surfaces must be sealed with a sealer coat, such as gesso, before applying composition leaf. A soft bristle brush is recommended if applying sealer to a picture frame or dimensional surface.

Sizing which accompanies composition gold leaf products is a liquid size which is made from rabbit-skin glue. Some sizing requires 30 minutes to 6 hours before it is ready to work. Quick size is workable in 5 minutes. Aerosol sizing can be worked in 1 to 2 minutes. Be sure to check the time requirements on the product you buy. The label will also tell you how long the size remains tacky to allow you to apply the leaf.

Liquid gold leaf is a different product. It is a liquid solution and contains pigment, styrene resin, and xylol. It is applied by brushing the liquid gold onto the surface. The product is thinned with xylol, which is a type of alcohol. Be cautioned that the paint can destroy your brush, or at least leave residue on the bristles.

APPLYING COMPOSITION GOLD LEAF Mark off a 2"-wide border on the outside edges and tape off with 1" masking tape. With a bright flat brush, paint gold leaf quick sizing (which is the tacky glue) onto the black gesso. Immediately wash the brush or leave it to soak in water for a few minutes. Remove the masking tape. After five minutes you can begin placing the gold leaf over the sizing.

The gold leaf comes in a packet with tissue paper between each leaf. It is easier to handle the leaf if you pick it up with the piece of tissue. First find the center fold of the packet and cut through all the layers on the fold. Lift out one leaf and one piece of tissue. Carefully tear the leaf and tissue into 2" strips. This is an approximate size since it is difficult to tear evenly. Tearing the leaf gives a better edge than cutting. Notice in the sample how the torn edge of the leaf looks on the inside edge. Use the tissue to help you place the leaf onto the sized area. Be careful not to get sizing on your fingers because the leaf will stick to your skin. Continue adding gold leaf until the whole area is covered, discard the tissue, and allow the leaf to dry. When dry, gently brush off the excess leaf with a soft bristle brush or a piece of cotton, and discard. Seal the gold leaf with acrylic matte medium, which may slightly darken the leaf.

PAINTING THE CENTER PANEL   Tape off a 12" x 12" area in the center of the banner. In an aluminum pie pan make a mixture of white opaque paint. You can add to this mixture iridescent pearl white paint and a touch of Setacolor Transparent buttercup to make a lively white. **OPTIONAL:** *Other paint colors can be added for accent. With a bright flat brush paint this mixture onto the 12" square, completely covering the whole black center area.*

If you like, take a crumpled piece of paper towel and dab it into a small amount of purple paint. Press this onto the black background at the edge of the center white square. Do the same with blue paint and iridescent gold on another side. This just adds a bit of interest to the black surface and is optional.

Remove the tape from the edges of the center square. When this is completely dry, you can use acrylic matte medium to adhere a silk organza photocopy to the center square. The project uses the Carbon Transfer method described on pages 52-54 and seen in lower right of photograph on page 55.

STAMP NUMBERS   The numbers four, five, six were stamped onto the black gesso by carefully hand applying acrylic paint, instructions on pages 41-42, to the surface of antique printing-press type and rubber stamps. Various pieces of painted silk organza, the foil, and the gold seal were applied to the surface using acrylic matte medium with a size 8 round brush.

A final application of acrylic matte medium was painted over the whole surface.

Cennino also offers a method for gilding fabric. "If you have to work on velvets, or to design for embroiderers, draw your works with a pen, with either ink or tempered white lead. If you have to paint or gild anything, take size as usual, and an equal amount of white of egg, and a little white lead; and with a bristle brush put it on the pile, and beat it down hard, and press it down thoroughly flat. Paint and lay gold in the way described, but just mordant gilding. But it will be less trouble for you to work each thing out on white silk, cutting out the figures or whatever else you do, and have the embroiderers fasten them on your velvet."[15]

So Special   This banner celebrates a wedding anniversary. The images are copies of Victorian illustrations, which were purchased from an antique store. The banner appears here with unfinished edges to illustrate the effects of black gesso on the white duck fabric. To complete the banner, the edges could be turned over artist stretcher bar frames or hemmed on the machine.

So Special. BANNER HAS UNFINISHED EDGES TO ILLUSTRATE COMPLETE COVERAGE OF BLACK GESSO.

PAINT, SUPPLIES, AND EQUIPMENT

Cotton Duck: white 32" x 27"

Plastic drop cloth

Bob Ross black gesso

Squeegee: 4" wide

Masking tape: 1" wide

Brushes: acrylic bright flat about 1" wide, size 8 and size 4 rounds

Liquitex acrylic matte medium

Opaque paint: white

Setacolor Transparent: buttercup

Liquitex artist paints: magenta, Iridescent gold and pearl

64-oz. water bottle to wash brushes

Aluminum pie pan or disposable dish to mix white paints

Pearlescent Liquid Acrylic: sundown magenta, macaw green

Rubber stamps: alphabet in size $1^1/_2$" font

Stencil: 1" grid and rose

Stencil brush: $^1/_2$"-wide tip

Photocopy of Victorian figures onto paper

Cotton batiste: white for transferring images

Turpentine

Paper towels

Newspaper

Tissue paper

Iron

Metallic pen: gold

PAINTING THE BACKGROUND   Lay the cotton duck on a plastic drop cloth and with a 4" squeegee cover the surface with black gesso; let this dry. See *Four Five Six* on page 135.

PREPARING THE CARBON TRANSFERS   Make copies of the Victorian pictures on paper and follow the directions for transferring images onto fabric using Carbon Transfer method found on pages 52-54. Use the cotton batiste fabric or a thin white broadcloth.

      OPTIONAL: *Since this will be a banner and not a quilt, you could simply adhere the paper copies of the images onto the surface of the banner using acrylic matte medium to glue them on.*

PAINTING THE CENTER PANEL   With masking tape, tape off areas on the black gesso that will be large enough to accommodate the size of the copied images. See instructions for mixing opaque white found on page 137.

      Remove the tape from the opaque white areas and, when completely dry, use a size 8 round brush and acrylic matte medium to adhere the images to the white areas.

RUBBER STAMPS   Follow directions for rubber stamping with acrylic paint on pages 41-42. Use the magenta artist acrylic paints to cover the alphabet stamps. The artist paint is opaque and the lettering will stand out on the black surface. Stamp the message of your choice. Be sure to clean the stamps after stamping with acrylic paint. When the paint is dry, use the size 4 small round brush and accent the letters with sundown magenta Pearlescent Liquid Acrylic.

STENCILING   Use iridescent gold paint, a stencil brush, and a 1" grid stencil and paint the top right edge and the left lower edge.

      Use magenta artist paint, macaw green Pearlescent Liquid Acrylic, and the rose and leaves stencil to paint the rose and leaves. Highlight these if necessary with more paint or Liquid Acrylic using the size 4 brush.

METALLIC PENS AND MOUNTING   Draw a single gold metallic pen line on the edges of the banner. The banner then can be stretched on an artist stretcher bar frame or taken to a framer to be professionally mounted; or you could use an aerosol artist's adhesive available at an art or craft store to glue the banner on a piece of cardboard. Then tape the raw edges of the duck to the back of the board.

END NOTES

1 Cennino d'Andrea Cennini. *The Craftsman's Handbook*, "*Il Libro dell' Arte*." Translated by Daniel V. Thompson, Jr. New York: Dover, 1960. page 3
2 Ibid, page 1
3 Ibid, pages 70—71
4 Ibid, page 21
5 Ibid, page 35
6 Ibid, page 24
7 Ibid, page 27
8 Ibid, page 31
9 Ibid, pages 32, 33
10 Ibid, page 52
11 Ibid, pages 22—23
12 Ibid, page 34
13 Ibid, page 67
14 Ibid, page 68,69
15 Ibid, page 107

BIBLIOGRAPHY

Cennini, Cennino d'Andrea. *The Craftsman's Handbook, "Il Libro dell' Arte."* Trans. Daniel V. Thompson, Jr. New York: Dover, 1960.

Colour. Marshall Editions, Ed. Helen Varley, London: Marshall Editions Limited, 1983.

Itten, Johannes. *The Art of Color.* Originally published in Germany under the title *"Kunst der Farbe."* Ravensburg, Germany: Otto Maier, 1961 and 1973. Trans. Ernest van Haagen. New York: Van Nostrand Reinhold, 1973.

Liquitex® *How To Mix & Use Color.* Easton, PA: Binney & Smith, 1993.

Mayer, Ralph. *A Dictionary of Art Terms and Techniques.* New York: Barnes & Noble Books, 1981.

OTHER FINE BOOKS FROM C&T PUBLISHING

RESOURCE GUIDE

Fabric

FABRIC TRADITIONS
1350 Broadway
New York, NY 10018
(800) 538-0668
Dyer's Cloth: 2 weights, 68" x 68"
and 60" x 60" (sheeting)

P & B FABRICS (wholesale)
646 N. Eckhoff Street
Orange, CA 92668
(800) 351-9087
(800) 247-3457 (west coast)
Dyer's cloth, muslin, batiste, Deco
Glaze

TESTFABRICS, INC.
P.O. Box 420
Middlesex, NJ 08846
(732) 469-6446
Large selection of fabrics without
sizing

EXOTIC SILKS (wholesale)
1959 Leghorn
Mountain View, CA 94043
(800) 845-SILK (outside California)
(800) 345-SILK (inside California)
(415) 965-0712 (fax)
Silk fabrics

Thai Silks (retail)
252 State Street
Los Altos, CA 94022
(800) 722-SILK (outside California)
(800) 221-SILK (inside California)
(415) 948-3426 (fax)
Silk fabrics

Fabric Paint and Dye

Pro Chemical & Dye Inc.
P.O. Box 14
Somerset, MA 02726
(800) 2-BUY-DYE
Ask for catalog

RUPERT GIBBON & SPIDER, INC.
Jacquard Products
P.O. Box 425
Healdsburg, CA 95448
(800) 442-0455 (U.S. and Canada)
(707) 433-9577
Ask for catalog

Art Paint

LIQUITEX U.S.A.
Binney & Smith Inc.
1100 Church Lane
P.O. Box 431
Easton, PA 18044-0431
(800) 272-9652

LIQUITEX U.K.
Binney & Smith Europe Ltd.
Ampthill Road
Bedford, MK429RS
England
(011) 44-1234-328009

LIQUITEX AUSTRALIA
Binney & Smith (Australia) Pty. Ltd.
599 Blackburn Road
Clayton North 3168
P.O. Box 4684
Mulgrave 3170
Victoria, Australia
(011) 613-9560-5633

LIQUITEX CANADA
Binney & Smith (Canada) Ltd.
15 Mary Street West
P.O. Box 120
Lindsay, Ontario K9V-4R8
(705) 324-6105
(705) 324-3511 (fax)

Pens

EK SUCCESS (wholesale)
611 Industrial Road
Carlstadt, NJ 07072
(800) 524-1349
Zig textile markers

Rubber Stamps

HERO ARTS (wholesale)
1343 Powell Street
Emeryville, CA 94608
(800) 822-HERO
(510) 652-6055
Ask for catalog

STAMPENDOUS (wholesale)
1357 South Lewis Street
Anaheim, CA 92805
(800) 869-0474
Ask for catalog

RUBBERSTAMPMADNESS, INC.
408 S.W. Monroe #210
Corvallis, OR 97330
(541) 752-0075
(541) 752-5475 (fax)
Request for issues send to:
P.O. Box 610
Corvallis, OR 97339-0610

STAMPA BARBARA
at Paseo Nuevo
505 Paseo Nuevo
Santa Barbara, CA 93101
(805) 962-4077

Embellishments

EVENING STAR DESIGNS
69 Coolidge Avenue
Haverhill, MA 01832
(508) 372-3473
(800) 666-3562
Ask for catalog

ELSIE'S EXQUISIQUES
208 State Street
St. Joseph, MI 49085
(800) 742-SILK
(616) 982-0449

WESTRIM (wholesale)
P.O. Box 3879
9667 Canoga Avenue
Chatsworth, CA 91311
(818) 998-8550
Ask for catalog

GICK CRAFTS (wholesale)
9 Studebaker Drive
Irvine, CA 92618
(800) 854-3368
Ask for catalog

Ribbon

RIBBON CONNECTIONS
969 Industrial Road, Suite E
San Carlos, CA 94070
(415) 593-5221
(415) 593-6785 (fax)

THINGS JAPANESE
9805 N.E. 116th Street,
Suite 7160
Kirkland, WA 98034-4248
(425) 821-2287
(425) 821-3554 (fax)
Ask for catalog

Mail Order Art and Quilt Supplies

CLOTILDE INC.
4301 N. Federal Hwy, Suite 200
Fort Lauderdale, FL 33308-5209
(800) 772-2891
Ask for catalog

Dharma Trading Company
P.O. Box 150916
San Rafael, CA 94915
(800) 542-5227
Ask for catalog

NASCO ARTS & CRAFTS
901 Janesville Avenue
Fort Atkinson, WI 53538
(800) 558-9595
(414) 563-2446
Ask for catalog

NASCO ARTS & CRAFTS
4825 Stoddard Road
Modesto, CA 95356
(800) 558-9595
(209) 545-1600
Ask for catalog

JERRY'S ARTARAMA
P.O. Box 58638
Raleigh, NC 27658
(800) U-ARTIST
Ask for catalog

INDEX

Yvonne Porcella has been working as a fiber artist since the early 1960s. At first she gained considerable local acclaim for her painting in acrylic and oils. Later, as a result of a lifelong interest in sewing and knitting, she learned the art of hand weaving as a means to create special fabrics. Self-education in textiles and fibers eventually led her to the discovery of folk costume construction. Yvonne began designing simply structured garment patterns to use with special woven fabrics. These patterns were also suitable for all types of embellishment: stitchery, woven fabric, patchwork, and collage.

Many instructional fiber books published during the next few years included the work of Yvonne Porcella, featuring her hand-woven textiles, stitchery, and patchwork.

As an adjunct to her handwovens she began to piece fabrics together to use in garments. In 1972 she had her first gallery exhibition of wearable art, which included patchwork garments and hand-woven textiles. At the time she was using ethnic textiles, ribbons, and trims as well as calico prints to create vivid garments. Today many of these early garments are in the collection of the Oakland Museum of California in Oakland, California, and the Fine Arts Museums of San Francisco, California.

As a teacher and author, her work has influenced other artists to work in the field of wearable art. Her books, beginning in 1977, offered easy patterns for construction of blouses, dresses, and vests. In the early 1980s she became interested in hand painting her own fabrics and included painting techniques in her 1986 book *A Colorful Book*.

Colors Changing Hue, published by C&T Publishing in 1994, is a process and project book using textile paints to color silk and cotton fabrics. Again Yvonne shows quilters how easy it is to create their own fabrics and use the fabric in innovative quilts and garments.

In this new book Yvonne expands the color palette to include darker and more vibrant colors, and again brings the reader new and interesting projects to expand their understanding of color.

Color has been a dominant feature of Yvonne's work. Her quilts using bold colored commercial fabrics have been exhibited worldwide. Her work has been collected by major museums as well as private collectors. Her quilt *Takoage* made in 1980 is included in the 150th anniversary exhibition of 300 artifacts selected from the collections of the sixteen Smithsonian Museums. In this exhibition she represents all contemporary quilters by having her quilt displayed in this auspicious event along with the Smithsonian's other treasures.

She is a wife, mother of four, and grandmother of ten. She and her husband live in central California. She continues to teach and lecture in the United States and abroad. Her art quilts are available through the Connell Gallery in Atlanta, Georgia.